Parents and Schools

Creating a Successful Partnership for Students with Special Needs

Anne M. Bauer
University of Cincinnati

Thomas M. Shea
Emeritus, Southern Illinois University–Edwardsville

Merrill
Prentice Hall

Upper Saddle River, New Jersey
Columbus, Ohio

Library of Congress Cataloging-in-Publication Data

Bauer, Anne M.,
  Parents and schools : creating a successful partnership for students with special needs /
Anne M. Bauer, Thomas M. Shea.
    p. cm.
  Includes bibliographical references and index.
  ISBN 0-13-018540-X (paperback)
    1. Children with disabilities—Education. 2. Parent-teacher relationships. 3. Home and
school. I. Bauer, Anne M. II. Title.

LC4019.S45 2003
371.91—dc21   2002024621

Vice President and Publisher: Jeffery W. Johnston
Editor: Allyson P. Sharp
Editorial Assistant: Penny Burleson
Production Editor: Sheryl Glicker Langner
Production Coordination: Emily Hatteberg, Carlisle Publishers Services
Design Coordinator: Diane C. Lorenzo
Photo Coordinator: Cynthia Cassidy
Cover Designer: Bryan Huber
Cover Art: Superstock
Production Manager: Laura Messerly
Director of Marketing: Ann Castel Davis
Marketing Manager: Amy June
Marketing Coordinator: Tyra Cooper

This book was set in Novarese by Carlisle Communications Ltd. It was printed and bound by R.R.
Donnelley & Sons Company. The cover was printed by The Lehigh Press, Inc.

Photo Credits: pp. 2, 8, 23, 64, 82, 169, 185 by Anne Vega/Merrill; pp. 16, 47, 102, 132, 164, 187, 205 by
Scott Cunningham/Merrill; p. 38 by Larry Hamill/Merrill; p. 52 by Ken Karp/PH College; pp. 58, 71, 85, 128,
196 by Anthony Magnacca/Merrill; p. 106 by Nick Cassidy; p. 116 courtesy of the Ganz family;
p. 135 courtesy of the Diesel family; p. 148 by Barbara Schwartz/Merrill; p. 151 by Todd Yarrington/
Merrill; p. 157 courtesy of the Foley family; p. 175 courtesy of the Humler family; p. 178 courtesy of the
Bauer family; p. 207 courtesy of the Ulrich family.

Pearson Education Ltd.
Pearson Education Australia Pty. Limited
Pearson Education Singapore Pte. Ltd.
Pearson Education North Asia Ltd.
Pearson Education Canada, Ltd.
Pearson Educación de Mexico, S.A. de C. V.
Pearson Education—Japan
Pearson Education Malaysia Pte. Ltd.
Pearson Education, *Upper Saddle River, New Jersey*

Merrill
Prentice Hall

10 9 8 7 6 5 4 3 2 1
ISBN: 0-13-018540-X

In memory of Dolores,
best friend, beloved spouse, and mother
"the wind beneath my wings"
tms
amb

Preface

The majority of teacher preparation programs in colleges and universities have a course about families. A few have a course, or at least a part of a course, related to families with members with disabilities. All students entering general and special education teacher preparation programs have personal experience as a member of a family. A few of these students have experience in a family with a member with a disability.

Many students have preconceived notions about how they will engage families in the education of their children. These notions are often based on personal experiences with their teachers or the experiences of their parents and family. Such experiences may positively or negatively bias their approach to families. They may have preconceived ideas about how they will conduct their first open house, welcome families and children to their classroom, and so on. They may have vague ideas of how they will write their first parent letter, conduct their first conference, and make their first home visit. They may dread one or all of these difficult but necessary and required activities due to a lack of understanding and preparation with regard to families in general, and family members with disabilities in particular.

Many students will work with families who are very dissimilar from their own family. Not only must they work with families from diverse racial, cultural, and linguistic groups and with families with members with disabilities, but they frequently work with single-parent families, blended families, foster families, and other family constellations. In addition, present-day teacher education students will work in classrooms and schools as well as live and work in communities very unlike those in which they were raised. They will be teaching children from backgrounds and with life experiences that diverge greatly from theirs.

This text focuses on the uniqueness of each family that challenges teachers as they practice in public schools. We strive to communicate to the reader the contribution each child and family can make to the community of learning. We write from a social systems perspective, which offers insight into the developmental contexts of each child and each family. Engaging families in the education of their children is not a simple task. There is no philosopher's stone or recipe. By taking a developmental perspective, we demonstrate the changing needs of families as their children with disabilities progress from infancy to adulthood.

This text presents the voices of real parents as they communicate the pleasures and problems of raising and educating a family member with disabilities. The text is based not only on the professional literature but also on our experiences as parents and professionals. We encourage the reader to empathize with those raising children with disabilities and challenge the reader to understand the complexities of working with families. As we researched and prepared this text, we were constantly amazed by the tenacity and resilience of the families represented here.

In the first section of the text, we provide background information into working with families on behalf of their children. In Chapter 1, we describe the role of context and the unique settings in which each child develops. In Chapter 2, we further explore the aspects of the developmental context, with a discussion of diversity related to family involvement. Chapter 3 describes a different aspect of the context for families with members with a disability, that is, their legal rights and responsibilities. Chapter 4 covers some of the persistent assumptions related to the impact of identification and diagnosis of disability on families. The literature is discussed and integrated in the social systems perspective.

In the next two chapters, we shift the focus of the discussion to implementation of parent engagement. Chapter 5 presents a model for family involvement. This is accomplished through the systematic application of a case study to the various steps in the model. Chapter 6 provides information on the challenges of collaboration, and increasing the potential for effective communication.

The second section of the text provides a developmental perspective on family involvement. Each of the chapters in this section uses the voices of parents as they tell the story of their engagement in their child's education. Chapter 7 describes the issues of early intervention services and working with parents of very young children with disabilities. Chapter 8 addresses the families of children in preschool and kindergarten, and the significant changes that occur in families in the transition to kindergarten and first grade. Subsequent chapters, 9 through 12, each infused with the voices of families, address primary grades, middle and junior high school, secondary school, and families of adults with disabilities.

We owe a considerable debt to the families who lent their voices to this project. Sally Gantz, Mef Diesel, Franky and Carl Foley, Riley Humler, Paul Bauer, and Mary Ulrich opened their hearts and experiences to us on behalf of other families of children with disabilities and those professionals preparing to work with families of children with disabilities. We thank them most sincerely for their openness, honesty, and commitment. We would also like to thank our friend and editor, Ann Davis, who has consistently and over many years and texts been supportive and made significant contributions to our efforts on behalf of children, adults, and families. Finally, we wish to thank our reviewers—Greg Conderman, University of Wisconsin, Eau Claire; Robert Oritz, California State University–Fullerton; and Alec F. Peck, Boston College—for their help.

Anne M. Bauer
Thomas M. Shea

Discover the Companion Website Accompanying This Book

THE PRENTICE HALL COMPANION WEBSITE: A VIRTUAL LEARNING ENVIRONMENT

Technology is a constantly growing and changing aspect of our field that is creating a need for content and resources. To address this emerging need, Prentice Hall has developed an online learning environment for students and professors alike—Companion Websites—to support our textbooks.

In creating a Companion Website, our goal is to build on and enhance what the textbook already offers. For this reason, the content for each user-friendly website is organized by topic and provides the professor and student with a variety of meaningful resources. Common features of a Companion Website include:

FOR THE PROFESSOR—

Every Companion Website integrates **Syllabus Manager™,** an online syllabus creation and management utility.

- **Syllabus Manager™** provides you, the instructor, with an easy, step-by-step process to create and revise syllabi, with direct links into Companion Website and other online content without having to learn HTML.
- Students may log on to your syllabus during any study session. All they need to know is the web address for the Companion Website and the password you've assigned to your syllabus.
- After you have created a syllabus using **Syllabus Manager™,** students may enter the syllabus for their course section from any point in the Companion Website.

- Clicking on a date, the student is shown the list of activities for the assignment. The activities for each assignment are linked directly to actual content, saving time for students.
- Adding assignments consists of clicking on the desired due date, then filling in the details of the assignment—name of the assignment, instructions, and whether or not it is a one-time or repeating assignment.
- In addition, links to other activities can be created easily. If the activity is online, a URL can be entered in the space provided, and it will be linked automatically in the final syllabus.
- Your completed syllabus is hosted on our servers, allowing convenient updates from any computer on the Internet. Changes you make to your syllabus are immediately available to your students at their next logon.

FOR THE STUDENT—

- **Topic Overviews**—outline key concepts in topic areas
- **Characteristics**—general information about each topic/disability covered on this website
- **Read About It**—a list of links to pertinent articles found on the Internet that cover each topic
- **Teaching Ideas**—links to articles that offer suggestions, ideas, and strategies for teaching students with disabilities
- **Web Links**—a wide range of websites that provide useful and current information related to each topic area
- **Resources**—a wide array of different resources for many of the pertinent topics and issues surrounding special education
- **Electronic Bluebook**—send homework or essays directly to your instructor's email with this paperless form
- **Message Board**—serves as a virtual bulletin board to post—or respond to—questions or comments to/from a national audience
- **Chat**—real-time chat with anyone who is using the text anywhere in the country—ideal for discussion and study groups, class projects, etc.

To take advantage of these and other resources, please visit the *Parents and Schools: Creating a Successful Partnership for Students with Special Needs* Companion Website at

www.prenhall.com/bauer

Contents

CHAPTER 3
Legal Rights and Responsibilities of Parents and Families   39

CHAPTER 4
The Impact of Identification and Diagnosis of Disability on the Family   53

CHAPTER 8
Engaging Families of Preschoolers and Kindergarten Students with Disabilities   129

CHAPTER 9
Engaging Families During the Primary Years   149

CHAPTER 10
Engaging Families in Middle School and Junior High School   165

CHAPTER 11
Secondary Students and the Transition to the Community   179

Note: Every effort has been made to provide accurate and current Internet information in this book. However, the Internet and information posted on it are constantly changing, so it is inevitable that some of the Internet addresses listed in this textbook will change.

CHAPTER 1

The Role of Context

I knew parenting a child with a disability was going to be different. I guess I just wasn't prepared for how difficult it was going to be.

It took me a while to realize that our experience as a family was going to be vastly different from those of the families in our neighborhood. For example, the moms were talking about how they were dreading summer vacation. I love summer vacation. With my kids, for whom school is hell, summer vacation is wonderful. No notes from teachers, no homework, no conferences, no check sheets, no trying to educate teachers who should know what's going on. Give me summer vacation any day.

I look at what I have learned from my child and really think she was a gift.

Three different families, three very different stories. Any time we discuss families, we have to do it with great caution. Each family, not only those with a child with a disability, is unique. Each family has a unique experience of parenting and of disabilities. In this chapter, we'll explore how parents currently engage in the education of their children. We'll take a social systems perspective and review the role of context in child development. The chapter will conclude with the assumptions on which the materials presented in this text are based.

Learning Objectives

After completing this chapter, you will be able to discuss these topics:

1. Parent and family engagement in education
2. The role of context in child development
3. Assumptions regarding the social systems perspective and family engagement

PARENT AND FAMILY ENGAGEMENT IN EDUCATION

This book is about working with parents and families on behalf of their children with disabilities. However, before confronting that challenge, we must first identify "who" or "what" is the family. The United States Census Bureau (1999) defines a family as, "a group of two people or more related by birth, marriage, or adoption and residing together" (p. 3). When you reflect on the comments of the family members presented in the introduction to this chapter, this definition seems too simple, too easy. Pipher (1996), providing a softer description, suggests that families are collections of people who pool their resources, helping each other over the long haul, loving even when it requires sacrifices, remaining cohesive even when they disagree. Sargent (1983) provides a very open definition, suggesting that a family is a group of people with common ties of affection and responsibility who live in proximity of each other. The Vanier Institute of the Family (1994) suggests that families provide for physical maintenance and care of family members, add new members, socialize children, exercise social control over members, produce, consume, and distribute goods and services, and provide love and nurturance.

The word family is not descriptive of one reality, though media seems to depict a family as a white, middle class, father-at-work, mother and children-at-home, living in a single-family house in the suburbs, a minivan in the garage, and a dog in the yard (Gestwicki, 2000). About 3% of all families are indeed headed by a working husband with a dutiful wife and two children at home (Roberts, 1993). Answering the question "What is a family?" actually depends on who responds to the question. Diem (1997) suggests that:

- Those interested in the structure and function of patterns in society emphasize the reciprocal obligations of family and society;
- Those interested in institutions in society focus on the role of mother, father, and child to define family;
- Those interested in relationships define families in view of the voluntary assumption of family-related roles;
- Developmentalists focus on the growth and maturity and chronological age of the members to define family;
- Economists focus on production and consumption.

Whatever definition one chooses to use for family, the parents and family exert influence or exercise authority over important factors related to the education of their children. These factors are: (a) student absenteeism, (b) the variety of reading materials in the home, and (c) television viewing habits. These three factors explained nearly 90% of the differences in the eighth-grade mathematics test scores across 37 states and the District of Columbia on the National Assessment of Educational Progress (Barton & Coley, 1992). In "Profile of the American Eighth Grader," the Office of Educational Research and Improvement (1990) reported that approximately 65% of parents said they had not talked to school officials about the academic program being pursued by their eighth-grade child. Only half of the parents had attended a school meeting since the beginning of the school year, and 52% said they have never asked about or discussed their child's grades with a teacher or school administrator. Forty-two percent of the parents said they had not contacted the school about their child's academic performance, and only 29% had visited their child's classroom.

For professionals then, engaging parents in the education of their children is, and will continue to be, a significant challenge. Professionals sometimes make the mistake of suggesting that parent involvement in school activities is the same as parent involvement with their children. Parent involvement in their children's education goes far beyond engaging in classroom and teacher-directed activities. Epstein (1995) suggests that there are six areas of parental involvement in their children's education:

1. **Basic parenting or the basic obligations of families.**   Positive home conditions are the responsibility of families; schools can help families become informed and skillful at understanding their children and supporting learning at home.
2. **Basic obligations of schools.**   This includes communicating with families about school programs and children's progress, through notices, phone calls, visit, report cards, and conferences.
3. **Involvement at school.**   Parents assist teachers, children, or other school personnel.
4. **Involvement in learning activities at home.**   Teachers request and guide parents who monitor and assist their children at home.
5. **Involvement in decision-making, governance, and advocacy.**   Parents serve in participatory roles and become active in advocacy groups; schools help parents become leaders through training, involving them in meaningful decision-making, and providing information to advocacy groups.
6. **Collaboration and exchange with community organizations.**   Schools collaborate with agencies, businesses, cultural organizations, and other groups to share responsibility for the education of children.

From her review of the knowledge base of family engagement, Epstein (1995) drew several conclusions. She argues that families care about their children, want them to succeed, and want to work with schools and communities as partners in their children's education. In addition, she suggests that nearly all teachers and administrators would like to involve families, but many professionals just don't know how to build a positive and productive parent-professional program. She describes a "rhetoric rut" in which educators are stuck talking about the need for partnerships with parents and families, yet are unable to put those partnerships in place. Finally, Epstein argues that almost all students, at all levels, want their families to be more knowledgeable partners about schooling and are willing to help in communication between home and school.

All family engagement or involvement takes place within a social context. In order to discuss family engagement in depth, we must first analyze the role of context in child development.

THE ROLE OF CONTEXT IN CHILD DEVELOPMENT

Throughout this book we assume a social systems perspective. This perspective views each individual as developing in dynamic relation with, and as an inseparable part of, the many social contexts or settings in which the individual directly functions. It also recognizes the social systems which may affect those social contexts. Bronfenbrenner (1979) viewed this as an "ecology of human development." He proposed that the individual interacts within several nested environments. The relationships of these nested contexts are presented in Figure 1.1.

In the social systems perspective, development is a lifelong process of continual adaptation of the individual within the ever-changing environment. The social systems perspective goes beyond the child's relationship to his or her parents and home and considers larger, interpersonal, and community structures. Bronfenbrenner (1979) compares these relationships to a three-legged stool. If third parties outside the parent-child relationship, such as the extended family, community, and schools, are absent or if they play a disruptive rather than a supportive role, then the child's development may break down. Like a three-legged stool, it topples if one leg is broken or shorter than the others. Bronfenbrenner extended Piaget's (1990) "construction of reality," to include the child's conception of the environment and his or her relationship to it as well as the child's growing ability to discover, sustain, and change aspects of the environment. Bronfenbrenner, speaking of the ecology of human development, describes development as a progressive, mutual accommodation between an active, learning child and the changing settings in which he or she lives. These settings are nested, similar to the way Russian dolls fit within and are encased by one another. The settings include one-to-one relationships (the microsystem), the interrelations between settings (the mesosystem), the settings that don't involve the child as an active participant but which affect those settings such as the parent's workplace, siblings, friends, and neighborhood (the exosystem) and cultural and societal beliefs and values (the macrosystem). Bronfenbrenner argues that in the social systems perspective, human development is the process through which the child acquires a more extended, differentiated, and valid concept of the setting. He or she also becomes motivated and able to engage in activities that clarify, sustain, or restructure that setting. Development increases the child's power to make sense out of and manipulate the setting.

The Ontogenic System

Bronfenbrenner (1979), true to his belief in the ecology of human development, began his discussions with familial relationships. Belsky (1980), however, suggests that the individual has specific characteristics which have a significant impact on development. Belsky referred to this context as the ontogenic system or the individual. The system takes into account the individual differences that each person brings to his or her primary personal relationships and settings, including the family and the parenting role. Among the personal characteristics which impact the individual's function-

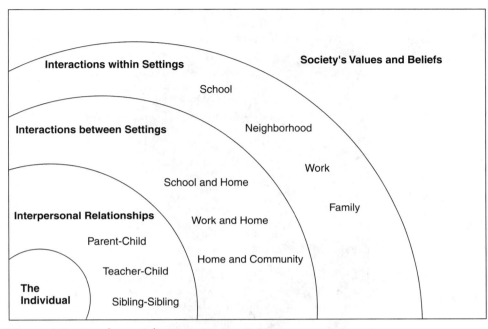

Figure 1.1 *Developmental contexts.*

ing are intelligence, personality, gender and other factors such as self-worth, religion, and the nature of the child's disability.

The Microsystem

The microsystem focuses on relationships within the family. It represents the complex interrelationships within the immediate family setting and includes mother-father, parent-child, and sibling-child relationships.

One of the most salient points Bronfenbrenner makes about the microsystem applies directly to parenting. Bronfenbrenner states that learning and development are facilitated when the child participates in more complex patterns of reciprocal activities with someone with whom the child has a strong and enduring emotional attachment. In addition, the balance of power between the child and the individual with whom they are attached must gradually shift the balance of power toward the child. In other words, in order for the child to have the greatest opportunities to learn and develop, "Somebody has got to be crazy about that kid!" (Bronfenbrenner, 1978, p. 774). In addition, the child must be encouraged and allowed over time to take control of his or her life.

Ideally the person to whom the child becomes attached is the parent. However, this essential person may be a foster parent, older sibling, relative, or other individual. With increasing frequency, the person that is crazy about the kid is a grandparent. Sandler, Warren, and Raver (1995) reported that even when they are not the primary

caregivers, grandparents frequently provide assistance through baby-sitting, buying clothing, and providing social support. When grandparents are the primary caregivers, a child's family experience may differ from that of children in other families. In their study of grandparents as primary caregivers, Bell and Smith (1996) found that 90% of the grandparents who served as guardians, had been appointed by the courts. The grandchildren for whom they cared dressed differently than their peers at times, and were dressed for warmth and growth. None of the grandparents had adequate financial resources to parent again; assistance was needed in accessing resources. Grandparents also talked about the need and desire to spend time with each other, rather than spending all of their time parenting the grandchild.

Parenting style influences the one-to-one relationships between parent and child. Baumrind (1991) suggests that parenting styles are normal variations on parents' attempts to control and socialize their children. Normal parenting revolves around the issue of control. Although parents vary in how they try to socialize their children, they assume that the primary role of all parents is to influence, teach, and control their children. Baumrind describes four parenting styles:

1. Indulgent, permissive, or nondirective parents are nontraditional and lenient. These parents may be further divided into two types: democratic parents, who are more conscientious, engaged, and committed to the child, and nondirective parents, who are more distant.

Table 1.1   Situation: An eight-year-old child wants to stay up past bedtime to watch a movie that may not be developmentally appropriate.

Parenting Styles	
Style	*Interaction*
Indulgent, permissive, democratic parents	"Okay, but remember, tomorrow morning you're going to be tired climbing on that school bus. And if it gets too violent, close your eyes or call me and I'll sit with you."
Indulgent, permissive, nondirective	"Okay, but remember your bedtime is really 9:00 p.m."
Nonauthoritarian-directive	"Come on, honey, you need to go to bed. It is your bedtime, and the movie is for mature audiences."
Authoritarian-directive	Turns off the television. "I said it's your bedtime. Go."
Authoritative	"It's hard to get up to get on the bus. When you don't get enough rest, it's also hard to pay attention at school. You need to go to bed so you'll be ready for school tomorrow."
Noninvolved	Does not interact with child. Allows the child to watch.

2. Authoritarian parents are demanding, directive, and expect their orders to be obeyed without explanation. Rules are clear and the home is structured. The two subtypes of this style include nonauthoritarian-directive parents, who are directive but not autocratic, and authoritarian-directive parents, who are intrusive and autocratic.

3. Authoritative parents are demanding and responsive. They are supportive rather than punitive, and are assertive in managing their children.

4. Noninvolved parents are neither responsive nor demanding. In extreme cases, they are rejecting and neglectful of the child.

A sample interaction between parent and child in each of these styles is presented in Table 1.1.

Children whose parents are authoritative rated themselves as more socially and instrumentally competent than other children. Children whose parents are uninvolved performed the most poorly in all areas. Children from indulgent homes are more likely to have problem behavior and behave less well in school, but they have higher self-esteem, better social skills, and lower levels of depression than their peers (Baumrind, 1991).

One-to-one relationships in the microsystem may vary when the child has a disability. For example, if a child is hospitalized for the first three months of life, the normal bonding between parent and child may be challenged. Early reciprocal activities between parent and child may not occur in the same way as for children who have had more typical experiences. Professionals should recognize that because of a parent's unique one-to-one relationship with their child, the parent knows the child best, and is the child's best advocate.

The Mesosystem

The mesosystem is concerned with the interrelationships of major settings in which an individual actually participates. These settings contain the individual at a specific point in his or her life. They include relationships between school and family and between family and social agencies.

In the mesosystem, Bronfenbrenner suggests that the developmental potential of new environments is enhanced if the child enters the setting in the company of one or more individuals with whom he or she has participated in prior settings. Parent involvement in schools enhances the developmental potential of the school for the child. Parent engagement in transitions from one setting to another further supports the child's development. This context includes, at the professional practice level, parent-teacher collaboration and the child's transition to new educational settings.

Epstein (1995) describes two different ways of viewing the spheres of influence in family, school, and community partnerships. She suggests that an external model of overlapping spheres of influence recognizes the three major contexts in which students learn and grow: the family, the school, and the community. These three components may either be drawn together or pushed apart depending on the quality of the partnership. An internal model, she suggests, shows where and how complex and essential interpersonal relationship are within the mesosystem. The social relationships within the mesosystem may be at the institutional level (for example, when a school invites all families to an event or sends the same communication to all families) or an individual level (for example, when a parent and a teacher meet in a conference or talk on the phone).

Epstein argues that one of the positive aspects of recognizing such interactions in the mesosystem would be more family-like schools. These schools would recognize each child's individuality and make each child feel special and included. Family-like schools welcome all families, not only those who are easy to reach. In partnership with the family-like school, the families become more "school-like", recognizing that their child is also a student.

Roberts, Behl, and Akers (1996), reporting the results of their national survey, described a variety of successful strategies to facilitate integrated services at the community level. However, they also reported limited coordination among hospitals, medical specialists, and mental health services. The survey identified a lack of funding for lower caseloads and compensations for services' coordination efforts as the greatest barriers to system integration efforts.

The Exosystem

The exosystem provides the context in which events occur that affect the individual's immediate environment—that is, the individual's microsystem (Bronfenbrenner, 1979). Settings within the exosystem may include work, church, neighborhood, school, and community. Significant factors within this context may include professionals, social interactions, and external social supports.

Bronfenbrenner suggests that direct and indirect links to power settings related to allocation of resources and decision-making enhance the developmental potential of settings. Parents who are active in the parent-teacher organization, for example, may enhance the developmental potential of school for their child because of their link to power settings. Bronfenbrenner also suggests that the developmental potential of a setting decreases as the number of connections to the power setting decreases. Lack of parent involvement may have a negative rather than a neutral effect on the child's development.

Epstein's (1995) review of partnerships in practice provides additional insight into the exosystem. It is suggested that, in general, affluent communities currently have more positive family involvement, unless the schools and teachers in economically distressed communities have been involved in conscious efforts to build positive partnerships with their students' families. Schools in more economically depressed communities make more contacts with families about problems and difficulties children are having than do schools in affluent communities. On average, single parents, parents who are employed outside the home, and parents who live far from the school are less involved unless explicit efforts are made to connect with them.

Child care is one aspect of the exosystem that has a great impact on families with children with disabilities as well as children who are developing typically. Booth and Kelly (1999) studied the impact of disability and risk-related characteristics of infants on their mothers' employment and child care characteristics and decisions. Mothers' employment plans and child care decisions were affected by their children's special needs, and were related consistently to the child's diagnosis. For example, infants diagnosed with Down syndrome were more likely to be in child care centers and to receive lower quality care than children whose developmental delays were of unknown origin. In families of infants who required the most intensive care, it was virtually impossible for mothers to return to the level of employment they needed or desired due to limited choices with regard to the availability and quality of child care. Herman and Thompson (1995) found that the need for child care was a significant issue. Though parents saw their basic resources for daily life as adequate, they reported that time, discretionary money, and child care resources were not adequate for caring for a child with a developmental disability. The need for flexible support services for families emerged.

The Macrosystem

The macrosystem is concerned with the cultural beliefs, values, and attitudes surrounding family life and disability in society. Bronfenbrenner (1979) defines this context as the generalized patterns, overarching ideology, and organization of the social institutions common to a particular culture or subculture. Rather than referring to specific ecological contexts, the macrosystem refers to the general patterns of values and beliefs that exist in any culture or subculture. These patterns influence the structure and activities occurring in that culture or subculture. The macrosystem includes the institutional patterns in which the microsystem, mesosystem, and exosystem are imbedded.

Development, Bronfenbrenner suggests, is related to the extent to which opportunities in various settings are open or closed to the developing person. For example, if a school does not provide inclusive settings, then the child with a disability attending that school has limited opportunities. The school or district's belief that children with disabilities are best served by special educators limits the child's opportunities.

Elkind (1995) argues that schools, which serve as mirrors of society and the family, have undergone a major transformation in response to changes in society. He contends that the shift from modernism (a belief in progress, predictability, and universal laws) to postmodernism has significantly impacted the modern school. Elkind suggests that, whereas modernity celebrated reason and paid homage to the ideals of individual freedom and liberty, postmodernism venerates language and honors human diversity as much as human individuality. Themes of difference, particularity, and uniqueness are increasingly transforming society and schools. In the postmodern family, society recognizes shared parenting, urbanity, and autonomy as a learned process. Children are viewed as competent, rather than as property or trophies.

Transactional Development

Another key aspect of the social systems perspective is transactional development. Sameroff (1975) suggests that contact between individuals and the environment is a transaction in which each is altered by the other. In parent involvement, for example, the behavior of the teacher toward parents influences the parents' reaction to the teacher, which then evokes a response on the part of the teacher. Interactions among parent, students, teacher, and school are reciprocal.

Keough (1999), in a discussion of families of children with learning disabilities, acknowledges the powerful contributions made by families to both their children's development and problems. Parent-child transactions contribute substantially to children's development and learning. These interactions are imbedded in the context of daily living—in their routines. Families construct these routines to meet their own individual needs. Living with a child with learning disabilities or other special needs affects a family's daily routine and specific adaptations and accommodations emerge in response to them.

According to Johnson, Bullock, and Ashton-Schaefer (1997), the perspective of transactional development emphasizes a personal strengths model. The personal strengths model is based on the premise that all individuals have the capacity to learn, grow, act, and manage their own lives. This model promotes the positive power of each child and family, focusing on strengths that far outweigh weaknesses or disabilities. As the teacher works with the family, he or she is a facilitator or collaborator who focuses on strengths, supports decision-making, and helps parents access and take advantage of environmental/community resources. Using leisure as a context, Johnson et al. suggest that teachers:

- Individualize assessment to determine the student's cognitive, emotional, motivational, and coping skills and work to uncover unique qualities and strengths;
- Assess students' abilities and strengths with normative activities in natural contexts;
- Identify and use social and cultural norms to guide the plan of action;
- Evaluate and use community supports and opportunities;
- Further the goal of expanding the students' community membership and acceptance.

The personal strength model is applicable to all facets of child and family life.

ASSUMPTIONS REGARDING THE SOCIAL SYSTEMS PERSPECTIVE AND FAMILY ENGAGEMENT

As stated in the introduction to this chapter, this text is grounded in the social systems perspective. As such, we assume that in order to change an individual's behavior, one must change the environment. In other words, if one wants parents to be engaged in their child's education, then the school must change in ways that encourage parent involvement. For example, parent-teacher conferences may need to be held during the evening. Letters may need to be sent home in a language other than English, that is, the primary language of the parents and family. Parents may be invited to a "pizza-with-your-child" evening or to work as, or with, an "artist in residence" in the school or classroom.

Even the school or district settings in which the parents may not directly engage may need to be changed. The school district may need to implement an "open access" policy, for example. Such a policy would open the school to parents and families, as well as children.

The social systems perspective also assumes that, because of the nature of the nested context in which the individual develops, cause and effect relationships between events and behavior can rarely be identified. The complexity and multiple variables that impact the individual's behavior are recognized. The social systems perspective assumes that there is no "cookbook" with "recipes" for parent engagement. Parent engagement activities must involve a careful study of the family's situation. From the social systems perspective, the response to the question "How do you engage parents in their child's education?" is "It all depends." This text focuses on the *how* of the "it all depends" of parent engagement.

Throughout this text, we have grounded our discussion in research. Readers are cautioned, however, that there are significant challenges in research on parent involvement. While most practitioners, school districts, and researchers support increased parent involvement, there is little agreement about what constitutes effective involvement (Baker & Soden, 1998). Baker and Soden suggest that there are methodological issues, inconsistent definitions of parent involvement, and difficulties in isolating the effects of parent involvement. Yet practical wisdom, theory, and related areas of research (such as research on the influence of the home literacy environment on language development) suggest that parent involvement is vital, even though research evidence is scant and conflictive.

We hope you, the student-reader, will bear with the complexity of the social systems perspective and the many ways it informs parent engagement. Throughout this book we celebrate the incredible diversity among children and their families and the uniqueness of each individual. We welcome you to study the complexity of parent engagement in the education of a child with a disability.

SUMMARY

- Engaging parents in the education of their children with disabilities is a significant challenge.
- Parent involvement takes several forms, from providing for their child's basic needs to collaborating with community agencies.
- In the social systems perspective, development is a lifelong process of continual adaptation of the individual within the environment. Development occurs within a series of nested contexts.
- In any environment, interactions between individuals are a transition in which each is altered by the other.
- The social systems perspective recognizes the complexity and multiple variables that impact individuals' behavior.

REFERENCES

Baker, A. J. L., & Soden, L. M. (1998). *The challenges of parent involvement research*. ERIC/CUE Digest No. 135. New York: ERIC Clearinghouse on Urban Education.

Barton, P. E., & Coley, R. J. (1992). *America's smallest school: The family*. Princeton, NJ: Educational Testing Services.

Baumrind, D. (1991). The influence of parenting style on adolescent competence and substance use. *Journal of Early Adolescence, 11*(1), 56–95.

Bell, M. L., & Smith, B. R. (1996). Grandparents as primary caregivers: Lessons in love. *Teaching Exceptional Children, 28*(2), 18–19.

Belsky, J. (1980). Child maltreatment: An ecological integration. *American Psychologist, 35*(4), 320–35.

Booth, C. L., & Kelly, J. F. (1999). Childcare and employment in relation to infants' disabilities and risk factors. *American Journal on Mental Retardation, 104*(2), 117–130.

Bronfenbrenner, U. (1978)."Who needs parent education?" *Teachers College Record*, 79 773–774.

Bronfenbrenner, U. (1979). *The ecology of human development*. Cambridge, MA: Harvard University Press.

Diem, G. N. (1997). The definition of family in a free society. *Formulations*, 4(3), 7–9.

Elkind, D. (1995). School and family in the postmodern world. *Phi Delta Kappan*, 77(1), 8–14.

Epstein, J. L. (1995). School/family/community partnerships: Caring for the children we share. *Phi Delta Kappan*, 76(2), 701–712.

Gestwicki, C. (2000). *Home, school, and community relations* (4th ed). Albany, NY: Delmar.

Herman, S. E., & Thompson, L. (1995). Families' perceptions of their resources for caring for children with developmental disabilities. *Mental Retardation*, 33(2), 73–83.

Johnson, D. E., Bullock, C. C., & Ashton-Schaeffer, C. (1997). Families and leisure: A context for learning. *Teaching Exceptional Children*, 30(2), 30–34.

Keough, B. K. (1999). Revisiting families of children with learning disabilities. *Learning Disabilities: A Multidisciplinary Journal*, 9(3), 81–85.

Office of Educational Research and Improvement. (1990). A *profile of the American eighth grader*. Washington, DC: U. S. Department of Education, OERI.

Piaget, J. (1990). A *child's conception of the world*. New York: Littlefield Adams.

Pipher, M. (1996). *The shelter of each other: Rebuilding our families*. New York: G. P. Putnam's Sons.

Roberts, R. N. (1993). Early education as community intervention. *American Journal of Community Psychology*, 21, 521–535.

Roberts, R. N., Behl, D.D., & Akers, A. (1996). Family-level service coordination within home visiting programs. *Topics in Early Childhood Special Education*, 16(3), 302–321.

Sameroff, A. (1975). Transactional models in early social relations. *Human Development*, 18, 65–79.

Sandler, A. G., Warren, S. H. & Raver, S. A. (1995). Grandparents as a source of support for parents of children with disabilities: A brief report. *Mental Retardation*, 33(4), 248–250.

Sargent A. J., III, (1983). The family: A pediatric assessment. *The Journal of Pediatrics*, 102(6), 973–987.

U. S. Census Bureau. (1999). *Current population survey (CPS)—definitions and explanations*. Washington, DC: Author.

The Vanier Institute of the Family. (1994). *Profiling Canada's families*. Ottawa, Ontario: Author.

CHAPTER 2

Issues of Diversity

I get so tired of the excuses. I get so tired of hearing statements like, "Black males often begin to have trouble about fourth grade" and comments like "Is his father involved?" Of course his father is involved. We are married professionals. We work with him every night. He is fine at home. Don't talk to me about "children like him" because you all are frustrated as teachers.

The social systems perspective recognizes and celebrates the role of diversity in children's development. Yet, dealing with the incredible diversity which exists in any school is a challenge. Thorp (1997) suggests that diversity is especially challenging for special educators, who are typically from the majority culture and poorly prepared to deal with diverse student populations. An additional challenge emerges because families may have already had a negative experience with the school and educators—including the overrepresentation of children from minority groups in special education and stereotypes about family participation—which make them hesitant participants. Thorp recommends that teachers explore their own cultural experiences, values, and attitudes. Professionals should learn as much as possible from the families with whom they are working. Classrooms and curricula should be evaluated through a cultural and linguistic lens. The whole educational system should be examined for opportunities for family involvement.

Jordan, Rayes-Blanes, Peel, Peel, and Lane (1998) concur, arguing that the rich diversity of today's special education services challenges traditional patterns of communications between schools and families. Diversity demands communication patterns sensitive to all parents, particularly to those responsive to cultural and ability differences. Educators are challenged to become personally aware and use culturally responsive interaction practices. Diversity goes beyond culture and ethnicity. Individuals' interactions vary by gender and age. Individuals living in poverty, or who are homeless have a unique experience. In this chapter we recognize diversity beyond race or cultures.

Learning Objectives

After completing this chapter, you will be able to discuss these topics:

1. Issues of gender and age related to families with members with disabilities
2. Issues of ethnicity, culture, and language related to families with members with disabilities
3. Issues of poverty related to families with members with disabilities
4. Issues of supporting parent involvement

GENDER AND AGE

Gender

Gender affects all interactions. In studies of both gender and race, it was found that students the most likely to receive teacher attention were white males; second most likely were minority males; third most likely were white females; and the least likely to receive teacher attention were minority females (Sadker, 1994). Boys did not only receive more attention, but were more likely to be praised or to receive constructive criticism. Girls, on the other hand, received bland and imprecise feedback such as "O.K."

Girls begin school outperforming boys on almost every measure. By middle school, girls' test scores begin to decline and are eventually overtaken by boys' scores. While girls are behind boys on standardized tests that measure achievement, females are ahead when it comes to report card grades. Boys are raised to be active, aggressive and independent and enter schools that want them to be quiet, passive, and conforming. When teachers are asked to remember their most outstanding students, boys' names dominate the list (Sadker, 1994).

Mann (1994) reports sharp and important differences in the physical play of fathers and sons versus fathers and daughters. Fathers typically come home from work and scoop up their sons, toss them in the air, and roughhouse. They play with little girls by gathering them in their laps. Boy babies and girl babies are even held differently: boys are often pointed outward and girls inward. Little girls are prompted to smile and cuddle, whereas little boys are prompted to be tough and adventurous. As boys' lives expand, girls' lives contract.

Gender biases have been observed as early as preschool. Little girls are clustered close to the teacher during group activities while boys sit or stand in the back of the circle or cluster. Girls play dress up and cook; boys play at building or constructing. In elementary schools, boys are eight times more likely than girls to call out and demand attention. Boys gain practice interrupting others while girls practice waiting to speak. Throughout elementary school, boys' achievement-oriented toys become increasingly more complicated. Boys build with sophistication and skill—constructing models, rockets, and playing team sports. As early as kindergarten, girls who are asked to draw a picture of a scientist sketch a picture of a white male. Mann suggests that educational strategies that take into account girls' core values of sharing and cooperation, as well as their need for close relationships, will produce a more supportive school environment. Schools, however, continue to emphasize the self-reliance associated with the white male culture.

Girls in the 10th and 11th grades are quite similar to boys in plans to work outside the home and in the anticipated importance of the careers. Boys exceed girls in their aspirations and plans for future educational and occupational attainments. Boys are clearly advantaged with respect to their feelings of efficacy regarding future work and are less likely to plan to marry and have children. Boys from single-parent households more frequently plan to remain single than boys from two-parent families (Dennehy & Mortimer, 1993).

Fathers, Mothers, and Child Care.   Some research has been conducted on the differences in child care responsibilities and stress between fathers and mothers. Roach, Orsmond, and Barratt (1999) reported in their study of children with Down syndrome that parents perceived more caregiving difficulties, more stress related to the child's distractibility, demandingness, and unacceptability, and more parent-related stress than parents of typically developing children. Mothers who reported more responsibility for childcare perceived more difficulties with health, role restrictions, and support from their spouses. Fathers who reported more responsibility for childcare perceived fewer difficulties with attachment and parental competence. Fathers who share day-to-day aspects of childcare may not only help the mothers' childcare burden, but may also experience a greater feeling of competence in their parenting roles and fewer difficulties in attachment with their children. In another study, Willoughby and Glidden (1995) found that greater father participation in child care was related to higher marital satisfaction for both parents of children with disabilities; high family income was related to higher marital satisfaction for fathers only.

In a study of families with older children, Dyson (1997) compared the stress, family functioning, and social support of parents of school-aged children with and without identified disabilities. In this study, when wives perceived greater family emphasis on personal growth of family members, the fathers had lower stress. As mothers experienced and perceived greater social support, fathers reported less stress. When husbands reported more social support, a positive family relationship, and greater family emphasis on personal growth, mothers indicated lower stress levels.

Fathers are critical members of the family system. Flynn and Wilson (1998) suggest that, though fathers influence their children and families in unique ways, the priorities and concerns of mothers are typically the focus of researchers or educators. Even the initial response of fathers to the diagnosis of disability is different. Fathers tend to set aside the emotional response and try to plan while mothers call friends and relatives and share feelings. These differences persist throughout the child's life—with fathers more concerned about the future, and mothers concerned about managing day-to-day. Fathers who participate in domestic routines, leisure activities, or learning and enrichment experiences may have more positive perceptions of their children with disabilities.

Teenage fathers have an even more challenging role than older fathers. These young fathers may initially react to parenthood with denial, fear, and a desire to escape. Teenage fathers face family rejection and potential barriers to contact with the child and mother. They might not be able to contribute financially and, in addition, an inability to envision future achievements makes it difficult for them to function effectively as a father. Teenage fathers may also believe that they are simply unwelcome and inadequate as parents.

Fathers give financial as well as emotional support. Assumptions are sometimes made that some men refuse to support children even when they have the means to do so. Addressing these assumptions, Stier and Tienda (1993) studied fathers in Chicago's inner city. They found that fathering children out of wedlock was particularly common among Chicago's inner-city African American men, where nearly three out of four men acknowledged an out-of-wedlock child. There were great differences among the number of fathers in other ethnic groups as well—about 50% Puerto Rican men, 8% of white men, and 25% of Mexican men acknowledged having children outside of marriage. Half of all African American and one third of all Puerto Rican fathers indicated they had dependent children who did not live with them. Stier and Tienda reported low marriage rates among African American men, which they attributed to their weak labor market standing, high rates of joblessness, and low earnings. The nature and level of support fathers gave to children with whom they did not live varied greatly in regularity and amount provided. Fathers most often contributed in-kind supports such as toys and clothes. Economic support of any kind was more frequent than direct interaction with children, though African American fathers visited their children more than any other ethnic group. Fathers who were currently employed were almost three times more likely to support their children than those who were not working. In addition, high school graduates were 20% more likely to support their children than those who did not complete high school. Stier and Tienda concluded that fathers are not marginal to the family, and that noncustodial fathers, on the whole, make great efforts to maintain ties with their children.

The roles fathers serve in children's lives has also been studied. Cohen (1993) suggests that traditionally there has been overwhelming acceptance of the male economic provider role as the appropriate male model. Cohen reports, however, that becoming a father often has a dramatic impact on the father's life. Men reported that they found themselves taking more precautions about their wives and going out of their way to be more conscientious. The men Cohen studied had concerns about being good fathers and were more anxious about being good fathers than providing financially. Men reported that their reaction to becoming fathers included having new priorities, less freedom, and less free time. Fathers reported that their relationships with their peers were restricted, and their relationships with their wives diminished. When asked about their role in the family, fathers most commonly responded that they were role models or teachers in socialization and nurturance of their children rather than financial providers. Though the fathers in the sample displayed more involvement than anticipated, they remained the secondary caregiver. Their involvement in the family was controlled by (a) their commitment to fathering, (b) their wives' need for respite, and (c) their work schedules. Men were consciously trying not to replicate with their children the kind of relationships they had with their fathers. They wished to be more conscientious, nurturing fathers.

ACTION STEPS 2.1: *WORKING WITH FATHERS*

Involving fathers in their children's education may require specific strategies. In working with fathers it is important to:

- Critically examine your personal values and viewpoints related to biases about fathers. Do you see them as active partners in their child's education? In their child's care?
- Reflect on your personal perspectives about the roles and expectations of fathers. Do you expect them to come to conferences? Do you ask for them when you make a call to the home?
- Identify and acknowledge your level of comfort with fathers. How do you feel when a father enters your room? Volunteers to help on a field trip? Asks to volunteer? Approaches you about their child?
- Recognize any personal cultural, racial, ethnic, or linguistic biases toward fathers. Are you uncomfortable talking with fathers? Do you have preconceived notions about fathers from specific cultural, racial, linguistic, or ethnic groups?
- Reflect on the input sought from fathers as compared to mothers. Do you specifically approach fathers about their opinions?
- Review how many times fathers were involved in the past month's family contacts. Do you approach fathers as often as mothers?
- Insure that materials distributed by the program are as likely to engage men as women. Are your materials generic or do they appeal to one gender over another? Do you send information to both parents? Do you call for fathers as often as mothers?

Source: Flynn & Wilson, 1998; Freif, DeMaris, & Hood, 1993.

Working with Fathers.   It is essential that educators insure that parents understand the importance of fathers' interaction with their children with disabilities and the value of gender-specific approaches to play and interaction (Flynn & Wilson, 1998). In addition, professionals should recognize that fathers may experience discomfort when talking with women about their children. Action Steps 2.1 presents ways of working with fathers.

Single fathers have some unique parenting challenges. In a study by Freif, DeMaris, and Hood (1993), most of the single fathers had difficulty balancing the demands of work and parenthood. The fathers who were successful found cooperative work situations and support networks.

Older Parents.   The general population is waiting longer to marry and have children. As a result, educators are more frequently working with older parents. Smith, Tobin, and Fullmer (1995) interviewed mothers, ages 58 to 96, who cared for their adult children with mental retardation at home. They found that the mothers were likely to be engaged in permanency planning, appointing guardians, and making financial arrangements if they already used social agencies or services. These older mothers did not cope by avoidance, but they did see themselves being affected by age-related change. There were many other indirect influences on the older mothers' making plans for their adult children. Mothers were more likely to make plans if they perceived a need for services. The extent of care giving tasks, the offspring's disability, and the mother's disability also influenced the mothers' planning.

In the United States Census (2001), 2,350,477 grandparents were responsible for their grandchildren of less than 18 years of age. Of these, 839,000 had been responsible for more than five years (U.S. Census Bureau, 2001). Grandparents are more frequently parenting their grandchildren with disabilities. The courts often appoint grandparents legal guardians of their grandchildren (Bell & Smith, 1996). The experiences of children raised by their grandparent differ from the experiences of those raised by their biological parents. Among the children in the sample, Bell and Smith found that the children dressed differently from other children. Grandparents reported financial needs related to caring for their grandchildren. They required assistance to complete the application for "provisional foster homes." Grandparents also reported a desire to spend some time with each other without their grandchildren.

Alternative Families.   The term "alternative families" is often used to describe gay and lesbian households in which both "parents" are of the same gender. There are few bodies of research that can inform teachers related to the education of children from alternative families. Casper and Schultz (1999) reported that teachers may view homosexuality as a threat to the inherent goals of early childhood education, even though teachers of young children provide experiences that may contribute to how children understand families. Wellhousen (1993) reported that teachers often use biased language in their classroom that fails to reflect the diverse and changing nature of today's family structure, and may portray disapproval of alternative families. There is, however, no evidence that the development of children of gay and lesbian parents is compromised in any way relative to the development of children of heterosexual parents (Patterson, 1992).

ETHNICITY, CULTURE, AND LANGUAGE

Though it is often recommended that teachers know characteristics unique to each family's culture, Bailey, Skinner, Correa, Arcia, Reyes-Blanes, Rodriguez, Vasquez-Montilla, and Skinner (1999) caution teachers about making generalizations about a particular group that may not pertain to every individual in that group. In their study of Latino parents, for example, they found that the family heritage varied widely in terms of awareness, use, and satisfaction with services. In addition, family characteristics commonly believed to influence these outcomes generally did not appear to be related.

One challenge to celebrating diversity in school is the availability of the anti-bias curriculum. Educators often use a "tourist" curriculum in which diversity is trivialized by organizing activities around holidays or foods, having one black doll, or having a single book about a cultural group. Derman-Sparks, and the A.B.C. Task Force (1989) suggest that teachers avoid disconnecting cultural diversity from daily classroom life through, for example, reading books about children of color only on special occasions or teaching a unit on a culture and never discussing that culture again. Teachers sometimes fall into a trap of misrepresenting American ethnic groups. Teachers

sometimes present pictures and books about Mexico to teach about Mexican Americans, and Japan to teach about Japanese Americans, though each group's experiences in their country of origin and the United States are vastly different.

Harry, Rueda, and Kalyanpur (1999) urge teachers to recognize their own cultural values as they apply the normalization principle to families from various ethnic, cultural, and linguistic groups. Teachers need to assume a posture of "cultural reciprocity" (p. 125) which examines the cultural beliefs from which their service ideas arise and looks for the cultural grounding of those beliefs rather than assuming that they represent universal values. Self-awareness can help teachers identify potent and pervasive biases which may affect interactions between teachers and families (Hyun & Fowler, 1995).

When working with families from various cultural, ethnic or linguistic groups, professionals should identify parents' perceptions of the special education process. Linan-Thompson and Jean (1997) suggest that there may be differences between professionals' and family members' understanding of disability, the process of dealing with disability, and methods of communication. To facilitate the families' understanding, educators must listen with care to family members and explain the results of the evaluation to them in comprehensible language. Families who are unsure of the impact of the disability on the child's ability to learn may seek other solutions or explanations for the child's difficulty in school. In terms of assessment, Linan-Thompson and Jean suggest that the assessment of all students should include the use of informal as well as formal tools. In order to address variations in methods of communications, the teacher should identify the family's preferred method of communication and may need to use phone calls, informal meetings, and personal notes in addition to the forms and meetings required by the school district.

Educators must avoid making assumptions about who wishes to be involved in what way. In their sample of African American and Latino families, Chavkin and Williams (1993) found that parents said they wanted to be more involved with their children's education, help with homework, and have more influence in the school. Ninety-seven percent said they cooperate with their children's teachers. These parents showed strong interest in attending school performances, helping children with homework, and assisting in school events (Chavkin & Williams, 1993).

Hourcade, Parette, and Huer (1997) use issues related to assistive technology as an example of the role culture plays in a family's participation in their child's education. If the family is not involved in the selection and implementation of selective devices, the devices are often "abandoned" by the family. In order to address this concern, there has been a recent emphasis on the use of informal assessment, which requires that the special educator have a high level of sensitivity toward the family. Specifically, they recommend that professionals:

- Understand family needs for information about assistive technology devices;
- Recognize the impact on, and changes in, family routines that assistive technology may cause;
- Consider the extent to which family members desire themselves or their children be accepted in community settings.

Professionals should understand that families and teachers may have very different perceptions and values related to technology based, in part, on their differing cultural backgrounds.

Though we reiterate that there is great variability among individuals within ethnic, cultural, or linguistic groups, some general information about specific groups may be helpful as teachers engage families in the education of their children. Guild (1994), for example, cautions educators that "Generalizations about a group of people have often led to naive inferences about individuals within that group" (p. 16). The following information related to the four largest cultural groups with whom educators interact in the schools should be considered in view of Guild's caution. In addition, we will discuss the unique experience of multiracial and immigrant families.

African American Families

Harry (1992) argues that two traditions have combined to challenge the participation of African American parents in the education of their children. First, there is a deficit view of African American families that combines with the deficit view of children's learning on which special education is based. These traditions diminish the roles of African American parents as full participants in decision-making. Harry contends that we must develop roles for African American parents beyond that of "consent-giver."

African American parents can be engaged in assessment—beyond simply giving the family's and child's social history—by including them as active members of the assessment team. Parents can present reports and provide information that becomes part of the official record. Parents may also become policymakers with membership on active parent advisory committees and become advocates and peer supports for other families.

Differences between majority culture and African American families may be noted in their approach to discipline. Nweke (1994) reported that, though African American parents and Euro-American parents punish the same misbehavior of their children, the time and place of the punishment differs. African American families may address behaviors in public that would be addressed in private among Euro-American families. In African American families, the mother is most often responsible for discipline (87.54% of the sample). In Euro-American families, only about half of the mothers were responsible for discipline.

In their study of culturally relevant factors, Boykin and Bailey (2000) used multiple measures to investigate the home socialization experiences, values, practices, and preferences of African American students from low-income backgrounds. Their findings suggest that the children reported a prevalence of communal, movement-expressive attitudes and practices that are cultivated by family members in the home environments. "Verve," described as intensity and liveliness, variability, and density of stimulation, was also evident in attitude and practice. The children endorsed learning orientations, and preferred classroom practices and learning contexts consistent with communalism, movement-expressiveness, and verve. Boykin and Bailey found a positive relationship between the children's perceptions of these Afro-cultural themes cultivated in the home environment and their preferences for practices in the classroom.

More than 70% of the children in this study preferred activities that:

- Promoted the communal aspects of learning. These include sharing knowledge and materials, and working and studying together in groups so that all members can achieve;
- Allowed for music and movement opportunity and expressiveness;
- Employed a variety of vervistic, high-energy pedagogical and learning strategies.

Because these themes are promoted and preferred in the home, it would seem appropriate that parent and family engagement activities would also promote communal aspects of learning, expressiveness, and verve.

Ellison, Boykin, Towns, and Stokes (2000) suggest that these cultural factors are often in opposition to mainstream culture. Whereas these children and their families are oriented toward movement, verve, and communalism, mainstream culture accentuates individualism, competition, and bureaucratic orientation. Individual aspects of culture—such as the personality and demeanor of the teacher, an emphasis on time and time management, and a "cult of quietness"—conflict with the children's cultural preferences. Ellison et al. found verve to be the least expressed of the cultural themes in the classroom.

Hispanic American Families

In the home, Latino children are usually nurtured by a large number of relatives. Generally, these family members do not extend their interaction to the school. Teachers may have misread the reserve and nonconfrontational manner of Latino parents to mean they are not interested in their children's education, leading to a cycle of mutual distrust (Inger, 1992).

Bailey et al. (1999) explored the needs and supports of Latino parents related to raising a child with a disability. These parents reported more support from family and formal sources than from friends and informal sources. English language proficiency accounted for differences among families in terms of the support they needed to navigate the social services system. There was a great deal of individual variation in the supports families reported needing to assist their child with a disability.

The role of the school and education in a child's socialization is more family-centered among Latinos. Many Latino families are reluctant to send their children to preschool (Lewis, 1993). They do not accept that their children will benefit from being in an early childhood education program. At home, Hispanic children are usually nurtured with great care by large numbers of relatives, and parents are hesitant to extend the care giving role to their children's schools (Nicolau & Ramos, 1990). Many low-income Latino parents may view the United States school systems as "a bureaucracy governed by educated non-Hispanic whom they have no right to question" (p. 13).

Zetlin, Padron, and Wilson (1996) studied five Latino families' experience with the special education system. All parents indicated they were committed and involved, but their responses varied in terms of how well they understood the Individualized Education Program (IEP) process, their awareness of rights and options, and their willingness to challenge the district's decisions concerning the child. Zetlin et al. reported that parents felt that the district was in compliance when notifying families in Spanish and providing an interpreter. The school district was not always in compliance with regard to the availability of the IEP in Spanish, nor were parents fully informed of their child's level of functioning and program options. All mothers were concerned about their child's education and worried about teachers' indifference, Spanish/English confusion, their child's potential, and the best placement.

In another study in which researchers interviewed Latino parents, Bailey et al. (1999) found that mothers were more aware of, and received more, services than fathers. However, family and child variables bore little relationship to awareness, use, and satisfaction of families with services. Program variables were more likely to be determinants of service use and satisfaction than family factors alone. In other words, the nature of relationships with the professionals providing services had a greater impact on family satisfaction than family or service characteristics.

In a study of Puerto Rican families caring for an adult with mental retardation, Magana (1999) reported evidence of "familism"—a cultural value including interdependence among nuclear and extended family members for support, loyalty, and solidarity—for mothers with adult children with mental retardation living at home. Better maternal well-being was related to larger social support networks, greater satisfaction with social support, and more minor children living in the household. Unfortunately, these mothers faced socioeconomic challenges and were in poor health, in addition to parenting an adult with mental retardation. Skinner, Bailey, Correa, and Rodriguez (1999) using narratives, found that in the Latino families with whom they were working, having a child with a disability raises key questions that are revisited as the child develops. These questions include (a) how to teach the child to maximize his or her development; (b) how to assure that the child receives needed services; and (c) how to cope with the demands and expectations of having a child with a disability. Other questions were more existential in nature—reflecting issues such as making sense out of the disability and why it happened to the child, what the disability meant for the parent and his or her life, and the meaning of disability in the larger world.

Bailey et al. (1999) found that Latino families may be somewhat less satisfied with early intervention and preschool services than their majority culture peers. With Latino families, there can be a very real language and communication barrier. Practitioners are cautioned that they should not assume that the traditional characteristics described in the literature are applicable to today's families.

Asian American Families

Asian Americans are an incredibly heterogenous group. There are, however, three general ethnic groups within the Asian community: (a) Pacific Islanders—mostly Hawaiians, Samoans, and Guamanians; (b) southeast Asians—Indochinese from Vietnam, Thailand, Cambodia, Laos, Burma, and the Phillippines; and (c) east Asians—including the Chinese, Japanese, and Korean. These cultures vary within, as well as among, each other. For example, some Vietnamese may be literate and find work with ease in contrast to the Hmong who have no written language (Schwartz, 1994).

In Asian culture, parents view teachers as professionals with authority over the child's schooling; parents are not to interfere. Teachers who ask for help may be viewed as incompetent. In addition, Asian families may have difficulty accepting the existence of learning disabilities and depression because psychological distress is an indication of organic disorders and shameful to the family and the individual. In terms of interaction, Asian culture generally perceives time as a process that lets things happen simultaneously whereas in western culture, time is measured. Communication in Asian culture is generally high context, and does not require verbal expression. It relies instead on shared assumptions, nonverbal signals, and the situation. Asian parents may seem polite to the point of appearing submissive (Schwartz, 1994).

Asian parents differ from Anglo-European families in their adaptation to the birth or diagnosis of children with disabilities. In their study, Raghavan, Weisner, and Patel (1999) found that South Asian families often lacked the family support that was available to Anglo-European families. Gender roles were clearly demarcated, with women providing the care for the child. Families reported a challenge to their cultural identity and feelings of fear. They referred to the United States as the "golden prison."

Many Asian families have the additional challenge of being refugees from their native country. In a study of Cambodian refugee parents, Scheinfeld (1998) found reports of widespread fatigue and depression from relentless economic pressures and cultural alienation. Under stressful conditions, the Cambodian practice of physical punishment sometimes became extended and exaggerated. In addition, intergenerational tensions emerged because of a parental culture that emphasized absolute parental knowledge and child deference to that knowledge, as well as traditional standards for child behavior. In addition, there is a relative lack of information on the part of many Cambodian parents about American culture and society. The supports on which families traditionally relied (for example the community, the extended family, and the Buddhist temple), are not available in American culture.

Native American Families

Native American families have experienced significant challenges to their identity, including removal from the family for boarding schools and foster placements, high school dropout rates (60% among children attending boarding school), overidentification as special education students, a high incidence of alcohol and drug abuse, high suicide rates, chronic health problems, and low income (Grimm, 1992).

Native American families may experience a sense of alienation (LaFramboise & Low, 1989). Spindler and Spindler (1994) describe several general responses among the Native American population to this sense of alienation. These responses include reaffirmation, withdrawal, constructive marginality, biculturalism, and assimilation. Among the Menominee people, reaffirmation was represented by a group of cultural "survivors" from the past and a larger number of younger people who had interacted with Euro-American culture in school and the workplace. This group was trying to recreate and sustain a recognizable Native American way of life. Another group of Native Americans, those who withdrew, were so torn by cultural conflict they could identify with neither traditional Native American nor Euro-American cultural symbols or groups. This group withdrew into either self-destruction through substance abuse or apathy.

Some Native Americans exhibited "constructive marginality," described by Spindler and Spindler (1994) as the forming of a personal culture that was instrumentally productive but composed of several different segments, some of which were Euro-American. Among those who assimilated into the Euro-American culture, two groups emerged: (a) those who were more "respectable" than most Euro Americans and denigrated Native Americans who did not conform, and (b) those who were undifferentiated culturally from Euro Americans, but were interested in Native American traditions in a distant or detached way. Bicultural Native Americans were equally at home in both their traditional culture and the Euro-American culture. Spindler and Spindler describe these cultural strategies as defensive reactions resulting from the threat to the self-esteem of the Native American people.

Multiracial Families

The term "multiracial" is used to indicate individuals of mixed racial, ethnic, or cultural ancestry. In addition to children who are born to mixed-race couples, many monoracial children who were adopted by parents of a different race often consider themselves multiracial (Schwartz, 1998a). A key issue for children who are multiracial is how they are labeled by themselves, their families, and the community (Root, 1996).

Many multiracial children keep home separate from school. They may feel pressured by peers and teachers, their family, and even the forms they fill out to choose a race. These children may choose a single racial identification publicly while privately remaining "multicultural." (Okun, 1996). Poston (1990) describes meshing a personal identity with a reference group orientation, and proposes that families usually follow one of these options:

- The family labels themselves as "human," which simplifies listing components of their heritage.
- The family labels themselves multiracial, which helps children develop their biracial or multiracial identity based on the components of their particular background. Others, however, may consider themselves multiracial but not identify themselves by every component of their heritage.
- The family labels themselves monoracial, with single parents opting to use their culture or their race when their child resembles them. Families argue, for example, that when one part of the child is African American, society will treat them as an African American.

Families may help their children develop a multiracial identity that promotes equal pride in all components of their heritage. Families may also choose to emphasize their own race and foster a monoracial identity. Parents may foster a monoracial identity because their children more closely resemble members of a certain race or because parents are only knowledgeable about one heritage. In addition, some parents of children with African ancestry raise them as black in order to prepare them for the treatment they will receive in society (Schwartz, 1998b). Schwartz has these recommendations for teachers:

1. Consider your personal views on race and multiculturalism to see how the child views the world. Teachers should examine their own personal values, recognizing the unique characteristics of each child. Do you see the child, or do you see parents of two races?
2. Elicit information from multiracial families. Ask parents how they identify their children and how the children see themselves before the question emerges, or another child asks.

Teachers should determine how to meet the developmental needs of their students, helping them develop the skills and confidence needed to protect against verbal and physical abuse.

Families of Immigrants

During the 1980s, the largest and most diverse group of immigrants arrived in the United States since the beginning of the century. In their study of the schooling needs of immigrant students, McDonnell and Hill (1993) concluded that immigrant education is not a visible policy issue. Yet immigrant children and youth are heavily concentrated in a few areas of the country; for example, in Los Angeles and Miami city schools immigrant students represent 20% of the total enrollment. The quality of schooling the immigrant students receive largely depends on the capacity of the local communities to provide for them. The needs of students who do not speak English are so great and instructional resources generally so scarce that few districts are able to offer any native-language instruction. McDonnell and Hill suggest that students who are immigrants have unmet educational needs that are unique to their newcomer status.

POVERTY

Many families living in poverty lack the literacy skills defined by American mainstream culture. Though Taylor (1993) contends that these families are able to solve complex problems related to their own survival in difficult situations, deficiencies in traditional literacy skills exacerbate the problems these families confront trying to function in society. Taylor suggests that, rather than approaching these families from the perspective of a deficit model, the schools should appreciate and use those skills that the parents and children bring to the situation. The families' innate and experience-based knowledge is a building block for additional development.

Poor people care about their children. Thompson (1992) suggests that if these families are asked to be involved but not given any real decisions to make, they're not likely to become involved. On the other hand, if people are asked to become involved and given a chance to make a real difference in their school, they respond in great numbers and stick with it, to make a difference.

For a significant number of families, the challenges of poverty, substance abuse, and exposure to violence are daily concerns (Hanson & Carta, 1995). Families living in poverty have more than just financial issues to address. In addition, they feel stress associated with poverty, suffer from poor parental care and nutrition, sense they lack control over their living situation, and harbor hope for success in the future. A combination of individual and family or environmental protective factors are at work for these children and may help them become resilient. Resilient children have strong cognitive skills, are curious and enthusiastic, can set goals, and have high self-esteem. Their parents set rules at home, show respect for their children's individuality, and are responsive and accepting of children's behavior. In addition, toys and materials are available to the child, as is space for exploration and privacy.

About 80% of teenage mothers who have a baby drop out of school, and only slightly over half of these young women finally graduate from high school (Armstrong & Waszak, 1992). Teenage mothers will make only half the lifetime earning of a mother who waited until at least 20 years of age to have her first child. Their children often have difficulty with school. The Educational Testing Service (1992) reports that, after controlling for socioeconomic differences between one- and two-parent families, students living with both parents perform better academically in school. Only 1 in 10 low-income parents belongs to a parent-teacher organization, with adolescent parents being especially hard to reach (Educational Testing Service, 1992).

One effort to break down the barriers that interfere with access to children's mental health services demonstrates the innovative thinking that must be employed to meet the needs of low income parents. Koroloff, Elliott, Koren, and Friesen (1996) reported on the use of paraprofessionals to provide families with information, emotional support, and tangible assistance. The paraprofessionals worked with parents to provide respite care, transportation, and recreational activities. Concrete services, such as paying for utilities, child care, helping parents with daily living tasks, and providing clothing, food, and contact with other parents were provided. Families involved with the paraprofessionals reported higher levels of empowerment in working with their child.

Substitute Care

Children who are growing up in families other than their biological family are another group that requires special consideration by teachers. Meese (1999) contends that teachers must be sensitive to the special needs of adopted students with disabilities in the classroom so as to avoid overreacting to learning and behavioral difficulties which may be temporary responses to adoption issues in children's development. She suggests that teachers take time to understand the family, and help all of the children learn that families are formed in many ways. Teachers should use positive adoption language, avoiding terms such as "real parent" (birth parent) or "gave away" (made an adoption plan). Classroom assignments, such as bringing in a baby picture, may also need to be adapted. The adopted child may not have such a picture.

Schwartz (1999) suggests that adults choose to become foster parents for many reasons. She contends that all believe they have something to offer children and want to provide a strong home for children who otherwise may not have one. Some have been foster children themselves; others want to fulfill their need to be a parent. Some may want companionship, while others erroneously believe it can provide them with financial support.

A high percentage of children in foster care receive special education services. In their study of school-related problems Smucker, Kauffman, and Ball (1996) reported that, not surprisingly, students who were in foster care and programs for students identified as having emotional/behavioral disorders demonstrated the most school-related problems. However, students who were in foster care more closely resembled other children who were in special education programs in terms of their school-related problems rather than children who were not in special education or foster care. Students presented challenges for teachers because of lying and stealing, anger and aggression, attention problems, poor peer relationships and social skills, feelings of fear, helplessness, and depression, poor self-image and the need for structure. Benzola (1997), an adult who "survived" foster care, reported that even as a successful adult, many carry various scars into adult life and relationships.

Schools can support foster children and foster families by providing stability. Schwartz (1999) suggests several school practices to support foster children and foster families including:

- A plan for enrolling and integrating foster students on a short notice;
- Working with social service agencies to develop a mechanism for maintaining an educational profile on foster children;
- Providing educational supports that increase foster children's skills, self-esteem, and commitment;
- Using instructional activities that recognize the many different configurations of families;
- Providing early intervention;
- Providing teacher education in view of the problems of children and families, and discussing how these problems may impede learning and behavior;
- Facilitating parent participation.

Children Who Are Homeless

Teachers rarely have information about children who are homeless. In recent study, almost half of the homeless children living in shelters had positive screening results for at least one disability requiring special education services (Zima, Forness, Bussing, & Benjamin, 1998). Emotional/behavioral disorders were the most common finding. There is a significant concern that children in homeless shelters, due to their chaotic lives, face the dual challenge of being at risk for problem behavior and learning difficulties while having limited access to special education programs.

Goins and Cesarone (1993) indicate that homeless children vary in their resilience and their experience. The length of time they have been without a home, the reasons for homelessness, age, gender, and temperament all contribute to each individual child's reaction. Individual children may be depressed, aggressive, or withdrawn. The most typical feelings are those of shame or embarrassment. Though there is federal legislation which assists in providing education for children who are homeless, challenges remain. Educating all children about homelessness and encouraging empathy is essential. Schools may need to provide a place for homeless children to go between the time school closes and the shelter opens. Tracking children's educational and health records may be challenging and interfere with students' enrollment in school.

PARENTAL INVOLVEMENT

School practices are more predictive of family engagement than family characteristics. Dauber and Epstein (1993) reported that various family characteristics, such as parental education, family size, marital status, socioeconomic level, or student grade level did not determine whether or not parents got involved in their child's education. Rather, the attitudes and practices of the schools determined the family's involvement. White-Clark and Decker (1996) contend that many parents who are "hard to reach" are, in fact, self-sufficient, motivated, and involved in their children's education. Many parents experience significant hardships but, through determination, have overcome enormous obstacles to achievement including domestic violence, abandonment, illness, and drug abuse.

Interviewing

Dennis and Giangreco (1996) examined culturally sensitive practices in family interviewing and developing Individualized Education Plans. They suggested several keys to conducting culturally sensitive interviews. They suggest that professionals appreciate the uniqueness of each family, and be aware of the impact of the professional role. In addition, you should acknowledge your own cultural biases, and seek new understanding and knowledge of various cultures. Professionals should develop an awareness of cultural norms, and learn with the families with whom they are working. To improve their practice, professionals should seek help from "cultural interpreters" before the interview. They should carefully ascertain the literacy and language status of family members. Family members should be involved in planning the interview, and the interview should be previewed with family members. Teachers should be responsive to the family's interaction style, and adapt the time frame to meet the needs of the family. Professionals should also carefully examine the nature of the questions they ask, seeking to avoid any discomfort or culturally loaded value systems. When working with Asian families, for example, it may be necessary to explain that it is a tradition in American education that parents be involved in their children's education (Schwartz, 1994).

Nicolau and Ramos (1990) have several suggestions for working with Latino parents. First, teachers should make it easy for parents to participate, for example, by providing interpreters and transportation. In addition, they suggest face-to-face conversations with parents in their primary language in the home in order to initiate involvement. Personalizing the invitation to be involved helps project the idea that the school wishes to understand and address concerns of the family. In addition, every meeting should respond to some need or concern of the parents. Teachers should consult with parents regarding agenda and meeting formats, and then include other information which the school considers vital eventually.

Freedman, Ascheim, and Zerchykov (1989) describe several factors that inhibit the involvement of parents from diverse cultural, ethnic, and linguistic groups. School practices, they report, do not accommodate the diversity of families served. Events and opportunities to be involved are often held at inconvenient times. Communications are written in language that is inappropriate for the families. Parents may not be given information or materials they can use at home, and school staff may consciously or unconsciously convey the attitude that under-involved families have little to contribute and do not care about their child's education. An additional factor Freedman et al. report is that of time and child care constraints. Negative experiences with schools, and having been unsuccessful themselves, may make parents cautious about becoming involved. The importance of basic needs—that is, making sure the family has food and shelter—may also decrease the amount of time or availability of parents to be involved in the school.

With the complexity of addressing the needs of families from various ethnic, cultural, or language groups, educators may not always be successful in engaging all families. Some families may appear hard to reach. White-Clark and Decker (1996) describe several "rules" for involving hard to reach parents:

- Believe in the importance of parental involvement. Teachers should recognize that parents are the primary educators of their children, and educational programs are incomplete without a parent involvement component.
- Embody an ethic of caring. Express caring and concern by helpings families overcome difficulty.
- Disregard stereotypes by recognizing that your assumptions change your behavior toward parents.
- Develop high expectations for all parents, demonstrating to parents that their participation is valued, and you have confidence in their potential impact.
- View parents as partners, collaborators, and problem solvers.
- Be an educator with clear expectations, roles, and responsibilities which are communicated to parents.
- Be willing to address personal concerns and work actively to involve parents.
- Understand the purpose and function of involving parents and your place in that involvement.
- Work to improve parent involvement by experimenting and being open to new ideas.

SUMMARY

- The diversity of today's schools challenge the traditional patterns of communication between home and school.
- Issues of gender affect all interaction, and challenge special educators in terms of educating girls and involving fathers.
- Teachers should be careful in making generalizations about members of ethnic, cultural, or linguistic groups that may not pertain to every individual in the group.
- Teachers must recognize their own cultural values and recognize that families from various ethnic, cultural, and linguistic groups should be allowed to function in ways typical for their group.
- Issues of poverty and homelessness have a significant impact on the education of children and on the involvement of their parents.
- Rather than identifying families as hard-to-reach, teachers should recognize that school practices may not accommodate the diversity of families served.

REFERENCES

Armstrong, E., & Waszak, C. (1992). *Teenage pregnancy and too-early childbearing: Public costs, personal consequences*. Washington, DC: Center for Population Options.

Bailey, D. B., Jr., Skinner, D., Correa, V., Arcia, E., Reyes-Blanes, M. E., Rodriguez, P., Vazquez-Montilla, E., & Skinner, M. (1999). Needs and supports reported by Latino families of young children with developmental disabilities. *American Journal on Mental Retardation, 104*(5), 437–45.

Bell, M. L., & Smith, B. R. (1996). Grandparents as primary caregivers: Lessons in love. *Teaching Exceptional Children, 28*(2), 18–19.

Benzola, E. J. (1997). Surviving foster care and its emotional roller coaster. *Journal of Emotional and Behavioral Problems, 6*(1), 19–21.

Boykin, A. W., & Bailey, C. T. (2000). *The role of cultural factors in school-relevant cognitive functioning.* Baltimore: Center for Research on the Education of Students Placed at Risk.

Casper, V., & Schultz, S. B. (1999). *Gay parents/straight schools: Building communication and trust.* Williston, VT: Teachers College Press.

Chavkin, N. F., & Williams, R. (1993). *Families and schools in a pluralistic society.* Albany, NY: State University of New York Press.

Cohen, T. F. (1993). What do fathers provide? Reconsidering the economic and nurturant dimensions of men as parents. In J. C. Hood (Ed.), *Men, work, and family* (pp. 1–22). Newbury Park, CA: Sage.

Dauber, S. L., & Epstein, J. L. (1993). Parents' attitudes and practices of involvement in inner-city elementary and middle schools. In N. Chavkin (Ed.), *Families and schools in a pluralistic society* (pp. 53–72). Albany, NY: State University of New York Press.

Dennehy, K., & Mortimer, J. T. (1993). Work and family orientations of contemporary adolescent boys and girls. In J. C. Hood (Ed.), *Men, work, and family* (pp. 87–107). Newbury Park, CA: Sage.

Dennis, R. E., & Giangreco, M. F. (1996). Creating conversation: Reflections on cultural sensitivity in family interviewing. *Exceptional Children, 63*(1), 103–116.

Derman-Sparks, L., & The A. B. C. Task Force (1989). *Anti-bias curriculum: Tools for empowering young children.* Washington, DC: National Association for the Education of Young Children.

Dyson, L. L. (1997). Fathers and mothers of school-age children with developmental disabilities: Parental stress, family functioning, and social support. *American Journal on Mental Retardation, 102*(3), 267–279.

Educational Testing Service. (1992). *America's smallest school: The family.* Princeton, NJ: Author.

Ellison, C. M., Boykin, A. W., Towns, D. P., & Stokes, A. (2000). *Classroom cultural ecology: The dynamics of classroom life in schools serving low-income African American children.* Baltimore: Center for Research on the Education of Students Placed at Risk.

Flynn, L. L., & Wilson, P. G. (1998). Partnerships with family members: What about fathers? *Young Exceptional Children, 2*(1), 21–28.

Freedman, S., Ascheim, B., & Zerchykov, R. (1989). *Strategies for increasing the involvement of underrepresented families in education.* Quincy, MA: Massachusetts Department of Education.

Frief, G. L., DeMaris, A. & Hood, J. C. (1993). Balancing work and single fatherhood. In J. C. Hood (Ed.), *Men, work, and family* (pp. 176–194). Newbury Park, CA: Sage.

Goins, B., & Cesarone, B. (1993). *Homeless children: Meeting the educational challenges.* Urbana, IL: ERIC Clearinghouse on Elementary and Early Childhood Education.

Grimm, L. L. (1992). The Native American child in school: An ecological perspective. In M. J. Fine & C. Carlson (Eds.), *The Handbook of Family-School Intervention: A Systems Perspective* (pp. 102–118). Boston: Allyn & Bacon.

Guild, P. (1994). The culture/learning style connection. *Educational Leadership, 52,* 16–21.

Hanson, M. J., & Carta, J. J. (1995). Addressing the challenges of families with multiple risks. *Exceptional Children, 62*(3), 201–212.

Harry, B. (1992). Restructuring the participation of African-American parents in special education. *Exceptional Children, 24,* 123–131.

Harry, B., Rueda, R., & Kalyanpur, M. (1999). Cultural reciprocity in sociocultural perspective: Adapting the normalization principle for family collaboration. *Exceptional Children, 66*(1), 123–136.

Hourcade, J. J., Parette, H. P., Jr., & Huer, M. B. (1997). Family and cultural alert! Considerations in assistive technology assessment. *Teaching Exceptional Children, 30*(1), 40–44.

Hyun, J. K., & Fowler, S. A. (1995). Respect, cultural sensitivity, and communication: Promoting participation by Asian families in the individualized family service plan. *Teaching Exceptional Children, 28*(1), 25–28.

Inger, M. (1992). *Increasing the school involvement of Hispanic parents.* ERIC/CUE Digest No. 80. New York: ERIC Clearinghouse on Urban Education, Teachers College, Columbia University.

Jordan, L., Reyes-Blanes, M. E., Peel, B. B., Peel, H. A., & Lane, H. B. (1998). Developing teacher-parent partnerships across cultures: Effective parent conferences. *Intervention in School and Clinic, 33*(3), 141–147.

Koroloff, N. M., Elliott, D. J., Koren, P. E., & Friesen, B. J. (1996). Linking low-income families to children's mental health services: An outcome study. *Journal of Emotional and Behavioral Disorders, 4*(1), 2–11.

LaFramboise, T.D., & Low, K.E. (1989). American Indian children and adolescents. In T. Gibbs & L.H. Huang (Eds.). *Children of Color: Psychological Interventions with Minority Youth* (pp. 138–149). San Francisco: Jossey Bass.

Lewis, M. C. (1993). *Beyond barriers: Involving Hispanic families in the education process.* Washington, DC: National Committee for Citizens in Education.

Linan-Thompson, S., & Jean, R. E. (1997). Completing the parent participation puzzle: Accepting diversity. *Teaching Exceptional Children, 30*(2), 46–50.

Magana, S. M. (1999). Puerto Rican families caring for an adult with mental retardation: Role of familism. *American Journal on Mental Retardation, 104*(5), 466–482.

Mann, J. (1994). *The difference: Growing up female in America.* New York: Warner Books.

McDonnell, L. M., & Hill, P. T. (1993). *Newcomers in American schools.* Santa Monica, CA: Rand.

Meese, R. L. (1999). Teaching adopted students with disabilities: What teachers need to know. *Intervention in School and Clinic, 34*(4), 232–235.

Nicolau, S., & Ramos, C. L. (1990). *Together is better: Building strong relationships between schools and Hispanic parents.* Washington, DC: Hispanic Policy Development Project.

Nweke, W. (1994). *Racial differences in parental discipline practices.* ERIC Document Reproduction Services No. ED 388 741.

Okun, B. F. (1996). *Understanding diverse families: What practitioners need to know.* New York: Guilford.

Patterson, C. J. (1992). Children of lesbian and gay parents. *Child Development, 63*(5), 1025–1042.

Poston, W. S. C. (1990). The biracial identity development model: A needed addition. *Journal of Counseling and Development, 69*(2), 152–155.

Raghavan, C., Weisner, T. S., & Patel, D. (1999). The adaptive project of parenting: South Asian families with children with developmental delays. *Education and Training in Mental Retardation and Developmental Disabilities, 34*(3), 281–291.

Roach, M. A., Orsmond, G. I., & Barratt, M. S. (1999). Mothers and fathers of children with Down syndrome: Parental stress and involvement in childcare. *American Journal on Mental Retardation, 104*(5), 422–436.

Root, M. P. P. (1996). A significant frontier. In M. P. P. Root (Ed.), *The multicultural experience: Racial borders as the new frontier* (pp. xiii–xxvii). Thousand Oaks, CA: Sage.

Sadker, M. D. (1994). *Failing at fairness: How America's schools cheat girls.* New York: Charles Scribners' Sons.

Scheinfeld, D. R. (1998). *New beginnings: A guide to designing parenting programs for refugee and immigrant parents.* New York: International Catholic Child Bureau, Inc.

Schwartz, W. (1994). *A guide to communicating with Asian American families.* NY: ERIC Clearinghouse on Urban Education, Teachers College, Columbia University.

Schwartz, W. (1998a). *The identity of multiracial youth.* ERIC/CUE Digest No. 137 EDO UD 98–7. New York: Clearinghouse on Urban Education.

Schwartz, W. (1998b). *The schooling of multiracial students.* ERIC Digest EDO UD 98–8. New York: Clearinghouse on Urban Education.

Schwartz, W. (1999). *School support for foster families.* NY: ERIC Clearinghouse on Urban Education, Teachers College, Columbia University No. ED O-UD-99–7.

Skinner, D., Bailey, D. B., Jr., Correa, V., & Rodriguez, P. (1999). Narrating self and disability: Latino mothers' construction of identities vis-à-vis their child with special needs. *Exceptional Children, 65*(4), 481–495.

Smith, G. C., Tobin, S. S., & Fullmer, E. M. (1995). Elderly mothers caring at home for offspring with mental retardation: A model of permanency planning. *American Journal on Mental Retardation, 99*(5), 487–499.

Smucker, K. S., Kauffman, J. M., & Ball, D. W. (1996). School-related problems of special education foster-care students with emotional or behavioral disorders: A comparison for other groups. *Journal of Emotional and Behavioral Disorders, 4*(1), 30–39.

Spindler, G., & Spindler, L. (1994). What is cultural therapy? In G. Spindler & L. Spindler (Eds), *Pathways to cultural awareness: Cultural therapy with teachers and students* (pp. 1–35). Thousand Oaks, CA: Sage.

Stier, H., & Tienda, M. (1993). Are men marginal to the family? Insights from Chicago's inner city. In J. C. Hood (Ed.), *Men, work, and family* (pp. 23–44). Newbury Park, CA: Sage.

Taylor, D. (1993). Family literacy: Resisting deficit models. TESOL *Quarterly, 27*(3), 550–553.

Thompson, S. (1992). Building on a foundation of respect for families and children: A round-table discussion. *Equity and Choice, 8*(3), 37–40.

Thorp, E. K. (1997). Increasing opportunities for partnership with culturally and linguistically diverse families. *Intervention in School and Clinic, 32*(5), 261–269.

United States Census Bureau. (2001). *American fact—Detailed tables.* Available at factfinder.census.gov.

Wellhousen, K. (1993). Children from nontraditional families: A lesson in acceptance. *Childhood Education, 69*(5), 287–288.

White-Clark, R., & Decker, L. E. (1996). *The "Hard-to-reach" parent: Old challenges, new insights.* Boston: Mid Atlantic Center for Community Education.

Willoughby, J. C., & Glidden, M. L. (1995). Fathers helping out: Shared child care and marital satisfaction of parents of children with disabilities. *American Journal of Mental Retardation, 99*(4), 399–406.

Zetlin, A. G., Padron, M., & Wilson, S. (1996). The experience of five Latin American families with the special education system. *Education and Training in Mental Retardation and Developmental Disabilities, 31*(1), 22–28.

Zima, B. T., Forness, S. R., Bussing, R., & Benjamin, B. (1998). Homeless children in emergency shelters: Need for prereferral intervention and potential eligibility for special education. *Behavioral Disorders, 23*(2), 98–100.

CHAPTER 3

Legal Rights and Responsibilities of Parents and Families

IEPs, IFSPs, ADA, 504 - *do you people speak in code?*

Collaborating with families with members with disabilities goes beyond the professional role of the teacher. Collaboration and the engagement of families are delineated in a series of federal laws. These laws include the Individuals with Disabilities Education Act (IDEA) of 1997 (Public Law 105–17), the Americans with Disabilities Act (ADA) of 1990 (Public Law 101–336), Section 504 of the Rehabilitation Act of 1973 (Public Law 93–112), and the Family Educational Rights and Privacy Act (FERPA) of 1974 (Public Law 93–380).

This chapter describes the legal rights and responsibilities of parents and families as mandated in the four federal laws above. It presents various aspects of these laws, which will serve as a basis for much of your practice as a special education professional. Later chapters will describe more specific information regarding engaging families in the education of their children with disabilities.

Learning Objectives

After completing this chapter, you will be able to discuss these topics:

1. Principles on which IDEA is based and the requirements of the law
2. The Americans with Disabilities Act and how it applies to schools
3. Section 504 of the Rehabilitation Act of 1973 and how it applies to schools
4. The requirements of the Family Educational Rights and Privacy Act
5. The responsibilities of parents related to these legal rights

INDIVIDUALS WITH DISABILITIES EDUCATION ACT

The Individuals with Disabilities Education Act is the primary special education law. The Act and its requirements are based on the principles presented below (National Information Center for Children and Youth with Disabilities [NICHCY], 1998a):

- Free appropriate public education
- Appropriate evaluation
- Individualized education program
- Least restrictive environment
- Procedural safeguards
- Parent and student participation in decision-making

These principles are used to structure our discussion of the Individuals with Disabilities Education Act which follows.

Free Appropriate Public Education

IDEA 97 guarantees that every eligible student with a disability will have a free, appropriate, public education. This education is provided at public expense without charge to parents or others responsible for the student, meets the state educational standards, and includes an appropriate preschool, elementary, or secondary school education as described in the student's Individualized Education Plan (IEP). The student's guaranteed "free, appropriate, public education" is implemented differently for each student documented in his or her IEP.

Appropriate Evaluation

"Appropriate evaluation" is a commitment that all students with disabilities are appropriately assessed in order to determine their eligibility for services, educational programming, and performance monitoring. Testing and evaluation materials must not be racially or culturally discriminatory. Appropriate evaluation assumes that (a) evaluators are knowledgeable and qualified, (b) a variety of instruments and procedures are used, and (c) tests or other procedures are not discriminatory. In addition, IDEA 97 contends that students should not be unnecessarily subject to tests and assessments, so the full battery of tests traditionally conducted every three years is no longer legally mandated. All assessment must provide relevant information that directly assists persons responsible for the child's treatment to determine his or her educational needs.

Individualized Education Program

Key to the individualization of the student's educational program is the Individualized Education Program, usually referred to as the IEP. IDEA 97 delineates specific components of the IEP. These components are presented in Figure 3.1.

IEP's include:

- The child's present levels of educational performance, including how the child is performing and progressing in the general curriculum;
- Measurable annual goals, with benchmarks or short-term objectives;
- The special education, related services, supplementary aids, and services provided for the student;
- The program modifications or supports that teachers and related services personnel will provide the child to advance toward meeting annual goals;
- Involvement in the child's progress in the general curriculum, including extracurricular and other nonacademic activities;
- An explanation of the extent to which the student will not participate with students without disabilities;
- Modifications to state or district-wide assessment programs, or alternative assessments;
- Projected date for the beginning of services, frequency, location, and duration of those services;
- Transition needs beginning when the student is 14 years-of-age and updated annually;
- Transition services when the student is 16 years-of-age or younger, when appropriate;
- A statement that the student was informed, at least one year before he or she reaches the age of majority under State law, of the rights that will transfer to the student;
- How the student's progress will be measured and how the students' parents will be kept informed.

Figure 3.1 *Components of the Individualized Education Program.* (National Information *Center for Children and Youth with Disabilities* [NICHCY], 1998b)

The IEP is developed by an informed team of individuals, including the parents of the child. This team includes at least one general education teacher and one special education teacher. A school district representative who can supervise the instruction and is knowledgeable about the general curriculum and availability of services must be present. Someone must be on the team who can interpret the instructional implications of evaluation results. In addition, at the discretion of the parents or the school, other individuals may be present. Whenever appropriate, the student is present. The IEP is the cornerstone of the special education process.

The IEP must consider the strengths of the child and the concerns of the parents for enhancing the education of their child, as well as the results of the initial or most recent evaluation. There are also several "special factors" which must be considered, including:

- Behavioral strategies and supports if the child's behavior impedes his or her learning or that of others;
- The child's language needs if the child has limited English proficiency;
- The provision of instruction in Braille and the use of Braille for students who are blind or visually impaired, unless inappropriate;

- The communication needs of the child, if the child is deaf or hard of hearing.
- Whether the student requires assistive technology devices and services.

Students who are younger than three years of age do not have an IEP. Rather, each of the parents and families is involved in writing an Individualized Family Service Plan (IFSP), developed by a multidisciplinary team including the parents. This IFSP includes:

- A statement of the child's developmental level;
- A statement of the family's strengths and needs as related to the child;
- A statement of the anticipated outcomes for the child and the family and the way in which progress will be measured;
- A description of early intervention services necessary to meet the needs of the child or family;
- Projected dates of initiation and duration of services;
- The name of the service coordinator;
- A plan for transition to preschool services.

The IFSP is reviewed semiannually and evaluated annually by the multidisciplinary team. Families are full partners in the development and review of the IFSP.

Least Restrictive Environment

The principle of the least restrictive environment assumes that the most appropriate educational setting for students is with their peers. Special classes and a separate school may only occur when the nature or severity of the disability is such that education in the general education setting cannot be achieved satisfactorily. Placement in the general education classroom is the first placement the IEP team may consider. If such a placement is not appropriate for the student, then other more restrictive placement may be considered.

Though IDEA 97 requires that placement in general education must be the first placement considered by the IEP team, a "cascade" (Reynolds, 1962) or "continuum of services" (Deno, 1970) has traditionally been described for students with disabilities. In addition to placement in general education classrooms and placement in general education with supplementary instruction, this traditional continuum includes:

- Students in general education classes part-time and special education part-time. These placements may be described as "pull-out programs" and have been related to increased anxiety on behalf of the students with disabilities who are concerned about social and transitional demands of these placements (Tymitz-Wolf, 1984).
- Students in full-time special classes. Though some districts maintain these placements, Algozzine, Morsink, and Algozzine (1988) found little difference between instruction in special classes and in general education classes.
- Students in special schools. These placements are quite restrictive, and serve few students.
- Students receiving homebound services. Homebound services are usually short-term interventions for students who are physically unable to attend school, or pose a significant danger to themselves or others.

Procedural Safeguards

Procedural safeguards are designed to protect the rights of parents and their child with a disability, and are a critical aspect of special education law. In addition to protecting rights, procedural safeguards serve as a mechanism for resolving disputes between the parents and the school (National Information Center for Children and Youth with Disabilities [NICHCY], 1998c)

Due Process.   Parents have the right to request a due process hearing on any matter with respect to the identification, evaluation, or placement of their children. Parents may request a due process hearing about the way in which the school is providing a free, appropriate, public education for the child. They have the right to a hearing conducted by an impartial hearing officer, to appeal the initial hearing decision to the appropriate state education agency, and, finally, to appear before the appropriate state or federal civil court.

Prior Written Notice and the Procedural Safeguards Notice.   IDEA 97 simplified the approach to delivering information to parents regarding the procedural safeguards under the law. This "procedural safeguards notice" is provided, at a minimum, at these specific times:

- When the child is initially referred for an evaluation;
- When parents are notified of an IEP meeting;
- When the agency proposes to reevaluate the child;
- Upon the registration of a due process complaint.

This document must be written in the native language of the parents unless it is clearly not feasible to do so. The information should be provided in a clear, understandable manner, and should include a description of procedural safeguards including:

- Independent educational evaluation;
- Prior written notice;
- Parental consent;
- Access to educational records;
- Opportunity to present due process complaints;
- Placement of the child pending a due process proceeding;
- Procedures for students who may be placed in an interim alternative educational setting;
- Requirements for placements by parents of children in private schools at public expense;
- The mediation process;
- Due process hearings, including requirements for disclosure of evaluation results and recommendations;
- State-level appeals and civil actions;
- Attorney's fees.

According to IDEA 97, there are two circumstances under which the parents must notify the school district: when they intend to remove their child from the public school and place the child in a private school at public expense, or when they intend to file a due process complaint.

Mediation.   IDEA 97 established mediation as a process that may be used to resolve differences. Under IDEA 97, mediation is an impartial system that brings individuals who have a dispute to confidentially discuss the disputed issues with a neutral third party. The goal of this discussion is to resolve the disputes in a binding, written agreement (Office of Special Education Programs [OSEP], 2000). The state must ensure that the mediation process is voluntary on the part of all the parties, is not used to deny or delay the parents' right to a due process hearing, or to deny any other rights afforded under IDEA 97. The state must assure that the mediation is conducted by a qualified and impartial mediator who is trained in effective techniques. The state must maintain a list of qualified mediators, and bear the cost of mediation. If parents choose not to use mediation, the school district or state may establish procedures to require the parents to meet with someone who would explain the benefits of mediation and encourage them to make use of the process.

Mediation was added to the law in an attempt to prevent conflicts from proceeding through formal due process and litigation. Mediation must be put in writing, remain confidential, and may not be used as evidence in subsequent hearings.

Discipline. An area of significant concern with regard to students with disabilities is discipline. One of the controversial issues related to discipline has been that of the "stay put" provision. The stay-put provision states that "...unless the state or local educational agency and the parents otherwise agree, the child shall remain in the then-current educational placement" (Section 615 j). Though this statement seems to insure that the child has the right to remain in his or her current placement while disputes are resolved, several questions remain—such as:

- What if school systems believe that keeping the child in the current placement may result in self-injury or injury to others?
- How can schools address behavior problems?
- With stay put, can students with disabilities be suspended or expelled?
- If students are suspended or expelled, is it a "change in placement?"

IDEA 97 clearly presents the requirements for students with disabilities who (a) violate a school rule or code of conduct subject to discipline, (b) carry a weapon to school or a school function, (c) knowingly possess, use, sell, or solicit a controlled substance while at school or a school function, or (d) who, if left in their current placement, are likely to injure themselves or others. IDEA 97 gives school personnel the authority to change the placement of a child with a disability to an appropriate alternative educational setting, other setting, or suspension for not more than ten days. However, this change in placement can only occur to the extent that this would be applied to children without disabilities. A student with a disability may not be removed for more than 45 days if the child carries a weapon or possesses, uses, sells, or solicits drugs or a controlled substance while at school or a school function. If a functional behavioral assessment had not been completed before the behavior that resulted in the suspension occurred, the school must convene an IEP meeting to develop an assessment plan. If there already is a plan, the IEP team reviews the plan and modifies it, if necessary, to address the behavior.

A hearing officer may order a change of placement to an interim alternative educational setting if the hearing officer determines that the school has provided substantial evidence that keeping the child in the current setting is likely to result in injury to the child or others. The hearing officer also considers the appropriateness of the child's current placement and whether the school has made reasonable efforts to minimize the risk of harm. The IEP team selects the alternative educational setting so that the student can continue to participate in the general curriculum in another setting and receive those services and modifications that will help the child meet the goals and objectives of the IEP.

One key issue in the application of discipline procedures with students with disabilities is that of the manifestation determination review. In general, if a disciplinary action is going to occur that will change the child's placement for more than 10 days (such as a suspension or expulsion), parents are to be notified and a review is conducted of the relationship between the student's disability and the behavior which is being addressed. The IEP team carries out this review, and considers the behavior, evaluation results and other relevant information, observations, and the IEP. The IEP team then determines whether the IEP and placement were appropriate and the services provided were those listed in the IEP, whether the student's disability did not impair the ability of the student to understand the consequences of the behavior, and whether the student's disability did not impair the ability of the student to control the behavior. If the behavior was not a manifestation of the disability, then the disciplinary procedures applicable to children without disabilities may be applied to the student in the same manner as it would be with a student without a disability. Parents may appeal the decision of the IEP team.

A final aspect of the procedural safeguards is attorneys' fees. IDEA 97 prohibits payment of attorney fees for participation in an IEP meeting or when mediation is conducted prior to the filing of a complaint. Legal fees may also be reduced whenever the court finds that the parent unreasonably protracted the final resolution, the amount exceeds a prevailing hourly rate, time spent seems excessive, or the attorney representing the parent did not provide to the school district the appropriate information in the due process complaint.

Parent and Student Participation in Decision-Making

IDEA 97 strengthens the role of parents, students, and educators to work as a team to improve student performance. In IDEA 97, parents retain right to prior notice when proposals or refusals initiating or changing the identification, evaluation, or educational placement of the student are made. In addition, parents have the right to inspect and review any education records relating to their child. Parents must consent to have a student evaluated for the first time, and have the right to obtain an independent educational evaluation, which, under certain circumstances, may be at public expense. Parents are members of the IEP team, and must consent to the student's initial special education placement. Parents also have the right to challenge or appeal any decision related to the identification, evaluation, or placement of their child (National Information Center for Children and Youth with Disabilities [NICHCY], 1998d).

IDEA 97 added several requirements to the parental involvement mandates of previous special education laws. Parents now have the right to participate in decision-making during the evaluation process and discussions of eligibility and placement. Parents have the right to consent or deny consent to the reevaluation, and to meet with the team with respect to identification, evaluation, and placement. Parents also have the right to receive reports on their child's educational progress. Parents must now notify the school of their intent to file a complaint.

IDEA 97 describes students' rights to participate in decision-making. During the transition planning process, transition services should be discussed with students. In addition, schools must notify students as to the rights, if any, that will transfer to them upon reaching majority.

AMERICANS WITH DISABILITIES ACT

The Americans with Disabilities Act of 1990 is a civil rights law, enacted to ensure the right to full participation of individuals with disabilities in American society. In addition to revising the definition of "disability," requirements were made in the areas of transportation, telecommunications, employment, and public accommodations for persons with disabilities and persons with acquired immunodeficiency syndrome (AIDS), and human immunodeficiency virus (HIV). Students who are not eligible for special education services under IDEA 97 may be provided with services and accommodations through the Americans with Disabilities Act.

The Americans with Disabilities Act requires that persons with disabilities have access to accommodations in employment, transportation, public accommodations, state and local government activities and communication. It defines disability as a physical or mental impairment that substantially limits one or more of the major life activities of an individual or the perception that such a disability exists. Because learning is identified as a major life activity, the Americans with Disabilities Act applies to education and schools. Students with disabilities may confront barriers such as inappropriately designed instruction or testing, long or complex directions, or distracting school settings. They may confront attitudinal barriers of impatient or inflexible teachers and a lack of empathy or understanding (National Joint Committee on Learning Disabilities, 1992).

According to the mandates of the Americans with Disabilities Act, school policies and practices must be modified when these impact on the functioning of students with disabilities. Policies that discriminate when reasonable accommodations and modifications would enable appropriate performance of students with disabilities must be addressed. For example, admission and placement procedures and policies

that do not allow for flexibility in curriculum and instruction may be identified as discriminatory. Promotion and retention policies may need to be addressed as well as school completion/graduation requirements that discriminate against individuals with disabilities (National Joint Committee on Learning Disabilities, 1992).

Title II of the Americans with Disabilities Act applies to placement in elementary, secondary, and postsecondary schools. In elementary and secondary schools, students with disabilities may be assigned to separate facilities or programs only when such a placement is demonstrated to be necessary to provide equal educational opportunity. Any separate facilities and the services provided in those separate facilities must be comparable to other facilities and services which the student would receive if not placed in the separate facility (U. S. Department of Education, Office of Civil Rights, 1998).

SECTION 504 OF THE REHABILITATION ACT OF 1973

Section 504 of the Rehabilitation Act of 1973 is also an equal rights law for individuals with disabilities. Section 504, however, only pertains to public institutions that receive federal funding—including public school systems. The eligibility requirements for accommodations is less stringent than that included in the Individuals with Disabilities Education Act. Like the Americans with Disabilities Act, to qualify for services under section 504, an individual must have a disability that interferes with one or more major life functions, including caring for oneself, walking, seeing, hearing, speaking, breathing, learning, and working. Students who do not qualify for services under IDEA 97 may qualify for services under section 504.

The basis of providing accommodations through Section 504 is the requirement that no one "...shall, solely by reason of his or her disability, be excluded from participation in, be denied the benefit of, or be subject to discrimination under any program or activity receiving federal financial assistance..." (19 U. S. C. sec. 794 (a)). If a student has already been evaluated under IDEA 97, that evaluation may be applied to determine eligibility under Section 504. In order to be eligible, the student must have a documented or diagnosed disability. A meeting is then held with the school's Section 504 representative to document the disability and determine eligibility. If the student is determined to be eligible, a 504 plan is written. This plan is developed to identify the students' needs and the accommodations required for equal access to educational programs and activities, school-sponsored events, and extracurricular activities (Wistech, 1999.)

Accommodations in a 504 plan are based on individual needs. These accommodations may include modifying written materials, using note-takers, or employing computers and assistive technology. Behavior plans that allow the student full participation in school-related activities may also be included. A health plan may be developed for students with chronic medical conditions (Wistech, 1999).

Section 504 has limitations. Schools do not need to make accommodations that fundamentally alter educational programs or cause financial hardship. For example, an academic honor society does not need to alter its educational standards to admit students with disabilities. The law requires, however, that programs be made accessible.

FAMILY EDUCATIONAL RIGHTS AND PRIVACY ACT

The Family Educational Rights and Privacy Act of 1974 (P. L. 103–382) applies to all records that schools or education agencies maintain about students, and protects both paper and computerized records. The act requires schools and local education agencies to annually notify parents of their rights, explain that parents may inspect and review records, and seek to amend inaccurate records. Parents have the right to consent or not consent to disclosures of personally identifiable information in the record. Custodial and noncustodial parents have equal access to student information unless there is a court order revoking those rights. Though the rights pass to students when they are 18 years old, parents retain access to student records of children who are their dependents for tax purposes (National Center for Education Statistics, 1997).

According to the Family Educational Rights and Privacy Act (FERPA) educational records include a wide range of student information. These records may be maintained in schools in any recorded way—handwriting, print, computer media, video or audiotape, film, or microfilm. Education records include:

- Date and place of birth;
- Parent/guardian addresses, including where the parent can be contacted in emergencies;

- Grades, test scores, courses taken, academic specializations and activities, and official letters regarding a student's status in school;
- Special education records;
- Disciplinary records;
- Medial and health records that the school creates, or collects and maintains;
- Attendance records, awards conferred, and degrees earned;
- Personal information such as a student's identification code, social security number, picture, or other information that would make it easy to identify or locate a student.

Personal notes made by teachers or other school officials that are not shared with others (such as a teacher's personal anecdotal records) are not considered education records. Law enforcement records created or maintained by a school are not considered education records.

Directory information is a part of the educational record that can be made public according to a school's student records policy. Directory information may include a student's name, address, telephone number, and other information typically found in school yearbooks or athletic programs. Names and pictures of participants in various extracurricular activities, recipients of awards, pictures of students, and height and weight of athletes may be considered directory information. Schools must notify parents of information considered directory information, and allow them to remove all or part of the information if they do not wish it to be available to the public without their consent.

If a parent finds education records inaccurate or misleading, they may request changes or corrections. Schools and education agencies must respond promptly. These requests must be made in writing. If the parent request is denied, the parent has the right to a hearing. If the disagreement concerning the record continues after the hearing, the parent may insert an explanation of the objection in the record. Schools may release information with prior written consent from parents (National Center for Education Statistics, 1997). Action Steps 3.1 presents issues that arise when working with families and the privacy of information.

PARENT RESPONSIBILITIES

Rights infer responsibilities. Knoblauch (1998) suggests that parents are responsible for developing a partnership with the school, and sharing relevant information about the student's education and development. In addition, it is the parents' responsibility to request clarification when needed and make sure they understand their child's educational program before signing the IEP. Parents have the responsibility to consider and discuss with the teacher how to more fully include the student in general school activities. They should monitor the student's progress and periodically ask for a report. They should discuss any problems that occur in the assessment, placement, or education program. Knoblauch "contends" that parents should keep records and join a parent organization.

ACTION STEPS 3.1: *WORKING WITH FAMILIES AND THE PRIVACY OF INFORMATION*

Alert families to the following issues:

- ❑ Custodial and noncustodial parents have equal access to student information unless there is a court order revoking that privilege.
- ❑ Parents retain the right to access the educational records of students who are eighteen-years-old or older if they are dependents for tax purposes.
- ❑ Personal notes that are not shared with others are not educational records.
- ❑ It is the responsibility of the school to communicate to the family the local definition of directory information.
- ❑ Families may request changes or corrections when they view educational records as being inaccurate or misleading.

SUMMARY

- The rights and responsibilities of parents and families of children with disabilities are delineated in a series of federal laws.
- The Individuals with Disabilities Education Act is based on the principles of (a) free, appropriate public education; (b) appropriate evaluation; (c) individualized education program; (d) least restrictive environment; (e) procedural safeguards; and (f) parent and student participation in decision-making.
- The Americans with Disabilities Act, a civil rights legislation, required that persons with disabilities have access to accommodations in employment, transportation, public accommodations, state and local government activities, and communication.
- Students who are not eligible for services under IDEA 97 may be eligible for service under Section 504 of the Rehabilitation Act of 1973 which is civil rights legislation.
- The Family Educational Rights and Privacy Act describes parents' rights with regard to access of records, defines "education record," and clarifies the maintenance of these records.
- Parental rights infer parental responsibilities in the education of their child with a disability.

REFERENCES

Algozzine, B., Morsink, C. V., & Algozzine, K. M. (1988). What's happening in self-contained special education classrooms? *Exceptional Children*, 55, 259–265.

Americans with Disabilities Act (ADA) of 1990, PL 101–336, 421 U.S.C. §§ 12191 et seq.

Deno, E. (1970). Special education as development capital. *Exceptional Children*, 37, 229–237.

Family Educational Rights and Privacy Act (FERPA) of 1974, PL 93–380, 20 U. S. C. §§ 1221 et seq.

Individuals with Disabilities Education Act (IDEA) Amendments of 1997, PL 105–17, 20 U. S. C. §§ 1400 et seq.

Knoblauch, B. (1998). *Rights and responsibilities of children with disabilities.* Reston, VA: ERIC Clearinghouse on Disabilities and Gifted Education.

National Center for Education Statistics (1997). *Protecting the privacy of student education records.* Washington, DC: Author.

National Information Center for Children and Youth with Disabilities, (1998a). *Office of Special Education Programs' IDEA Amendments of 1997 Curriculum: Module 3: Six principles of IDEA.* Washington, DC: NICHCY.

National Information Center for Children and Youth with Disabilities, (1998b). *Office of Special Education Programs' IDEA Amendments of 1997 Curriculum: Module 7: Individualized Education Program.* Washington, DC: NICHCY.

National Information Center for Children and Youth with Disabilities, 1998c). *Office of Special Education Programs' IDEA Amendments of 1997 Curriculum: Module 10: Procedural Safeguards.* Washington, D. C.: NICHCY.

National Information Center for Children and Youth with Disabilities, (1998d). *Office of Special Education Programs' IDEA Amendments of 1997 Curriculum: Module 9: Parent and student participation in decision-making.* Washington, DC: NICHCY.

National Joint Committee on Learning Disabilities (1992). *Learning disabilities and the Americans with Disabilities Act (ADA).* Washington, DC: Author.

Office of Special Education Programs, (2000). *OSEP Memorandum "Questions and answers on mediation."* Washington, DC: Author.

Rehabilitation Act of 1973, PL 93–112, 29 U. S. C. §§ 701 et seq.

Reynolds, M.C. (1962). A framework for considering some issues in special education. *Exceptional Children,* 28, 367–370.

Tymitz-Wolf, B. (1984). An analysis of EMR children's worries about mainstreaming. *Education and Training of the Mentally Retarded,* 19, 157–168.

U. S. Department of Education, Office of Civil Rights (1998). *Student placement in elementary and secondary schools and Section 504 and Title II of the Americans with Disabilities Act.* Washington, DC: Author.

Wistech, (1999). *Parents' guide to Section 504 of the Rehabilitation Act of 1973.* Madison, WI: Wisconsin Department of Health and Family Services.

CHAPTER 4

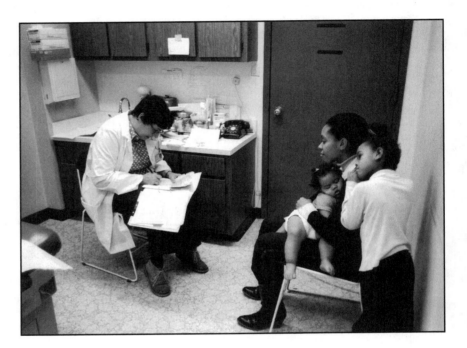

The Impact of Identification and Diagnosis of Disability on the Family

It is not a cliche when people talk about the loss of the child you carried for nine months.

It sort of came to me when we were at the community holiday tree lighting. All of the other kids were staring in wonder at the tree, oohing and ahhing over the tree. Their parents were all smiling and cuddling them. Our son was screeching, grasping me at the knees, beating my legs with both his small fists. I thought, "our life is not going to be like anyone else's here."

Perhaps the most controversial aspect of working with families who have members with disabilities is the impact of identification and diagnosis of disability on the families. Professionals have made assumptions related to stages, stress, and stigma. Parents have described parenting as stressful or as rewarding. Conflicting data are presented, depending on the researchers and the methodology. Though we feel that the activities and information we put forward in this book are valid for your work with families, there are many challenges in parent involvement research. Baker and Soden (1998) reviewed more than 200 research studies, and found many methodological limitations in terms of difficulty in design, the inability to separate the effects of the parent involvement from that of other programs, and inconsistent definitions of parent involvement.

In this chapter we will describe some of the persistent assumptions related to the impact of identification and diagnosis. We will then use an integrated perspective to present research related to families with members with disabilities.

Learning Objectives

After completing this chapter, you will be able to discuss these topics:

1. Traditional interpretations of the impact of identification and diagnosis of disability on the family
2. An integrated approach to the literature on family adjustment
3. Families' efforts toward normalization

TRADITIONAL INTERPRETATIONS

The birth of a child with disabilities has typically been accepted as a stressful event. Helff and Glidden (1998) reviewed 20 years of research to determine whether these studies reflected less negative and/or more positive conceptions of families with children with disabilities. They used two studies to independently rate 20 articles from each of three time periods; 1971–1975, 1976–1983, and 1983–1993. Results indicated that even though there was a general reduction in the negative tone of the papers, there was no real increase in a positive tone. Most investigators still write about family adjustment in a predominantly negative manner.

Scott, Atkinson, Minton, and Bowman (1997) studied the negative tone and assumption of stress among parents of children with disabilities. They compared distress levels of parents who had infants with Down syndrome to that of control parents of infants without an identified disability. The families were matched case-by-case on socioeconomic status. Although parents of infants with Down syndrome did demonstrate greater depression, Scott et al. cautioned that parenting an infant with Down syndrome may cause less distress than previously thought.

In addition to an assumption of stress, the most common interpretation of the adaptation of families to their children with disabilities has been that of stages. Parents were perceived to progress through the psychological stages of shock, denial, bargaining, anger, depression, and acceptance (Creekmore, 1988; Kroth & Otteni, 1985). Parents of children with disabilities were assumed to experience chronic sorrow (Kroth & Otteni) and grieving has been viewed by some professionals as a healthy way in which parents free themselves from the dream of having a "perfect" child (Hanline, 1991).

Though stage theory has been often described in the literature, there is little empirical evidence to support it. Blacher (1984) concluded that the stages reported are actually clinical judgments based on interviews, rather than an analysis of objective data. Allen and Affleck (1985) concurred, finding no support for stages in parents' reactions. Kratochvil and Devereaux (1988) argued that stage theory presupposes closure. Their data, however, suggested that despite overall adjustment, all parents experienced "down periods" triggered by unreached milestones, concerns about the future, and introspection.

AN INTEGRATED APPROACH

In an integrated approach to family adaptation, adjustment becomes a developmental process (Bauer & Shea, 1987; Shea & Bauer, 1991). Bronfenbrenner's (1979) ecological contexts form a framework for the simultaneous consideration of (a) interactions within the family, (b) variables in the larger social system in which the family is functioning, (c) interactions of these settings, and (d) society's overriding cultural beliefs and values.

Interactions Within the Family

Children with Down syndrome have been used as examples in family adjustment research because they are identifiable from birth, and form a heterogeneous group with regard to race, economic status, and other variables. Barnett and Boyce (1995) used a large sample of families of children with Down syndrome to study the effect of children with disabilities on parents' daily activities. In comparison with parents of children without identified disabilities, parents of children with Down syndrome devoted more time to child care and spent less time in social activities. Mothers of children with Down syndrome allocated less time to paid employment.

It is not surprising that mothers who observed more progress in their child's development reported less stress (Robbins, 1991) than mothers who noted little progress in their child. Parents of boys with disabilities with limited communication skills reported greater stress than parents of girls or those who could communicate effectively (Frey, Greenberg, & Fewell, 1989). Two-parent families experienced more positive adaptation to their children with disabilities than one-parent families (Trute & Hauch, 1988).

Lambie (2000) infuses the "normal traditional family life cycle" (Carter & McGoldrick, 1989) with the birth or diagnosis of a child with a disability. This effort is grounded in the recognition that diagnosis of a child with a disability is a significant life stressor that will affect the future development of the family at all levels (Hurtig, 1994). The first stage, "the newly married couple," typically involves the couple realigning their relationships with friends and family members and developing common goals and directions for the future. If one of the individuals is the sibling of a child with special needs, however, there may be additional challenges. Questions arise as to whether the couple will also have a child with a disability, or the role the sibling with a disability will have in the lives of the couple. The second stage, "families with young children," moves the couple from attending to each other to caring for an infant and realigning the marital system to include a child. When the child has a disability, there are the additional challenges of obtaining an accurate diagnosis, making emotional adjustments, and advising the rest of the family. In the third stage, families with elementary-aged children, typical families are emphasizing the growth needs of the child, and providing opportunities for the child to grow in independence. When there is a child with a disability, however, the family must address issues of school placement and services. In some families, difficulty in school may be the challenge that results in identifying a disability. Parents need to become educated and actively involved in the child's school placement. Balancing the functional and emotional tasks of the family becomes a major challenge.

The fourth stage of the "normal traditional family life cycle" (Carter & McGoldrick, 1989), involves families with adolescents, in which the couple must manage the child's increasing independence and refocus on middle-career and middle-marriage issues. Typical adolescents experience adjustment problems during this stage of the family cycle. This stage presents significant challenges for families with a child who has a disability, because these typical adjustment problems are exacerbated. Adolescents with disabilities have to come to grips with their limitations as they compare themselves to their peers. The challenges of planning for vocational development, difficult for all adolescents, are even more disconcerting for families of children with disabilities.

The fifth stage, families launching children, involves supporting independence and adult-to-adult relationships with grown children. Families of children with disabilities must recognize and adjust their continued responsibilities for children with disabilities. Depending on the child, parents may need to help find and fund an appropriate adult residence. The sixth stage, families in later life, forces the couple to redefine their roles, dealing with the death of friends and family members. Difficulties may arise as elderly individuals continue to be caregivers or support their child with a disability.

One of the most difficult times for parents is the diagnosis of a school-aged child. Ramp (1999) suggested that discussions with parents with a school-aged child with a disability should always start with a positive sharing of something the child can do well. Focusing on test scores can be difficult for both the teacher and the parent; providing work samples and demonstrating the child's strengths and weaknesses are more productive. Ramp contended that parents need time to assimilate, understand, and adjust to the diagnosis, and sometimes scheduling a second meeting or series of meetings is helpful.

Birth or diagnosis of a child with a disability has a profound impact on parent self-esteem, wellness, and sense of competence. Doberman (1998) reporting statements from several parents, indicated that one parent suggested that parenting an individual with a disability is like a tide; there are days when the tide of emotions is in, making the world seem overwhelming; on other days the tide is out and life is easier. Fatigue, the logistics of child care, and pessimism over the child's future seem insurmountable. On days when the tide is out, the world is under control, and the future appears more secure.

Stress of parenting a child with a disability is lower if parents' personal and family needs are being met. Doberman (1998) reports that sources of stress include practical financial problems, emotional ties within the family, modification and limitation on family activities, modification and limitation on family social life, and nurturing

ACTION STEPS 4.1: *HELPING PARENTS MAKE THEIR LIVES MORE MANAGEABLE*

Work with families to make their lives more manageable by suggesting that they

- ❑ set time aside for themselves;
- ❑ view their adult activities as a priority;
- ❑ set reasonable goals for themselves, spouses, and family, recognizing their personal skills and strengths;
- ❑ achieve a balance between work outside and inside the home;
- ❑ find and use professionals who recognize and accept the expertise of parents;
- ❑ take an active role as "parent expert" rather than a passive one when making decisions;
- ❑ seek clear and accurate information about possible outcomes for their children;
- ❑ understand that the nature of each child's disability and strengths and weaknesses will influence the type of adaptations necessary for the family to be successful;
- ❑ recognize the importance and comfort that a spiritual connection can bring to the family;
- ❑ prepare for life transitions for the child and the family;
- ❑ pick their battles with care, recognizing when it is time to "let go."

Source: Adapted from Doberman, 1998.

children who require skilled medical management. One parent described herself as part of a "4-F" family, with no friends, no fun, no furniture, and no free time. To make their life more manageable, Doberman has several suggestions for parents, presented in Action Steps 4.1.

Siblings.   Alper, Schloss, and Schloss (1995) suggested that brothers and sisters play a crucial role in the life of children with disabilities. Siblings can be models of appropriate behavior, "coaches" in daily activities, playmates, and can introduce the brother or sister with disabilities to other children. Brothers and sisters, however, need information to answer questions about their sibling's disability. They need information on dealing with their sibling's feelings and on meeting the needs of their brother or sister.

The relationship of a typically developing child with his or her sibling with a disability varies just as the relationship between any brother and sister varies. In a study of deaf-blind children, however, Heller, Gallagher, and Fredrick (1999) reported that relationships between siblings is unequal, with siblings primarily taking on a helping role. Siblings struggled to communicate with their brothers and sisters who were deaf-blind, and often did not implement the unique modifications needed to effectively interact with individuals who are deaf-blind. The relationships between siblings ranged from helping, playing, and teaching to avoiding them. Communication was a significant barrier in the development of sibling relationships.

In a study of children with learning disabilities, a substantial indicator of the impact of a child with learning disabilities on siblings was related to whether the child with learning disabilities had behavior problems. Those with few behavior

problems had more typical brother-sister relationships (Lardieri, Blacher, & Swanson, 2000).

The Larger Social System

External family supports may be found at work, at church, or in the community. Families who are able to use family and friendship network resources experience more positive adaptation (Trute & Hauch, 1988). Fujiuara (1998) conducted a survey utilizing a large sampling of families of individuals with mental retardation or developmental disabilities (91,000 individuals in 34,000 households). As a result of the profiles drawn from this study, Fujiuara reports that families remain the dominant form of support for individuals with mental retardation and developmental disabilities. A significant concern, however, is that a large cohort of individuals with mental retardation or developmental disabilities live in households headed by aging family members. In addition, significant economic disparities were found among subgroups of families, defined along gender and racial lines.

In a study of families of persons with cerebral palsy, Lin (2000) reported that more than two thirds of the variance in family coping was accounted for by positive family appraisal, support from concerned others, spiritual support, personal growth and advocacy, and positive social interaction. Once children entered school, families appeared to use more coping behaviors related to positive family appraisal and had better positive social interaction. Families of infants and preschoolers used more coping behaviors through seeking external sources.

Interractions Among Settings

Bronfenbrenner (1979) suggested that the developmental potential of a setting is enhanced if the individual's transition into that setting is made with one or more persons with whom he or she has participated with in prior settings. If families have appropriate information and advice from trusted professionals who follow them through transitions, then the transition will be more successful.

Society's Overriding Cultural Beliefs and Values

Parents must live with stereotypes regarding their children with disabilities. Cahill and Glidden (1996) described how children with Down syndrome are popularly thought of as having easy temperaments and agreeable personalities. In their study, they matched families raising children with Down syndrome and families raising children with other types of developmental disabilities. No differences were found between matched groups on various measures. The assumption that there is better adjustment in families of children with Down syndrome disappeared when the families were matched. Long-term, raising children with Down syndrome is comparable to raising other children with developmental disabilities.

Families with children with disabilities may be stigmatized and exhibit stress related to being categorized as a "family with a disability" (Darling, 1979). These feelings may be a "courtesy stigma" in which the parents' former social identity is changed after the birth or diagnosis of a child with a disability (Gallagher, Beckman, & Cross, 1983).

FAMILIES' EFFORTS TOWARD NORMALIZATION

Families can and do positively adapt to having a member with a disability. Lustig and Akey (1999) reported that social support, a family sense of coherence, and family adaptability are important resources for family adaptation. Families with higher levels of these resources are better able to function effectively when confronted with change. Dyson (1997) reported that fathers and mothers of children with developmental disabilities did not differ from each other nor from fathers and mothers of children without disabilities in parental stress, family social support, or family functioning. However, parents of children with disabilities did experience disproportionately greater levels of stress related to their children than did parents of children without disabilities.

Working with parents as soon as possible after the birth or diagnosis of the child's disability is important. Clare, Garnier, and Gallimore (1998) reported on a longitudinal study of parents' developmental expectations and child characteristics. They found that parents' expectations for their child's development remained fairly stable over time, declining as the child matured. Parents' developmental expectations were associated with child characteristics at age 3 and became increasingly correlated with child characteristics over time. Early child characteristics, rather than early parent expectations, appeared to be the best predictors of parents' developmental expectations and child outcomes when the child reaches 11 years of age.

Parents' interaction with their children remains fairly consistent over time (Floyd, Costigan, & Phillippe, 1997). Even as children develop, becoming more compliant and positive, parents persist in the intensity of their efforts at instruction and behavior. Floyd et al. suggested that effective parenting requires responsiveness to change and the development of abilities in the child.

Families are moving toward "normalization" and "social valorization" for their children. Wolfensberger (1980), when he first defined normalization, used it to describe the use of culturally valued efforts to enable people to live culturally valued lives. As the concept continued to develop, Wolfensberger (1983) moved toward using the phrase "social role valorization." He suggested that "the most explicit and highest goal of normalization must be the creation, support, and defense of valued social roles for people who are at risk for social devaluation" (p. 235). In other words, it is inadequate to focus on valuing the person and the family without also attending to the situation into which they are cast.

Normalization is the most common adaptation found among families of children with disabilities (Seligman & Darling, 1989). For some families, however, normalization remains elusive. For these families, Seligman and Darling suggested that other adaptations emerge. One alternative adaptation, crusadership, is a result of parents' attempts to bring about social change. Crusading parents engage in campaigns to increase public awareness regarding their child's disability, testify before committees, or wage legal battles with the school system or state department of education. They attempt to change the structures of services for their child and for other children.

Another adaptation, altruism, builds on normalization. Seligman and Darling (1989) indicated that some families who have achieved normalization remain active in organizations on behalf of other children, and represent successful role models for parents of younger children. A final pattern, resignation, includes families who never become involved in crusadership, altruistic activities, nor attain normalization. These parents become resigned to the status of "problem family" and lacking access to supportive resources, become isolated. Though these alternative adaptations gain much attention in research, most families attain normalization.

SUMMARY

- Professionals often make assumptions related to stress and grieving as families adapt to the birth or diagnosis of a child with a disability.
- An integrated approach to family adaptation recognizes the simultaneous contexts in which families develop.
- The birth or diagnosis of a child with a disability may modify the "normal traditional family life cycle" for some families.
- Stress in families is lower if family members' needs are met.
- External family supports may be found at work, at church, or in the community.

- Families with members with disabilities must live with stereotypes regarding their children, and may share a courtesy stigma.
- The most common adaptation for families with a member with a disability is normalization.

REFERENCES

Allen, D. A., & Affleck, G. (1985). Are we stereotyping parents?: A postscript to Blacher. *Mental Retardation, 23,* 200–202.

Alper, S., Schloss, P. J., & Schloss, C. N. (1995). Families of children with disabilities in elementary and middle school: Advocacy models and strategies. *Exceptional Children, 62*(3), 261–270.

Baker, J. L. & Soden, L. M. (1998). *The challenges of parent involvement research.* (Report No. EDO-UD-98-4). New York: ERIC Clearing House on Urban Education (ERIC Document Reproduction Service #9419030).

Barnett, W. S., & Boyce, G. C. (1995). Effects of children with Down syndrome on parents' activities. *American Journal on Mental Retardation, 100*(2), 115–127.

Bauer, A. M., & Shea, T. M. (1987). An integrative approach to parental adaptation to the birth or diagnosis of an exceptional child. *School Social Work Journal, 9,* 240–252.

Blacher, J. (1984). Sequential stages of parental adjustment to the birth of a child with handicaps: Fact or artifact. *Mental Retardation, 22*(2), 55–68.

Bronfenbrenner, U. (1979). *The ecology of human development.* Cambridge, MA: Harvard University.

Cahill, B. M., & Glidden, M. L. (1996). Influence of child diagnosis on family and parental function: Down syndrome versus other disabilities. *American Journal on Mental Retardation, 101*(2), 149–162.

Carter, B., & McGoldrick, M. (1989). Overview: the changing family life cycle—A framework for family therapy. In B. Carter & M. McGoldrick (Eds.), *The changing family life cycle: A framework for family therapy* (2nd ed., pp. 3–28). Boston: Allyn & Bacon.

Clare, L., Garnier, H., & Gallimore, R. (1998). Parents' developmental expectations and child characteristics: Longitudinal study of children with developmental delays and their families. *American Journal on Mental Retardation, 103*(2), 117–129.

Creekmore, W. N. (1988). Family-classroom: A critical balance. *Academic Therapy, 24*(2), 202–207.

Darling, R. B. (1979). *Families against society.* Beverly Hills, CA: Sage.

Doberman, F. J. (1998). Meeting the challenge. *Exceptional Parent, 28*(12), 38–40.

Dyson, L. L. (1997). Fathers and mothers of school-age children with developmental disabilities: Parental stress, family functioning, and social support. *American Journal on Mental Retardation, 102*(3), 267–279.

Floyd, F. J., Costigan, C. L., & Phillippe, K. A. (1997). Developmental change and consistency in parent interactions with school-age children who have mental retardation. *American Journal on Mental Retardation, 101*(6), 279–594.

Frey, K. S., Greenberg, M. T., & Fewell, R. R. (1989). Stress and coping among parents of handicapped children: A multidimensional approach. *American Journal of Mental Retardation, 94,* 240–249.

Fujiuara, G. T. (1998). Demography of family households. *American Journal on Mental Retardation, 103*(3), 225–235.

Gallagher, J. J., Beckman, P., & Cross, A. (1983). Families of handicapped children: sources of stress and its amelioration. *Exceptional Children, 50,* 10–19.

Hanline, M. (1991). Transitions and critical events in the family life cycle. *Psychology in the Schools*, 28(1), 53–59.

Helff, C. M., & Glidden, M. L. (1998). More positive or less negative? Trends in research on adjustment of families rearing children with developmental disabilities. *Mental Retardation*, 36(6), 457–464.

Heller, K. W., Gallagher, P. A., & Fredrick, L. D. (1999). Parents' perceptions of siblings' interactions with their brothers and sisters who are deaf-blind. *Journal of the Association for Persons with Severe Handicaps*, 23(1), 33–43.

Hurtig, A. L. (1994). Chronic illness and developmental family psychology. In L. L'Abate (Ed.), *Handbook of developmental family psychology and psychopathology* (pp. 265–283). New York: Wiley.

Kratochvil, M. S., & Devereaux, S. A. (1988). Counseling needs of parents of handicapped children. *Social Casework*, 69(7), 420–426.

Kroth, R. L., & Otteni, H. (1985). *Communicating with parents of exceptional children: Improving parent-teacher relationships* (2nd ed.). Denver: Love.

Lambie, R. (2000). *Family systems within educational contexts*. Denver: Love.

Lardieri, L. A., Blacher, J., & Swanson, H. L. (2000). Sibling relationships and parent stress in families of children with and without learning disabilities. *Learning Disabilities Quarterly*, 23(2), 105–116.

Lin, S. (2000). Coping and adaptation in families of children with cerebral palsy. *Exceptional Children*, 66(2), 201–218.

Lustig, D. C., & Akey, T. (1999). Adaptation in families with adult children with mental retardation: Impact of family strengths and appraisal. *Education and Training in Mental Retardation and Developmental Disabilities*, 34(3), 260–270.

Ramp, A. (1999). How to tell parents their child has a disability. CEC *Today*, 5 (8), 6.

Robbins, F. (1991). Family characteristics, family training, and the progress of young children with autism. *Journal of Early intervention*, 15(2), 173–184.

Scott, B. S., Atkinson, L., Minton, H. L., & Bowman, (1997). Psychological distress of parents of infants with Down syndrome. *American Journal on Mental Retardation*, 102(2), 161–171.

Seligman, M., & Darling, L. B. (1989). *Ordinary families, special children*. New York: Guilford Press.

Shea, T. M., & Bauer, A. M. (1991). *Parents and teachers of children with exceptionalities: A handbook for collaboration* (2nd ed.). Boston: Allyn & Bacon.

Trute, B., & Hauch, C. (1988). Building on family strength: A study of families with positive adjustment to the birth of a developmentally disabled child. *Journal of Marital and Family Therapy*, 14(2), 185–193.

Wolfensberger, W. (1983). Social role valorization: A proposed new term for the principle of normalization. *Mental Retardation*, 21, 235–239.

Wolfensberger, W. (1980). The definition of normalization: Update, problems, disagreements, and misunderstandings. In R. J. Flynn & K. E. Nitsch (Eds.), *Normalization, social integration, and community services* (pp. 71–115). Baltimore: University Park Press.

CHAPTER 5

A Model for
Engaging Parents

I've been to those parent meetings. I sit there, bored to tears, and think, "Why doesn't somebody ask me what I want to know?" But I'm scared to not come, not do face-time. I'm scared they won't think I'm a concerned parent.

Engaging parents is not easy. The American family has changed, increasing the complexity of interaction. Most often it is not a lack of interest that keeps parents from becoming involved in their child's education (State of Iowa, 1998), but the barriers of poverty, single-parenthood, non-English literacy, and cultural and socioeconomic isolation. A survey conducted by the National Parent-Teachers Association (1992) found that parents reported that they did not become involved in their child's education because of time (89%), feeling they had nothing to contribute (32%), not knowing how to become involved (32%), lack of child care (28%), feeling intimidated (25%), not being available during the time school functions are scheduled (18%), or not feeling welcome at school (9%).

Parent involvement shifts as children progress through school grades or programs. Both the quality and quantity of parent contact with the school decline as children get older, and the proportion of parents serving as school or classroom volunteers decreases (Puma, Jones, Rock, & Fernandez, 1993). By eighth grade, more than two thirds of all parents report that they have not talked to school officials about the academic program, approximately one half of the parents report that they have attended a school meeting, and less than one third had visited their children's classes (Office of Educational Research and Improvement, 1990).

Programs that have been successful in working with parents have similar characteristics. These programs tend to focus on prevention rather than treatment, and recognize the need to work with the entire family and community. Successful programs have a commitment to the family as an active participant in their children's education and to cultural diversity. In addition, successful programs focus on strength-based needs, programming, and evaluation and have flexible staffing (Dunst & Trivette, 1994).

There are several issues that emerge when working with parents. Kagan (1995) suggested that equity must be addressed, making sure that experiences are open to both families with limited access and resources and those with greater resources and access. Programs often struggle with the issue of being voluntary or involuntary, a characteristic that can change the whole intent and nature of the activities. Kagan argues that to work effectively with parents, professionals must be culturally competent. Finally, programs should be of high quality and should be specific in terms of their objectives.

In order to facilitate the involvement of parents in their child's education, we propose an integrated model. The model is grounded in the parents' assessment of their needs, and is outcomes-based. Activities emphasize positive child-rearing practices and behavioral supports that recognize each parent and child as an individual with unique abilities, needs, and environmental influences. The model involves cooperation, collaboration, and mutual problem-solving. Aversive interventions are inappropriate for this model. The primary goal of the model is to further the optimal development of the child and a positive quality of life for the whole family.

To illustrate our model, we will use the case of Cassia. Cassia is a fifth-grade student who was identified as having learning disabilities in third grade. She lives with her mother, who works full time, and grandmother, who provides after school care for her. Cassia is placed in the general education classroom, with accommodations and resource support from Mr. Kennedy, a special educator.

Learning Objectives

After completing this chapter, you will be able to discuss these topics:

1. An integrated model for engaging parents
2. Strategies for conducting the initial conference with the parent and family
3. Ways to help families identify their needs and identify goals and objectives for their participation
4. Ways to evaluate efforts to engage parents

AN INTEGRATED MODEL FOR ENGAGING PARENTS

Swap (1991) described four basic models of parent involvement. In the first model, the protective model, the goal is to reduce conflict between parents and educators, primarily through separating their functions, i.e., "protecting" the school from parent interference. The protective model assumes that parents delegate the education of their children to the school, and that the school is then accountable. There is little parent intrusion, and no structure is used for preventive problem solving. The second model is that of school-to-home transmission, in which the school enlists parents in supporting the objectives of the school. This model assumes that parents should endorse the importance of school expectations. Parents, however, are not equal partners, and differences in background may make teachers and parents feel uncomfortable.

The third model Swap (1991) proposed is that of curriculum enrichment, in which the goal is to expand and extend the school's curriculum by incorporating the contributions of families. In this model, parents and educators are assumed to work together to enrich curriculum objectives and content. Relationships are based on mutual respect. In the final model, parent-educator partnership, the goal is for parents and educators to work together to accomplish success for all children. This model assumes that a common mission requires collaboration between parents and educators. This is a true partnership based on collegiality. The model presented and discussed in this chapter is a partnership model.

Our proposed model for engaging parents consists of five phases: (a) intake and assessment, (b) selection of goals and objectives, (c) planning and implementation of activities, (d) evaluation of activities, and (e) review (Shea and Bauer, 1991). The model is depicted in Figure 5.1.

The "intake and assessment" phase is actually the first meeting between parents and teacher. During this meeting, the teacher works to establish a positive interpersonal relationship and to review and discuss the child's program and progress including the child's Individualized Education Plan. At this session, the teacher attempts to ascertain the parents' perception of the challenges confronting their child. The assessment aspect of the meeting focuses primarily on the parents' perception of their child and the child's disability. In the assessment process, the teacher determines the parents' capacity to attend to their child's disability and verifies their understanding of the information presented during the initial meeting. Through assessment (a) the parents provide their perspective on the child and the assessment of his or her abilities, and (b) the teacher and parents assess the parents' readiness, interest, willingness, capacity, and need for engagement in their child's program. This phase is completed when parents and teacher agree that they have sufficient information and understanding to continue to Phase 2: selection of goals and objectives.

Setting specific goals and objectives is one of the most crucial components of a model for parent engagement in their child's education. Dunst, Trivette and Deal (1988) suggested that the failure of efforts at engaging parents in their child's education is usually due to a lack of consensus on what is needed or what should be done. Selection of goals and objectives is a participatory process, in which parents and teacher synthesize their assessment data. Unmet needs are translated into program goals and objectives. Goals are general targets of the program, and state the desired outcomes of parent engagement. Objectives serve as benchmarks toward those goals,

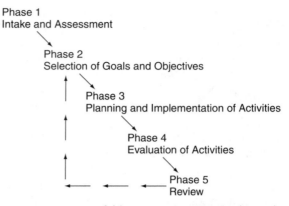

Figure 5.1 A *model for engaging parents.* (*Shea and Bauer,* 1987; 1991)

stating the behavior, knowledge, or skill the parent, child, or teacher will exhibit upon completing an activity. Goals and objectives should be selected independent of whether a suitable activity is presently available.

Teachers and parents frequently select more objectives than can reasonably be attained. Thus, they must organize objectives by priority. Teachers and parents should each have one of their high priority objectives selected for immediate attention.

In the third phase of parent engagement, activities are planned and implemented. Objectives are translated into activities. These activities may be viewed as occurring along a continuum. Activities vary by the amount of (a) time involved, (b) personal disclosure, and (c) personal commitment and involvement. For example, reading a written notice is far less involved than participating in a parent-to-parent conference or discussion group. Activities can be loosely grouped as follows:

1. Information-giving activities, such as newsletters, written notes, and periodic report cards, in which the family passively receives information;

2. Information-sharing activities, such as parent-teacher conferences, in which information is shared between parents and teacher;

3. Collaborative support for school programs, in which the family members work together to implement specific goals, objectives, or educational activities with the child in the home;

4. Collaboration in the school community, in which family members serve as volunteers, tutors, or preparing instructional materials;

5. Parent education, in which specific efforts are undertaken to increase parents' knowledge and skills;

6. Parent leadership, policy, and advocacy efforts.

A continuum representing these efforts is provided in Figure 5.2

Figure 5.2   *Continuum of family involvement activities.*

The fourth phase in the proposed model is the evaluation of activities. The most basic evaluation efforts address the following questions:

1. Is the activity available?
2. Is the activity offered as scheduled?
3. Are all parties participating in the activity at the agreed-upon level?

These questions assist teacher and parent in determining if they are maintaining their part of the agreement. For example, if an activity does not take place as scheduled and both parties had agreed that the teacher was to organize and conduct the activity, the person responsible for the problem is clear—the teacher. Alternatively, if an activity takes place and parents do not attend or participate, the issue is again clarified. The parents did not meet their responsibility.

A different level of evaluation is content evaluation, which responds to the question, "Are the participants learning the knowledge and skills promoted by the activity?" For example, teachers can examine parents' participation in a study group or observe the parent interacting with his or her child and determine if the parent has gained the knowledge and skill promoted in an activity.

The final phase of the model is review. This is conducted during a parent-teacher conference. Generally, parent engagement only ends when the parent or teacher leaves the school or community or when the student graduates from school or moves to another program, classroom, or teacher. However, parents and teacher should meet annually to review program plans. This step ensures that the program remains responsive to parent and teacher needs and that new goals and objectives are developed that support continuing engagement.

Date: 9/27/03
Student: *Cassia Santiago*

Parent(s): *Ms. Santiago; Mrs. Santiago (Grandmother)*

Teacher(s): *Mr. Kennedy*

Summary of Initial Meeting:

Ms. Santiago (Cassia's mother) and Mrs. Santiago (Grandmother) both attended the conference. An ecomap was generated and waking day interview was conducted. The purpose of the meeting was to identify goals and objectives, and all parties agreed that the meeting succeeded in addressing this purpose.

Goals and Objectives:

Cassia will decrease her distactibility at home.

Through using self-recording, Cassia will evaluate her attending to a request made by her mother and grandmother.

Activities:

Cassia will record if she completed the task first time asked, after a second request, or only after the threat of having privileges removed. After Cassia has accumulated ten "first time asked" checks, her mother will take her to the mall.

Ms. Santiago will return the checksheets the fifth of each month.

Due to involvement in church and other activities, further activities were not desired.

Evaluation:

After three checklists, Mr. Kennedy will contact Ms. Santiago and discuss the progress.

Figure 5.3   *Program development form.*

One essential part of parent engagement is to track the family's participation. The program development form (Figure 5.3) is useful in both evaluating and reviewing the parent engagement plan.

STRATEGIES FOR THE INITIAL CONFERENCE

Parents' initial conference with their child's teacher is a critical venture. In this chapter, we will describe some tools which will help educators work with parents during this initial conference. In Chapter 6, we will discuss basic skills related to communication and collaboration.

Interviews

Interviews are the primary assessment technique in parent engagement. Interviews, however, are only a means to an end—a way to gather information regarding the parents' needs. Kroth (1985) described five deterrents to effective interviews:

1. Fatigue, particularly if the conference takes place after a day's work
2. Strong feelings, which can interfere with how participants perceive situations
3. The use of emotionally loaded words or phrases
4. Teacher talking to the extent that the parent's participation is limited
5. The environment, which, if distracting or uncomfortable, limits the possibilities for a productive interview

During the interview, the teacher will generally ask questions for two purposes: (a) to obtain information, and (b) to redirect the interview when it strays from pertinent topics. The initial interview is key, and allows the teacher to do the following:

- Establish a positive working relationship between teacher and family members;
- Review and discuss the child's program;
- Review and discuss related services and accommodations;
- Review and discuss the role of the parents;
- Introduce the parents to engagement in their child's education.

Name: Cassia Santiago

Individual interviewed: Ms. Santiago, Mrs. Santiago

On the left side of the checklist, clarify the specific activities or events that occur in the family. On the right side, describe the child's behavior during that activity or event.

Waking up, dressing: Cassia takes a long time to dress, fixing and refixing her hair and deciding what to wear.

Breakfast: Cassia doesn't come when called the first time; messing with her cat; often late and running for the bus; Cassia says, "It's Lucifer—he's just too cute."

Getting ready for bus/transportation to school: Often runs for the bus, breakfast in hand.

After arrival home from school: Sets the timer for a 15-minute break; then starts homework, gets a drink, does a little more, talks to grandma about dinner.

Preparation for dinner: Helps set the table, uses the time to chat with grandma about school, boys, clothes, hair, etc.

Dinner: Sometimes has a snack and doesn't eat much; reminded not to snack.

After dinner: Begins homework, gets up for a drink; does another problem; turns on the radio; does a little more, plays with cat who sits on her lap—15-minute assignment can take all night.

Preparation for bed: Long, long bubble baths and showers; efforts to lay out clothes for the next day usually turn into "fashion shows."

Bedtime: Difficulty settling down to sleep; gets up and sits with mom; goes to the kitchen, etc.

Figure 5.4 *Waking day interview.*

This intake conference actually serves as an assessment. At this conference, several important issues can be clarified. The parents' need for information, support, services, and education may begin to emerge. In addition, parents may express concerns about their child's present and future. Parents' priorities also emerge.

The ecobehavioral interview (Barnett, Carey, & Hall, 1993) is an important assessment tool. This interview can be used to develop detailed descriptions of behaviors across the environments in which the child and family interact. The ecobehavioral interview can also be used to analyze specific situations in depth, and help identify the people, places, and things related to the issue of concern. Ecobehavioral interviews can take many formats, but are usually based on the "waking day interview" developed by Wahler and Cormier (1970). During this interview, the teacher asks the parent to describe the child's interactions and behavior in each of the settings or events that occur in the home. A sample home waking day interview is presented in Figure 5.4

By studying the results of the waking day interview, the teacher and parent can identify behaviors that cut across various environments. For example, the parent may indicate that a child has difficulty completing a simple task of setting the table, leaves "dirties" on the floor, and has difficulty staying with a game until it is finished. Rather than separate behaviors, these may all be indicators of distractibility.

An ecomap (Holman, 1983) is another strategy that can be completed during an interview. Ecomaps were originally used to help social workers assess individual family needs. These maps portray the child's developmental contexts, showing the interactions of members with outside resources including extended family members, schools, health services, friends, and work. The ecomap portrays the nature and flow of the relationships between family members and outside resources. In this way, it identifies areas of stress and support within the family system as well as areas where individual and family needs are unmet.

To provide the practitioner and family with a broad understanding of the family's perceptions of its ecological system, Holman (1983) suggested involving as many family members as possible in the ecomap development process. To develop an ecomap, the teacher sits with the family group around a large piece of paper or a posterboard, and asks nonintrusive questions such as "Who are the people who live together in your family?" In the ecomap, the nuclear family is drawn in a center circle with squares for males and circles for females, with generational mapping that is usually used in family mapping. Then, the family as a whole and individual members are connected with important extrafamilial systems. Different types of lines are used to illustrate the types of relationships involved; for example, unidirectional relationships are indicated by ⇨ or ⇦. Strong positive relationships may be depicted with a solid line (_____), tenuous relationships by dashed lines (- - - - -), and nontenuous relationships by (+ + + + +). An example of an ecomap is presented in Figure 5.5.

Ecomaps provide considerable information on the family's social environment, significant sources of stress, and available used and unused sources of social support. This assessment strategy is valuable during the initial conference because it generates a great deal of information in a brief period of time. The ecomap can be used to specify and individualize the stress, conflicts, and available resources within the family system and to generate a comprehensive family history.

At times, parents may feel more comfortable meeting the teacher during the initial conference after completing a needs assessment on their own prior to the meeting. Using a "parent(s) interest form" may be less threatening for some parents, and may be completed by the parent at his or her convenience. There are, however, a few problems with "fill-in-and-return" forms. Any such needs assessment requires a fair amount of English literacy on the part of the parent, and requires the ability to follow fairly complex written directions. In addition, such an effort impersonalizes the teacher's efforts to work with the parent. A sample interest form is provided in Figure 5.6.

In the case of Cassia, Mr. Kennedy invited both her mother and grandmother to the initial conference. During the needs assessment, they completed both an ecomap

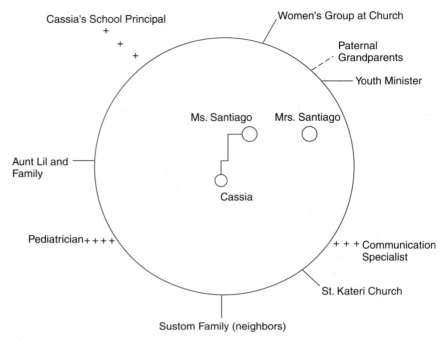

Figure 5.5 *Ecomap.*

and a waking day interview. The ecomap indicated that Cassia's family is highly involved in church activities, and that individuals from their church were quite supportive when Cassia's grandmother was recently hospitalized. The family has few interactions outside of those within the church but does have a fairly positive relationship with the school. However, both Cassia's mother and grandmother reported a tenuous relationship with the school principal, whom they perceive to be rigid and conservative and having little interest in families that are not comprised of "mom, dad, two kids, and a dog."

The waking day interview revealed that much of Cassia's daily supervision and care is conducted by her grandmother. Her mother, using public transportation to get to and from work, is usually out the door as Cassia comes to the kitchen for breakfast, and does not arrive home until dinnertime. Cassia's grandmother enforces rules and schedules because of mother's work schedule. On Thursdays, when Cassia's grandmother has her meeting at church, Cassia and her mother try to "do a girl thing" such as watch a video together, go shopping, go to a fast-food restaurant for dinner, or walk around the mall. Across environments, Cassia's "messing" (her mother's word) and "piddling" (her grandmother's word) was a consistent problem. Cassia would become distracted and play with her cat after being called for breakfast, often resulting with a grabbed piece of toast and a run for the bus. Cassia would begin

Date _____

Student _____

Parent(s) _____

Directions:

Listed below are concerns common to parents. These may or may not concern you at this time. Please complete only those items that currently concern you. This information will only be used to help plan ways to support you. All information is held in strict confidence.

1. Read each statement carefully.
2. Circle whether or not the concern is important to you.
3. Under each concern are several statements suggesting ways you may prefer to meet your stated needs. Check one or two of the four statements.
4. You may write any additional comments in the space provided.

1. I need to discuss my feelings about my child and his or   Important   Not important
   her learning with someone who understands the problem.

_____ I'd like to talk to a professional.
_____ I'd like to talk with a parent of a child who is similar to mine.
_____ I'd like to be referred to another agency for counseling.
_____ I'd prefer to read articles and books.
_____ I'd prefer _____
        _____.

2. I would like to learn more about my child's special needs.   Important   Not important

_____ I'd like to receive some written information.
_____ I'd like to observe teachers and other professionals working with my child and discuss my
        observations.
_____ I'd like an individual parent-teacher conference.
_____ I'd like a parent-teacher discussion group.
_____ I'd prefer _____
        _____.

3. I would like to learn more about how children develop   Important   Not important
   and learn.

_____ I'd like to receive some written information.
_____ I'd like to participate in a formal class.
_____ I'd prefer a parent-teacher discussion group.
_____ I'd prefer meetings with specialists.
_____ I'd prefer _____
        _____.

Figure 5.6   *Parent(s) interest form. (adapted from Shea & Bauer, 1991)*

4. I would like to learn more about how to help   Important   Not important
   my child at home.

_____ I'd like to observe my child at school.
_____ I'd like to attend a presentation on instructional methods.
_____ I'd like to work with the teacher in my child's classroom.
_____ I'd prefer to receive readings and newsletters.
_____ I'd prefer _____

_____.

5. I'd prefer _____.   Important   Not important

The following topics and activities may be of interest to parents of children with and without disabilities. Not all parents are interested in any single item, nor is any parent interested in all of the items. Please indicate any of the items that are of interest to you by placing a check mark next to the item.

_____ 1. Helping my child learn
_____ 2. Building my child's self-confidence
_____ 3. Selecting books, games, toys, and experiences to help my child learn
_____ 4. Teaching my child to better follow directions
_____ 5. Helping my child enjoy learning
_____ 6. Supporting my child's language development
_____ 7. Teaching my child problem-solving skills
_____ 8. Fulfilling my role as a parent to my child
_____ 9. Protecting my child from getting hurt
_____ 10. Caring for my child when he or she is sick or injured
_____ 11. Helping my child develop positive behavior
_____ 12. Dealing with my child's misbehavior
_____ 13. Teaching my child to express feelings in a socially acceptable manner
_____ 14. Teaching my child to live in harmony with the family
_____ 15. Developing a positive and productive relationship with my child
_____ 16. Developing my problem-solving skills

I am interested in learning more about

_____ Art, creative movement, and music activities for my child
_____ Educational games and activities
_____ Exercise, health, wellness
_____ Nutrition and diet
_____ Recreation and leisure
_____ Sleep
_____ Other: _____

Figure 5.6 (*Continued*)

homework, get up for a snack, do another problem, then turn on the radio to listen to a specific song, etc. until a 20-minute assignment became an all night event. Even when out with her mother and grandmother, Cassia would become distracted and messing.

In the written needs/interest form, Cassia's mother and grandmother had difficulty agreeing on some needs. Cassia's mother wanted more information about learning disabilities and wanted to talk with other parents. Cassia's grandmother felt that Cassia needed to work harder, and that her uncle, who now had a responsible job with the post office, had the same messing problems.

IDENTIFYING NEEDS, GOALS, AND OBJECTIVES

When given the opportunity, parents are quite active in setting goals (Powell, 1989). Identifying needs, goals, and objectives is usually completed through an additional parent-teacher conference. During this conference, all of the information gathered is reviewed. Presenting this information in a written format and reviewing it with the parent may be helpful. Rock (2000) suggested having butcher paper, an easel, a dry erase board, or chalkboard, with markers or writing instruments for all participants, to record ideas brainstormed at the meeting. In addition, copies of the student's individualized education plan should be available. Rock suggests having beverages and snacks to increase the participants' comfort during the meeting.

When discussing priorities and needs, sensitivity is necessary. The need for sensitivity may be heightened when there is a cultural mismatch between the teacher and parents. Dennis and Giangreco (1996) provided a series of suggestions related to conducting such an interview. They suggest that teachers seek help from "cultural interpreters" before the interview, and carefully ascertain literacy and language status of the individuals who will be participating. In addition, teachers should involve family members in planning the interview, and preview the interview with family members. The teacher should carefully examine the nature of the questions asked, and respond to the family's interaction style. Dennis and Giangreco presented several keys to conducting sensitive interviews, including:

- Appreciating the uniqueness in each family;
- Being aware of the influence of your role as a professional;
- Acknowledging your own cultural biases;
- Seeking new understanding and knowledge of cultures;
- Developing an awareness of cultural norms;
- Learning from families.

Parents' involvement is in the hands of the parents. Though their priorities may not match the educator's, using the parents' priorities initially may assist in introducing the teacher's priorities at a later time. Teachers must understand and respect the family's beliefs and values, and recognize the family members as experts with regard to their child and their family. Through recognizing the parents' goals and priorities, the teacher is showing support for and being empathetic to the family.

In the case of Cassia, both mother and grandmother agreed that something needed to be done about Cassia's distractibility, whether it be called messing or piddling. Though Cassia's mother wanted additional written information regarding this and about learning disabilities in general, her grandmother contended that she knew how to handle Cassia and if Cassia's mother would let her take things into her hands everything would be fine. Cassia's mother held firm, however, and asked if the self-recording form that was used at school could also be used at home. Because of their schedule and involvement with church, they didn't want parent group and support sessions at the school. Cassia's mother did state that on the fifth of every month she would return to the teacher the checksheet about how well Cassia was doing with her "messing."

EVALUATING EFFORTS TO ENGAGE PARENTS

Borden and Perkins (1999) suggested that there are specific themes or factors that should be evaluated in collaborative relationships. These questions can provide important self-evaluative information. The basis of self-evaluation is presented in Action Steps 5.1.

By reflecting on these factors, Borden and Perkins suggested that participants will better be able to attain their goals.

Kreider (1998), of the Harvard Family Research Project, suggested that parents should also evaluate their participation. She contended that parents should ask themselves:

- What is my relationship like with my child's teacher?
- How do I find out what the school expects from me and share with them what I want for my child from the school?
- How can I help my child learn at home?
- What can I tell my child's teacher about my child?
- How can I be most helpful to the school?
- How can I help educate teachers?

In the case of Cassia, the evaluation was based on the monthly checksheets that her mother returned. In addition, Cassia's mother responded to questions related to whether the written materials she was provided by the teacher were helpful, and if she would recommend them to other parents.

In addition to evaluating individual efforts to engage parents, the Wisconsin Department of Public Instruction (1996) suggested ways to evaluate the overall impact of parent engagement. They suggested three key areas of data. First, the levels of participation should be evaluated, gathering information regarding the number of participants in activities, number of parent contacts made by teachers, and the number of contacts initiated by parents. The second source of information, information about activities, should include written evaluations of all classes, workshops, and activities. In addition, pre- and post-assessment of children's learning resulting from specific

ACTION STEPS 5.1: *EVALUATING INTERACTIONS WITH FAMILIES*

Evaluate your interactions in the following areas by asking these questions:

- ❑ Communication: Is there open communication? Is a way of continuing the communication established?
- ❑ Sustainability: Does participation continue? Are the resources still available?
- ❑ Research and evaluation: Was there a needs assessment? Is information gathered about whether goals are being met?
- ❑ Political climate: Is there a positive history and environment surrounding power and decision-making?
- ❑ Resources: Are environmental, in-kind, financial, and human resources available?
- ❑ Catalysts: What can spark collaboration on a problem or a comprehensive approach?
- ❑ Politics/laws/regulations: Have policies changed in order to allow the collaboration to function effectively?
- ❑ History: Is there a history of working cooperatively and solving problems?
- ❑ Connectedness: Are participants connected? Are there informal and formal communication networks?
- ❑ Leadership: Does the leadership support team building, capitalize on diversity, and use individual strengths?
- ❑ Understanding community: Do participants understand the community, including its people, cultures, values, and habits?

Source: Adapted from Borden & Perkins, 1999.

kinds of activities in workshops should be conducted. Finally, information about participants and their perceptions should be gathered. This information includes parents' and family members' perceptions about (a) comfort level, (b) programs meeting their needs, (c) students' learning, (d) appropriateness of materials and supplies, (e) publicity and information about the activities, and (f) diverse ethnic, cultural, and linguistic groups feeling welcome.

SUMMARY

- An integrated model for engaging parents includes (a) intake and assessment, (b) selection of goals and objectives, (c) planning and implementation of activities, (d) evaluation of activities, and (e) review.
- Parent activities vary by the amount of time involved, personal disclosure, and personal commitment and involvement.
- Interviews are the primary assessment technique in parent engagement, and should be conducted with sensitivity.
- Efforts to engage parents should be evaluated in terms of levels of participation, evaluations of the activities themselves, and parents' or family members' perceptions about the involvement efforts.

REFERENCES

Barnett, D. W., Carey, K. T., & Hall, J. D. (1993). Naturalistic intervention design for young children: Foundations, rationales, and strategies. *Topics in Early Childhood Special Education*, 13(4), 430–444.

Borden, L. M., & Perkins, D. F. (1999). Assessing your collaboration: A self-evaluation tool. *Journal of Extension*, 37(2), 1–6.

Dennis, R. E., & Giangreco, M. F. (1996). Creating conversation: Reflections on cultural sensitivity in family interviewing. *Exceptional Children*, 67, 103–116.

Dunst, C. J., & Trivette, C. M. (1994). Aims and principles of family support programs. In C.J. Dunst, C. M. Trivette, & A. G. Deal (Eds.), *Supporting and strengthening families: Vol. 1 Methods, strategies and practices* (pp. 30–48). Cambridge, MA: Brookline Books.

Dunst, C. J., Trivette, C. M., & Deal, A. G. (1988). *Enabling and empowering families*. Cambridge, MA: Brookline Books.

Holman, A. (1983) *Family assessment: Tools and understanding for intervention*. Beverly Hills, CA: Sage.

Kagan, S. L. (1995). *The challenge of parenting in the '90s*. Washington, DC: The Aspen Institute.

Kreider, H. (1998). *Early childhood digest: Families and teachers as partners*. Washington, DC: National Institute on Early Childhood Development and Education, Office of Educational Research and Improvement.

Kroth, R. L. (1985). *Communicating with parents of exceptional children: Improving parent-teacher relationships* (2nd ed.). Denver: Love.

National Parent Teachers Association (1992). *Survey of parent involvement*. Washington, DC: Author.

Office of Educational Research and Improvement (1990). *A profile of the American eighth grader*. Washington, DC: U. S. Department of Education, OERI.

Powell, D. (1989). *Families and early childhood programs*. ERIC Document No. ED309872. Washington, DC: National Association for the Education of Young Children.

Puma, M. J., Jones, C. C., Rock, D., & Fernandez, R. (1993). *Prospects: The congressionally mandated study of educational growth and opportunity: Interim report*. Bethesda, MD: ABT Associates.

Rock, M. L. (2000). Parents as equal partners: Balancing the scales in IEP development. *Teaching Exceptional Children*, 32(6), 30–37.

Shea, T. M., & Bauer, A. M. (1991). *Parents and teachers of children with exceptionalities: A handbook for collaboration*. (2nd ed.). Boston: Allyn & Bacon.

State of Iowa, Department of Education (1998). *Parent involvement in education: A resource for parents, educators, and communities*. DesMoines, IA: Author.

Swap, S. M. (1991). *Developing home-school partnerships: From concepts to practice*. NY: Teachers College Press.

Wahler, R. G., & Cormier, W. H. (1970). The ecological interview: A first step in outpatient child behavior therapy. *Journal of Behavioral Therapy and Experimental Psychology*, 1, 279–289.

Wisconsin Department of Public Instruction (1996). *Organizing a successful family center in your school*. Madison, WI: Author.

CHAPTER 6

Collaboration and Communication

Communicating with teachers? I don't even think we speak the same language! I know we don't live the same lives.

The education of children with disabilities should be a joint venture between families and teachers (Spinelli, 1999). The National Standards for Parent/Family Involvement Programs (Lockett, 1999) emphasized collaboration between home and school, promoting and supporting parenting skills, the parent's role in student learning, and parents as full partners in decision-making and advocacy. Bauer, Joseph, and Zwicker (1998) related that the evolution of the word *partner* from the Middle English word *partaker*, one who shares, clarifies the meaning of the word. As in dance, partnerships imply a responsiveness in which both individuals support each other but are also allowed a solo, a moment in the spotlight. This notion of partners is the foundation of a collaborative environment. This collaboration supports the development of an integrated, coordinated social context to foster children's development (Epstein, 1995). Though it is emphasized throughout the literature and the media, "collaboration" frequently remains elusive.

The nature of parent-teacher collaboration may evolve as the child grows and learns. In this chapter, we discuss general information regarding collaboration and communication that applies across age groups.

Learning Objectives

After completing this chapter, you will be able to discuss these topics:

1. The nature of collaboration and partnerships with parents
2. Communicating effectively with families
3. Barriers to collaboration and participation

4. Attributes of effective parent/teacher collaboration
5. Communicating effectively with families from diverse cultural, ethnic, and linguistic groups

COLLABORATION AND PARTNERSHIPS

Collaboration is a process in which people with diverse expertise and experience work together to generate new solutions to mutually defined problems (Idol, Paolucci-Whitcomb, & Nevin, 1986). Collaboration occurs when power and authority are shared and where people are brought together to achieve common goals that could not be accomplished by a single individual or organization independently (Kagan, 1991). The end result of collaboration between families and teachers is better outcomes for children and families (Bruner, Kunesch, & Knuth, 1992). Bruner et al. suggested these characteristics of effective collaboration:

- All key players are involved;
- Realistic strategies are used that reflect the priorities of all involved;
- A shared vision is established;
- Collaborators agree to disagree during the process, and have a constructive problem-solving process to move forward;
- Make promises you can keep;
- Keep your eyes on the prize; don't let day-to-day operations and disagreements interfere with striving for better outcomes;
- Build ownership at all levels;
- Avoid "red herrings" and don't let "technical difficulties" impede the development of shared vision;
- Institutionalize your successes;
- Publicize your successes.

Collaborating with families requires a wide range of services. Cheney and Osher (1997) suggested that collaboration involves four dimensions. The first dimension is relationship and partnership building. Second and third are coordinating services and explaining service options, respectively. The final dimension is flexibility. Through these dimensions, professionals can assist families in their efforts to raise their children and provide self-help to strengthen their parental roles. A goal of this collaboration is maintaining the integrity of the family unit, and supporting parents as they struggle, in some situations, to survive.

Petit (1989) suggested that collaboration with families can involve monitoring, informing, and participating. In monitoring, schools make parents aware of the school situation. In informing, parents are made aware of the policies, procedures, aims, and expectations of the school and classroom. Participation, Petit's final level, involves active participation on the part of teachers. This participation may range from working with students in the classroom by sharing books or writings (Simic, 1991), to positive behavioral support across home and school (Fox, Vaughn, Dunlap, & Bucy, 1997), to participating in action research with parents pursuing their own research questions about their child's learning (Kay & Fitzgerald, 1997).

COMMUNICATING EFFECTIVELY WITH PARENTS

Communicating with families and students is an essential skill for teachers. In assessments of teachers' communication skills, 13 areas have been identified: oral language usage, fluency, feedback, speech mechanics, subject knowledge, explaining, emphasis, directing, questioning, using students' ideas, interacting with parents, enthusiasm, and nonverbal communication (McCaleb, 1987). In interacting with parents, both written and oral communication is used.

Humans communicate at several levels simultaneously: through verbal expressions (what they say); through body language (how they behave); and through emotional responses (how they feel). The more congruent these levels of expression, the more meaningful or understandable the message becomes. To fully interpret others' messages, an individual must listen to the words, and interpret both the accompanying body language and emotional content. Further, by understanding three important forms of language—descriptive, inferential, and evaluative—people can reduce the need to amend original messages.

Descriptive language relates information about things the communicator has observed using his or her senses of sight, hearing, taste, touch, and smell. Inferential

Table 6.1   Words and phrases to avoid and use.

Avoid	Use
Must	Should
Is lazy	Seems to need more effort
Is a troublemaker	Disturbs others
Is uncooperative	Needs help in working with others
Cheats	Let's others do his or her work
Is below average	Is working at his or her own level
Truant	Absent without permission
Impertinent	Discourteous
Steals	Takes without permission
Is dirty	Needs help in grooming
Disinterested	Complacent, not challenged
Is stubborn	Feels strongly about his or her own way
Insolent	Outspoken
Wastes time	Needs to make better use of time
Is sloppy	Could be neater
Is mean	Has difficulty getting along with others
Time and again	Repeatedly
Dubious	Uncertain
Poor work	Work is below his or her usual standard
Will flunk	Could be more successful if......

language describes patterns a person has become aware of through multiple observations. Such language is tentative, qualifying observations with words such as appears, seems, and maybe. Evaluative language communicates judgments and conclusions. Evaluations can be positive or negative statements because they refer to the speaker's values. Teachers should be able to relate objective information to parents about their child (descriptive language), communicate patterns that seem to emerge from observations (inferential language), and formulate conclusions (evaluative language).

Clarity of language when communicating with parents is essential. The use of clear language helps parents, especially parents from various ethnic, cultural, economic, or linguistic groups, by lessening their fear and anxiety (Marion, 1981). Table 6.1 offers examples of words that may be emotionally charged, and substitutes words that may communicate in a more positive manner.

Johnson and Noga (1998) suggested several barriers to effective communication during collaborative dialogues. Giving advice, rather than offering suggestions, implies that the advice is the correct and only option. When professionals give false reassurances, often well-meaning attempts to resolve another's concerns, partners are placed in difficult situations when problems are not resolved and minimize the group's motivation to work toward a resolution. Misdirected questions, another barrier, shift the focus to different aspects of the communication that interfere with meaningful dialogue. Changing the subject, also a communication problem, indicates inattention and disinterest in the topic at hand. Another challenge is using clichés, which raise questions about the validity of the program. Minimizing feelings and jumping to conclusions show an unwillingness to spend adequate time reflecting on an issue. Interrupting individuals during a dialogue drastically shifts the focus of the dialogue and can inhibit further conversation.

One aspect of communication that is frequently overlooked is listening. Teachers who are skilled active listeners state their understanding of what the parents said (the nonverbal language and feelings as well as the words), and provide feedback for the parents' verification and clarification. Active listening is not a mechanical process of hearing and repeating words. The active listener wants to hear and takes the time to hear what the parents are saying and wants to help them with the problems they confront. Teachers who are active listeners accept parents' feelings whether or not they concur with those feelings. Finally, they demonstrate faith in parents' capacity to solve their problems with assistance. Teachers who use active listening listen for the basic message in parents' communication and restate to the parents a brief, precise, summary of the verbal, nonverbal, and feeling tone of the message as they perceived it. They are sensitive to the parents' verbal or nonverbal cues to their restatement of the initial message and encourage parents to correct inaccurate perceptions. Active listening is further explored in Action Steps 6.1.

Conferences

True dialogue can transform teachers to educators, children to students, and parents to partners (Allan, 1997). Teachers and parents alike, however, often greet conferences with trepidation. Students are wary of the idea of parents and teachers discussing them behind closed doors (Clark, 1999). Conferences can be a regularly scheduled way of sharing a student's progress, or can be called to discuss a specific issue.

Open communication between parents and teachers can help to ensure that the issues that are raised in parent-teacher conferences are not surprises. Teachers can help parents prepare for the conference by sending home an information sheet such as the one provided in Figure 6.1. Teachers should plan for the conference by reviewing student information and preparing an agenda that is provided to the parents before the conference. Teachers may choose to cue themselves throughout the conference using index cards. These procedures will help to keep teacher, parents, and student, if present, on-task during the conference.

ACTION STEPS 6.1: *USING ACTIVE LISTENING EFFECTIVELY*

Active listening is a complex skill that requires practice. Brownell (1986) argued that active listening is comprised of six skill areas. In using active listening, professionals should attend to each of these areas:

1. **Hear the message**

   - Concentrate on what the speaker is saying
   - Take control of the listening environment, minimizing distractions and having everything you need at hand
   - Be ready when the speaker begins—pay attention from the first word
   - Look like a listener—sit up, look at the speaker, and nonverbally communicate that you are interested

   Example: A student's father has come by and asks to talk with you after school. You face the parent, inviting him to begin. The area is quiet and private. You are sitting up, nodding, and looking at the parent.

2. **Work at understanding the message**

   - Put your ego aside, paying attention to what the individual is saying rather than formulating your response
   - Monitor your behavior
   - Don't interrupt—it stops the speakers flow of thought and makes it harder to follow the message

   Example: Parent states, "This is the worst year my son has ever had in school." Rather than responding, you nod and wait for him to continue.

3. **Remember the message**

   - Repeat the content back to the speaker
   - Remain calm—it's hard to remember what is said if you are angry or stressed

   Example: You respond, "This has been a difficult year?" and look at the speaker encouragingly.

4. **Interpret the message**

   - Keep the speaker's background, goals, and role in mind
   - Think about the speaker's nonverbal communication
   - Watch for the relationship between verbal and nonverbal cues
   - Attend to the speaker's voice
   - Identify the level of communication: Is the speaker stating fact or opinion? Is the speaker communicating feelings?

   Example: You recognize that the father must be truly upset because this is the first time he has ever come to school. You notice that he is agitated and holding a note in his hand. His voice is trembling, and he has to stop to gather himself.

5. **Evaluate the message**

   ❏ Think about the speaker's credibility
   ❏ Try to follow the speaker's line of reasoning
   ❏ Consider the speaker's evidence or lack of evidence

   Example: The father states that he never knows what's going on with his son. He tries to talk to the child's mother, but doesn't seem to get any answers. He received a letter indicating that his son did not pass the proficiency test, and didn't even know he was taking the test.

6. **Respond to the message**

   ❏ Reflect the speaker's message, paraphrasing to check understanding
   ❏ Provide perception checks
   ❏ Continue a supportive listening climate
   ❏ Be physically alert, maintaining eye-contact, but minimize gestures and random movements

   Example: You reflect back to the parent: "You're concerned that you hadn't received earlier information about the test." "You were unaware that your son was taking the test."

Dear Parents:

Next week we will begin our quarterly parent-teacher conferences. We are excited to have this time together with you to discuss your child. During this meeting we will discuss your child's progress and interactions here at school. It would be helpful if you would reflect on these questions before the conference:

• What school activities does your child describe or discuss most often?
• What seems to be your child's favorite subject?
• Does your child talk about school friends?
• Does your child complete homework assignments independently?
• What is your child's greatest strength?
• What concerns you most about your child?

Please feel free to jot down any questions you may have for me. In addition, we have been talking with the children about these conferences, and it may be helpful if you would ask your child if there is anything he or she would like to have you ask.

We will have child care available each conference evening from 4:30 p.m.–7:30 p.m. Please use this child care (in Room 19) so that we may discuss your child without distraction. If you are unable to keep your appointment, please give me a call (555-3987) or e-mail me (kgriswald@schoolnet.org).

Thank you for your assistance. I am looking forward to meeting with you.

Sincerely,

Kristin Griswald

Figure 6.1   *Conference information for parents.*

When there are disagreements during the conference, Katz (1996) suggested that it is a good idea to refer to the school policy for handling conflicts and disagreements. In addition, it is important to use discretion about when and where children and their families are discussed. Children and parents should never be discussed by teachers with colleagues, friends, relatives, and others unauthorized to know about the child and parents. Parents and teachers should talk directly with each other about any problem that arises, and avoid criticizing each other in front of the children. An appropriate time and place for a discussion should be determined cooperatively by parents and teacher.

Rose (1998) suggested that teachers welcome the parent with warmth, and have a written outline and agenda (sent to the parent when scheduling the conference) available. As the teacher discusses the child's behavior and performance, he or she allows for the possibility of parent anger, and weighs his or her words with care. Parents' suggestions should be sought, and the teacher should have some concrete solutions in mind in response to concerns raised during the discussion. At times, it may be necessary to partner with the principal. Following the conference, the teacher should send a summary of the discussion, as the teacher understands it, to the parent. The parents should be encouraged to respond to the summary, if they feel it necessary. A copy of the summary is filed in the student's school record.

Written Communication

Written communication with parents may take many forms. Report cards are the most common written communication that parents receive. Grades, however, are often inadequate in communicating what the child has learned or accomplished (Wiggins, 1994). Writing comments give teachers the opportunity to reflect on the child's educational program and behavior, as well as to provide additional information to parents (Brualdi, 1998). The effective report card comments suggested by Shafer (1997) are summarized in Figure 6.2.

In addition to periodic reports, daily written reports may be used. More frequent feedback on students' academic and behavioral performance may be more likely to inspire continued positive performance. Any daily report system should be mutually agreed upon. If the system is used for all students in a classroom, a parent meeting may be useful for discussing the daily reports before implementation. If the system is individualized, a telephone call or conference would be an effective way of negotiating the manner in which the report will be used. Specific questions to address when developing and implementing a daily report card include:

- What is to be evaluated?
- What are the criteria for ratings used?
- What system will be used to make sure the report reaches the parents?
- How will parents follow through with the reports?

Some parents and teachers use a spiral notebook that serves as a dialogue journal. This notebook travels with the child to and from school and home. However, the use of such notebooks is time-consuming, and teachers may not feel that a descrip-

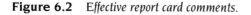

Phrases to promote a positive view:

thorough	caring
shows commitment	improved
has a good grasp	

Phrases to express concern:

could profit by	finds it difficult at times to
needs reinforcement in	requires support

Words to avoid:

unable	can't
won't	refuses
always	never

Figure 6.2 *Effective report card comments.*

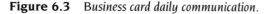

Marcella's Daily Communication Card

Today, Marcella:

Was prepared for class	Yes	No
Participated in class	Yes	No
Has written homework	Yes	No

Signature: Date:

Figure 6.3 *Business card daily communication.*

tion of daily routine is that helpful for the child. Bauer and Myree (2001) suggested the use of a "business card" to keep parents informed of students' performance in class (Figure 6.3). The teacher circles the appropriate response on the "business card" and gives it to the student to take home.

Written communication may also take the form of notes, letters, and notices. Teachers typically begin the year with a "welcome letter" that may include the following:

- A list of the year's scheduled subjects, activities, and events;
- An invitation to visit the school and class;
- An invitation to contribute to the class as a volunteer;
- "Who to call for what" information;
- A list of materials the child needs for school;
- Suggestions for parents wishing to help the child at home.

Dear Parents:

Welcome to another exciting school year at Demeter Primary School. Your child has been assigned to my second/third grade classroom.

I'd like to tell you a bit about myself. I am certified to teach pre-kindergarten through third grade for children who are developing typically and those with mild to moderate disabilities. I have taught for Europa City Schools for nine years. My first five years were spent in teaching kindergarten, and I am beginning my fifth year in the second/third grade multigrade classroom. Ms. Zoe Adams returns as our instructional assistant. We have nineteen students.

This is an exciting year for the students. We will work in collaborative learning groups, completing projects related to our science themes for the year, beginning with our first theme, "air." We will use a project approach, and invite you to our classroom to see our final presentations. We will work on completing the transition from manuscript to cursive handwriting, and the move from learning to read to reading to learn.

One of the programs that the students always enjoy in our classroom is that of Young Authors. We will be looking for parent volunteers to help the students in editing, illustrating, and publishing their books. We will have our annual "Literary Lemonade Party" as the students present these books.

Our business partner, Europa Office Machines, has donated composition journals and plan books for each student. The other supplies that your child needs are described on the attached list. In addition, you will find a "who to call for what" list to help you find the answers to school questions.

Thank you for your support — we're looking forward to a great year!

Yours in service,

Sarina Marks

Figure 6.4 *Welcome letter.*

A sample welcome letter for a primary classroom is included in Figure 6.4. Preschool, middle school, and secondary school letters would vary according to the program.

Teachers may also write to parents regarding specific events or "thank you notes" for their contributions to the program. Teachers should let children know the content of any notes, letters, or notices that go home to allay children's anxiety. Other written products teachers may share include weekly or monthly calendars, newsletters, or handbooks.

Technology

Technology can facilitate communication between parents and teachers. When using technology, teachers should recognize individual differences. They should be sensitive to individual differences with regard to gender, age, and cultural differences, as well as accessibility of technology (Colton & McGuire, 1999) to the individuals with whom they wish to communicate. In a study using voice mail, for example, Cameron and Lee (1997) reported that though parents of older students were satisfied with using voice mail to communicate with teachers, parents of younger students preferred traditional methods.

Lucas (1994) described several uses of classroom telephone lines for parent-teacher communication. Using a telephone system, parents may be connected through a password to their child's electronic grade book. Homework hot lines can help parents become aware of their children's home assignments. E-mail to parents and the use of an electronic bulletin board can provide both individualized and group information.

BARRIERS TO COLLABORATION AND PARTICIPATION

When parents and teachers collaborate, all students, particularly those with disabilities, grow academically, socially, and emotionally (Spinelli, 1999). Teachers and parents, however, often make assumptions that make collaboration more difficult.

Perhaps the most common assumptions about parent-teacher collaboration center around individuals who are poor. Thompson (1992) argued that if you ask poor people to become involved but don't give them any real decisions to make, they're no more likely to become involved than you would under similar circumstances. But, if you ask them to become involved and give them a chance to make a real difference in their school, then they respond in great numbers, remain involved, and make a difference.

When reviewing efforts to engage parents in the education of their children, some consistent patterns emerge. Ballen and Moles (1998) suggested four primary barriers to parent involvement that must be addressed in any plans for parent engagement:

- Time: With the increase in the number of families in which there is either one parent, both parents working, or parents working more than one job, children are often left alone. In these situations, both the parents and teachers—often working parents themselves—are strapped for time.
- Uncertainty: Parents are often uncertain about what to do and about their own importance. Parents are not only unsure of how to help, but may have had experiences in school that make them unlikely to return. Parents are intimidated and unsure of their collaboration.
- Cultural barriers: There may be difficulty in language or in communicating with schools because life experiences and perspectives are so different.
- Lack of supportive environment: Schools have not always tried to nurture families, and low income parents in particular may need support if they are to become involved. These parents need personal attention, literature and classes on parenting, and a resource center.

Identifying barriers may be helpful, but teachers need to implement ways to address those barriers. In a discussion of barriers identified by the National Parent Teachers Association (1992, cited in State of Iowa, 1998) offered these possibilities:

- Time: Be flexible with schedules, times, and days of the week. In addition, having meetings "off campus" at community centers, apartment buildings, or churches may be helpful.

- Feeling unvalued: Personally welcome parents, and actively seek ways for parents to use their talents to benefit the school.
- Unaware of how to contribute: Teachers can conduct a talent survey, and use those talents by encouraging parents to share information on careers, hobbies, pets, or other skills.
- Unaware of how the system works: Teachers can develop a handbook addressing rules, procedures, and where to find the answers to typical issues or questions.
- Child care: Find an available room in the school and ask older students to volunteer to baby-sit.
- Language: Have materials translated, using English on one side and another language on the other.
- Cultural difference: Increase your sensitivity to other cultures, values, attitudes, celebrations, and the views of the school with regard to these.
- Transportation: Visit parents in the home, or hold meetings in places more convenient to families.
- A sense of token invitations: Use parent meetings to address real issues to gather parents' ideas, and listen to and consider solutions. Listen to parents and use their ideas.
- A sense of being unwelcome: Work with the school staff to make parents feel welcome. Have a parents' room and post welcomes in various languages.
- Resistance to formal leadership: Ensure that all parents are involved in planning, policy making, and advocacy.
- Parents having limited literacy skills: Use the telephone to contact parents, and develop a family literacy plan.
- Snobbery: Actively seek new participants who represent various cultural, socioeconomic, and religious groups.
- Deal with the issue of the "out group": In some schools the strong leadership of a parent-teacher association is a detriment in that an "in group" and "out group" tend to emerge. Parents may be unwilling to participate if they feel that others are manipulating either the situation or are already meeting all of the needs of the school. Because children from at-risk homes may have the most to gain from parent involvement, programs that only meet the needs of the "in group" may be excluding the very group for which involvement could be most beneficial.

Though barriers are often discussed, elements common to successful programs have also been identified. Williams and Chavkin (1989) suggested that schools should have written policies, including vision and mission statements, which address the participation of parents in the school. Administrative support should make funds available, provide materials, space, and equipment, and identify specific individuals to help carry out the program. In addition, continuing professional education for teachers regarding parent involvement is necessary. In successful programs, a partnership approach is in place, involving joint planning, goal setting, and other strategies to help parents develop a sense of ownership. Successful programs utilize two-way communication, and help parents network. Finally, successful programs involve regular evaluation activities at key stages as well as at the end of the year.

ATTRIBUTES OF EFFECTIVE PARENT/TEACHER COLLABORATION

Specific parent and teacher attributes may support parent-teacher collaboration. Swick (1991) reported that parents who were happy in their marriage, had greater family harmony, were successful in earlier collaborations, and more open to others' ideas were more effective in partnerships with teachers. Schaefer and Edgerton (1985) noted that parents who are higher in self-esteem are more assertive in school involvement. Epstein (1984) reported that parents who have a positive self-image are more effective in school involvement. In addition, parents may become more supportive, responsible, and dependable through models provided by teachers (Lawler, 1991).

In terms of teacher attributes, Comer and Haynes (1991) described warmth, openness, sensitivity, flexibility, reliability, and accessibility as important to effective collaboration. In addition, a positive attitude, active planning to involve parents, professional development, and personal competence have been related to more effective parent involvement (Epstein, 1984; Galinsky, 1990).

Lightfoot (1978) suggested that an action-oriented philosophy of family-school support and nurturance are essential and create a positive learning environment. Such a philosophy assumes sensitivity to ethnic, cultural, and linguistic characteristics of the group being served. Teacher roles, critical to effective partnerships, include the family-centered roles of support, education, and guidance. Teacher activities should include nurturing, supporting, guiding, and decision-making. Parents' roles extend nurturing, teaching, and modeling cross contexts, and parents' ability to nurture and guide should be exploited in parent-teacher involvement (Swick, 1992).

Financial and human capital have been related to successful parent involvement in school. In an extensive study by the National Center for Educational Statistics (1997), parents with more financial resources were found to show greater levels of involvement. Even among single parents, greater income indicated greater involvement, though single mothers with the highest incomes were somewhat less involved, perhaps due to the demands of work. Parent involvement was higher for children in families living above the poverty threshold, and single fathers were more likely to be involved if they did not receive federal assistance. Home ownership was also found to be related to higher levels of involvement, perhaps because owning a home is usually indicative of family stability.

The National Center for Educational Statistics also reported that human capital was related to parental involvement. Parent involvement increases with education. Parents who are highly involved in their children's school are generally more likely to be involved at home, as well. Children in kindergarten through fifth grade who live in two-parent families or single-parent homes, in which their parent(s) are highly involved in their schools, are more likely to participate in educational activities at home. In the upper grades, children whose parents are involved in schools are more likely than parents who have low levels of involvement to have played a game, sport, or worked on a school project with other parents. Interestingly, parents who are highly involved in their children's schools are almost equally as likely to have shared in any given activity with other families outside of school. Their families are more likely to belong to a community group, church or synagogue, union, or professional organization. These data indicate that families who are involved together and with others outside of the school are those who are typically involved in schools. The challenge confronting teachers, however, is to involve parents who may not be as highly involved with their children at home and with others in the community and may not have the resources available for such involvement.

Teachers at times have difficulty recognizing the insights parents may have about their children. Stone (1997) found that among a group of adolescents with learning disabilities and their parents, the parents' ratings of their children were consistent with those of the teachers in most skill areas.

One critical group that has often been neglected in terms of parent collaboration is fathers. Flynn and Wilson (1998) suggested that teachers should ensure that fathers understand the importance of their interaction with their children with disabilities and the value of gender-specific approaches to planning and interaction. Teachers should understand that individuals are often more comfortable discussing personal matters with a person of the same gender. Consequently, fathers may be less comfortable talking to female teachers than a male teacher. Flynn and Wilson urge that teachers critically examine their personal values and views related to fathers, and seek to understand their personal perspectives about the roles and expectations of fathers in today's society. They also suggest that teachers spend time reflecting how they seek input from fathers as compared to mothers and review how many times fathers were involved in past parent-teacher activities. Materials should be reviewed to see if they are as likely to engage men as women, and information should be sent to both fathers and mothers when appropriate.

COMMUNICATION AND CULTURAL, ETHNIC, AND LINGUISTIC GROUPS

Unfortunately, there is continued overrepresentation of children from diverse ethnic, cultural, and linguistic groups in special education. Oswald, Coutinho, Best, and Singh (1999) reported that ethnicity base rates, i.e., the proportion of individuals from diverse ethnic, cultural, and linguistic groups in the general population, are an important factor in determining disproportionate representation. Districts with the lowest base rates of African American students identified a greater percentage of African American students needing special education services when compared to districts with higher base rates. The issues, however, are complex, and interrelated with socioeconomic status. Fujiura and Yamaki (2000) reported that when there are controls in place for poverty, there is no incremental risk for identification related to racial or ethnic status. However, there is significant risk in single-parent households and poverty for individuals to be identified as having disabilities. Rather than describing specifics related to each of several minority groups, we will review information from which generalizations related to working with various ethnic, cultural, and linguistic groups can be drawn.

Families from diverse ethnic, cultural, and linguistic groups are a challenge for many teachers. Thorp (1997) suggested that the teaching pool itself is not diverse, and few teachers are really prepared for the diversity they confront in the classroom and school through either life experience or education. Thorp suggests the following four-part approach for professionals:

1. Explore your own cultural experiences, values, and attitudes, recognizing the power role of the teacher. In order to teach, you must know your own story.
2. Learn as much as possible from families about their cultural experiences, values, and attitudes. Establish ongoing relationships, and use families as cultural guides.
3. Evaluate your classroom setting and curriculum strategies through a cultural and linguistic lens. Create a welcoming environment, and analyze the curriculum for relevance and bias.
4. Examine all components of your school for family involvement, making sure that there are leadership options for parents.

Holland (1987) used urban Appalachians as an example of the way in which communication can contribute to the participation of a specific cultural group. In effective communication, teachers assumed an active approach, with persistent follow-up. Teachers who communicated effectively with parents used personal communication, such as telephone calls, notes, and informal encounters, rather than formal letters and conferences. Effective communicators consistently communicated the message "We need to work together to help your child" rather than "Come in if you want." Teachers who used specific, frequent invitations rather than global statements, who were flexible with schedules, and who developed strong rapport were more effective with parents.

One essential consideration for teachers working with students from diverse ethnic, cultural, and linguistic groups is that of the variability within the group itself. For example, among Asian Americans, some Vietnamese may be highly educated and literate, whereas the Hmong, a Vietnamese ethnic group, have no written language and have a different home tradition than other Vietnamese (Schwartz, 1994). Latino families may be, for example, Puerto Rican, Cuban, or Mexican. Though all Latinos, the cultures of these groups vary greatly. Across all cultural groups, however, there are several factors that inhibit the involvement of parents. Freedman, Ascheim, and Zerchykov (1989) suggested that school practices do not accommodate the diversity of the families served, offer opportunities to be involved at inconvenient times, provide written communications in inappropriate languages or literacy levels, fail to provide useful information or materials, and unconsciously convey the attitude that families have little to contribute. In addition, child care constraints may be an issue, as may the parents' previous negative experiences with schools. Most important, the focus on meeting basic needs (food, clothing, and shelter) of some families may limit their ability to be involved in their child's education.

Families from groups that are often underrepresented in parent involvement, however, do want to be involved. In Chavkin and Williams' (1993) large research sample, African American and Latino families said they wanted to be more involved with their children's education, to help with homework, and to have more influence on the school. Teachers should recognize, however, that some cultures may have difficultly dealing with parent involvement. Some Asian American cultures may view teachers as professionals with authority over the child's schooling and feel that parents aren't supposed to interfere. In this light, teachers who ask for help may be judged incompetent (Schwartz, 1994). Latino families may be hesitant to send their very young children to preschool, and may not agree that children would benefit from such early separation from their loving family (Lewis, 1993). Some Latino families may view schools as bureaucracies that they should not question (Nicolau & Ramos, 1990). Families living in poverty may be quite able to solve complex problems related to their own survival in the most difficult of situations, yet have such difficultly with traditional skills that they are hesitant to approach teachers (Taylor, 1993).

From the literature related to families from diverse cultural, ethnic, and linguistic groups, several suggestions emerge:

- Make sure all meetings are relevant, and respond to some need or concern of parents. Consult parents with regard to agenda and meeting formats (Nicolau & Ramos, 1990). Provide relevant information (Felber, 1997).
- Make it as convenient as possible for parents to participate, including providing interpreters and transportation (Nicolau & Ramos, 1990).
- Personalize invitations, using face-to-face specific invitations (Holland, 1987; Nicolau & Ramos, 1990).
- Recognize parent and family strengths; avoid the deficit model. Appreciate and engage parents (Taylor, 1993; Bailey, Skinner, Correa, Arcia, Reyes-Blanes, Rodriguez, Vazquez-Montilla & Skinner, 1999; Harry, 1992). Avoid stereotyping parents (Felber, 1997).
- Explain that the tradition in American education is involvement, and that the parents' participation would be helpful for the child (Schwartz, 1994; Lewis, 1993).
- Provide multiple roles and options for parents, expanding beyond "consent-giver" to assessor, presenter of reports, policy maker, and advocate (Harry, 1992).
- Communicate to parents that you celebrate their child's individuality. Warn them about media portrayals of children with disabilities, and reach out to establish effective communication (Felber, 1997).

Attending to these suggestions will facilitate the parent-teacher partnership.

SUMMARY

- Collaboration between home and school requires recognizing parents' role in student learning and involving parents as full partners in decision-making.
- Humans communicate at several levels simultaneously, and these levels of expression may vary by culture.
- Collaboration occurs when power and authority are shared by people brought together to address common goals that could not be met by the individual.

- Technology, such as telephone communication and e-mail, can support parent-teacher communication.
- Time, uncertainty, cultural issues, and lack of support can affect parent-teacher communication.
- Educators must know their own culture before becoming culturally competent.

REFERENCES

Allan, L. L. (1997). Food for thought: Do you resent and stonewall parents? *Young Children*, 52(4), 72–74.

Bailey, Jr., D. B., Skinner, D., Correa, V., Arcia, E., Reyes-Blanes, M. E., Rodriguez, P., Vazquez-Montilla, E., & Skinner, M. (1999). Needs and supports reported by Latino families of young children with developmental disabilities. *American Journal on Mental Retardation*, 104(5), 437–451.

Ballen, J., & Moles, O. (1998). *Strong families, strong schools*. Washington, DC: U. S. Department of Education.

Bauer, A. M., & Myree, G. D. (2001). *Teaching in an inclusive high school*. Baltimore: Paul H. Brookes.

Bauer, A. M., Joseph, S. C., & Zwicker, S. A. (1998). Supporting collaborative partnerships. In L. J. Johnson, M. J. LaMontagne, P. M. Elgas, & A. M. Bauer (Eds.), *Early childhood education: Blending theory, blending practice* (pp. 63–82). Baltimore: Paul H. Brookes.

Brualdi, A. (1998). *Teacher comments on report cards*. ERIC/ARE Digest No. ED423309. Washington, DC: ERIC Clearinghouse on Assessment and Evaluation.

Bruner, C., Kunesch, L. G., & Knuth, R. A. (1992). *What does research say about interagency collaboration?* Oakbrook, IL: North Central Regional Educational Laboratory.

Cameron, C. A., & Lee, K. (1997). Bridging the gap between home and school with voice-mail technology. *Journal of Educational Research*, 90(3), 182–190.

Chavkin, N. F., & Williams, R. (1993). *Families and schools in a pluralistic society*. Albany, NY: State University of New York Press.

Cheney, D., & Osher, T. (1997). Collaborate with families. *Journal of Emotional and Behavioral Disorders*, 5(1), 36–55, 54.

Clark, A. (1999). Parent-teacher conferences: *Suggestions for parents*. ERIC Digest No. ED433965. Champaign, IL: ERIC Clearinghouse on Elementary and Early Childhood Education.

Colton, L., & McGuire, K. (1999). *Making the MOST of out-of-school time: Technology's role in collaboration*. Proceedings of the Families, Technology, and Education Conference. Champaign, IL: ERIC Clearinghouse on Elementary and Early Childhood Education.

Comer, J., & Haynes, M. (1991). Parent involvement in schools: An ecological approach. *Elementary School Journal*, 91, 271–278.

Epstein, J. L. (1995). School/family/community partnerships: Caring for the children we share. *Phi Delta Kappan*, 76(9), 701–712.

Epstein, J. L. (1984). School policy and parent involvement: Research results. *Educational Horizons*, 62, 70–72.

Felber, S. A. (1997). Strategies for parent partnerships. *Teaching Exceptional Children*, 30(1), 20–23.

Flynn, L. L., & Wilson, P. G. (1998). Partnerships with family members. What about fathers? *Young Exceptional Children*, 2(1), 21–38.

Fox, L., Vaughn, B. J., Dunlap, G., & Bucy, M. (1997). Parent-professional partnership in behavioral support: A qualitative analysis of one family's experience. *Journal of the Association for Persons with Severe Handicaps, 22*(4), 198–207.

Freedman, S., Ascheim, B., & Zerchykov, R. (1989). *Strategies for increasing the involvement of underrepresented families in education.* Quincy, MA: Massachusetts Department of Education.

Fujiara, G. T., & Yamaki, K. (2000). Trends in demography of childhood poverty and disability. *Exceptional Children, 66*(2), 187–199.

Galinsky, E. (1990). Why are some parent-teacher relationships clouded with difficulties?" *Young Children, 45*(2), 38–39.

Harry, B. (1992). Restructuring the participation of African-American parents in special education. *Exceptional Children, 24,* 123–131.

Holland, K. E. (1987). *Parents and teachers: Can home and school literacy boundaries be broken?* Paper presented at the University of Kentucky Conference on Appalachia. Lexington, KY: University of Kentucky.

Idol, L., Paolucci-Whitcomb, P., & Nevin, A. (1986). *Collaborative consultation.* Austin, TX: Proed.

Johnson, L. J., & Noga, J. (1998). Key collaboration skills. In L. J. Johnson, M. J. LaMontagne, P. M. Elgas, & A. M. Bauer (Eds.), *Early childhood education: Blending theory, blending practice* (pp. 19–43). Baltimore: Paul H. Brookes.

Kagan, S. (1991). *United we stand: Collaboration for child care and early education services.* New York: Teachers College Press.

Katz, L. G. (1996). *Preventing and resolving parent-teacher differences.* ERIC Digest No. ED401048. Champaign, IL: ERIC Clearinghouse on Elementary and Early Childhood Education.

Kay, P. J., & Fitzgerald, M. (1997). Parents + teachers + action research = real involvement. *Teaching Exceptional Children, 30*(1), 8–11.

Lawler, D. (1991). *Parent-teacher conferencing in early childhood education.* Washington, DC: National Education Association.

Lewis, M. C. (1993). *Beyond barriers: Involving Hispanic families in the education process.* Washington, DC: National Committee for Citizens in Education.

Lightfoot, S. L. (1978). *Worlds apart: Relationships between families and school.* New York: Basic Books.

Lockett, C. (1999). *The National PTA's National Standards for parent/family involvement programs.* ERIC Document No. ED430919. Memphis, TN: Annual Conference of the Center for the Study of Small/Rural Schools.

Lucas, L. W. (1994). *Say "yes" to telephone lines in the classroom.* ERIC Digest No. ED377829. Syracuse, NY: ERIC Clearinghouse on Information and Technology.

Marion, R. L. (1981). *Educators, parents, and exceptional children.* Rockville, MD: Aspen.

McCaleb, J. L. (1987). *How do teachers communicate?* ERIC Digest No. ED282872. Washington, DC: ERIC Clearinghouse on Teacher Education.

National Center for Education Statistics (1997). *Findings: Involvement of resident parents.* Washington, DC: National Center for Education Statistics, Department of Education.

Nicolau, S., & Ramos, C. L. (1990). *Together is better: Building strong relationships between schools and Hispanic parents.* Washington, DC: Hispanic Policy Development Project.

Oswald, D. P., Coutinho, M. J., Best, A. M., & Singh, N. N. (1999). Ethnic representation in special education. *The Journal of Special Education, 32*(4), 194–206.

Petit, D. (1989). *Opening up schools.* Harmondsworth, England: Penguin.

Rose, M. C. (1998). Handle with care: The difficult parent-teacher conference. *Instructor, 108*(3), 92–93, 101.

Schaefer, E. & Edgerton, M. (1985). *Parent and child correlates of parental modernity* (pp. 287–318). In B. Sigel (Ed.), Parental Belief Systems. Hillsdale, NJ: Lawrence Erlbaum.

Schwartz, W. (1994). *A guide to communicating with Asian American families*. NY: ERIC Clearinghouse on Urban Education, Teachers College, Columbia University.

Shafer, S. (1997). *Writing effective report card comments*. New York: Scholastic.

Simic, M. (1991). *Parent involvement in elementary language arts*: A program model. ERIC Digest No. ED326901. Bloomington, IN: ERIC Clearinghouse on Reading and Communication Skills.

Spinelli, C. G. (1999). Breaking down barriers—Building strong foundations: Parents and teachers of exceptional students working together. *Learning Disabilities*: A *Multidisciplinary Journal*, 9(3), 123–129.

State of Iowa, Department of Education (1998). *Parent involvement in education*: A resource for parents, educators, communities. Des Moines, IA: Author.

Stone, C. A. (1997). Correspondence among parent, teacher, and student perceptions of adolescents' learning disabilities. *Journal of Learning Disabilities*, 30(6), 660–669.

Swick, K. (1992). *Teacher-parent partnerships*. ERIC Digest No. EDO-PS-92-12. Champaign, IL: Clearinghouse on Elementary and Early Childhood Education.

Swick, K. (1991). *Teacher-parent partnerships to enhance school success in early childhood education*. Washington, DC: National Education Association.

Taylor, D. (1993). Family literacy: Resisting deficit models. TESOL *Quarterly*, 27(3), 550–553.

Thompson, S. (1992). Building on a foundation of respect for families and children: A round table discussion. *Equity and Choice*, 8(3), 37–40.

Thorp, E. K. (1997). Increasing opportunities for partnership with culturally and linguistically diverse families. *Intervention in School and Clinic*, 32(5), 261–269.

Wiggins, G. (1994) Toward better report cards. *Educational Leadership*, 52(2), 28–37.

Williams, D. L., & Chavkin, N. F. (1989). Essential elements of strong parent involvement programs. *Educational Leadership* (October), 18–20.

CHAPTER 7

Engaging Families of Infants and Toddlers

Isabel and Sally

I have been involved in special education and related services for twenty years. My jobs have included therapeutic recreation while attending college, earning my bachelor degree in education and teaching nine-to-twelve year-olds with special needs. Followed by receiving my master degree and becoming an Occupational Therapist. Throughout my various careers I have specialized in working with young children. During each phase of my career I have continued to gain insight from both parent and child. While working with numerous families, I have often been amazed with their resilience. Periodically, families have opened themselves up to me and shared their very private thoughts and emotions. I was always able to hear their words and empathize with them. The depth of my understanding grew with each phase of my life.

When my third child was born, nothing had prepared me for the depth of emotions that I experienced. As soon as she was placed on my chest, I knew she had Down syndrome. I did not need confirmation from the neonatal pediatrician, nurses, cardiologist, or geneticist. I knew. What I did not know was how it felt to be on that "roller coaster ride" of emotions, which I have heard parents speak of and I have spoken about over the years. My husband and I needed to grieve and were able to openly talk about all of our thoughts and feelings over the next few months. I also have a strong support network in my family and my friends. Getting through the early months was difficult at times. The most helpful were those who had experienced a loss in their own lives and able to understand our initial sadness. It is not a cliché when a person speaks of the loss of the child they were anticipating for nine months. (Gantz, 1999)

Learning Objectives

After completing this chapter, you will be able to discuss these topics:

1. Family adaptation and infants and toddlers with disabilities
2. Early intervention services

FAMILY ADAPTATION AND INFANTS AND TODDLERS WITH DISABILITIES

Although I was unprepared for my daughter's diagnosis, my work experience had prepared me for what immediate actions needed to occur. Each medical appointment during the first few weeks, (daily checks of her bilirubin count, for example) were reminders again and again of my daughter's special needs. These visits were at times exhausting, making sure I was asking all the right questions, as well as passing other parents in the hallways of the hospital with their typical children. I am fortunate to have a number of friends in the medical and special education fields that have made themselves available to me on a number of occasions. Also in the region where we live is an active Down Syndrome Association (DSAGC). Over time I have begun reaching out to other parents and gaining support from families walking down the same road. (Gantz, 1999)

The birth of any child changes the family. When the child has a disability, changes differ in intensity and degree, being greater and more demanding (Krahl, 1989). Talking openly within the family about the disability and providing a forum for family members to discuss the disability may be helpful (National Information Center for Children and Youth with Disabilities [NICHCY], 1994b). The family may be challenged by requiring services, addressing financial concerns, and future planning that they may not have previously considered.

As early intervention becomes the standard of practice, families may be dealing with issues of disability before the baby is even born. Helm, Miranda, and Chedd (1998) described the experiences of 10 mothers who received a prenatal diagnosis of Down syndrome and chose to continue their pregnancy. Although the mothers reported varied experiences, some of which were positive and reassuring, all of the mothers reported meetings with some health professionals, including obstetricians, nurses, technicians, and genetic counselors, who they felt did not support their decision nor try to understand why they chose to have the child. Printed materials about Down syndrome were reported to be helpful and supportive, and meetings and phone conversations with other parents were a great source of support and information.

There are often assumptions made about parenting a child with a disability. It has often been grounded in the belief that the experience leads to negative outcomes and processes for the family (Gallimore, Bernheimer, & Weisner, 1999). Harry (1992), however, suggests that these assumptions may be due to the measures used to evaluate them. She reported that when methods other than scales to measure depression, stress, or coping are used, families recall their initial responses and adaptations to disability, but do not focus on deficits or pathologies of the experience. Rather, parents speak about the child in a positive way, as a stimulus for learning, becoming more tolerant, and highlighting the child's strengths. In their study of Latino families, Skinner, Bailey, Correa, and Rodriguez (1999) found that a majority of mothers described notions of the child being a blessing or a gift from God. They described their child's disability and themselves in relation to it as a "quest," or self-transformation. Mothers related positive identities and experiences, giving voice to perspectives other than those rooted in despair, depression, stress, and coping.

Parents' lives with children with disabilities or chronic illness are often filled with strong emotion, difficult choices, interactions with many different professionals and specialists, and an ongoing need for information and services. However, the majority of families adapt to the stress and challenges that accompany having a child with a disability or chronic illness. As Emily Perl Kingsley (in Wesley, Dennis, & Tyndall, 1997) related, having a baby can be compared to planning a fabulous vacation to Italy. After months of eager anticipation, the day arrives, and, several hours later, the parent is told "Welcome to Holland." Rather than a horrible place, you are in a different place, a place for which you were not prepared. After you've been there a while, you begin to enjoy the sites and pleasures of Holland, but it still isn't the Italy for which you planned. However, professionals should understand and be prepared to assist some parents who may be angry, frightened, guilty, confused, or feel powerless (NICHCY, 1994b).

The problems that parents of babies with disabilities confront are the same problems that all parents confront though their challenges may be of greater intensity, duration, and frequency (Hodapp & Zigler, 1993). Though stages of shock, denial, grief, guilt, anger, and bargaining are often described as stages of adaptation for parents of a child with a disability, parent reactions are highly individualized, and there is no empirical evidence that the stages of adaptation exist (Blacher, 1989). In fact, the application of the stages of grieving to working with families with members with disabilities may in itself be counterproductive, leading professionals to label families as "in denial" or "in the anger stage" rather than addressing family needs and concerns (Bragg, Brown, & Berninger, 1992). McGill-Smith (1992) suggested that some educators apply the grieving literature to the extent that they have strong personal beliefs about how each family should "grieve," their steps for involvements, and how they fit in to the professional's perception of helping.

Crises may occur when the child is initially identified as having a disability and at times of transition (Seligman & Darling, 1992). Even before starting school, there are several transitions that may challenge parents and family. The parents and family may need to transition into being a family with a member with a disability. They must confront the transitions involved in finding, entering and attending early intervention, preschool, and kindergarten services.

Stress

In addition to questions related to adaptation and stages of grieving, assumptions have been made related to stress in families with infants with disabilities. Some situations, such as hospitalization in neonatal intensive care units, have been described as stressful by parents. In their study of mothers' and fathers' perceptions of stress

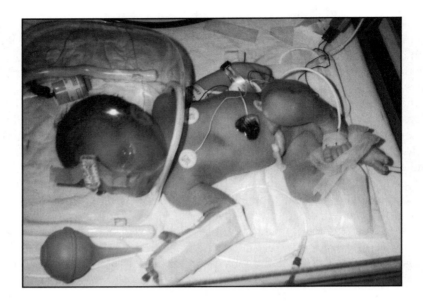

during the initial few weeks of their preterm infant's intensive care hospitalization, Hughes and McCollum (1994) reported that mothers identified more stressors than fathers, and found the intensive care experience more stressful on the whole than fathers. Yet, the differences between mothers' and fathers' perceptions were often of degree rather than type. No fathers reported feelings of guilt when asked the reasons for the premature birth; fathers either listed medical reasons or said they didn't know why. However, 21% of the mothers said they felt guilty in some way or wondered if they could have somehow prevented the problems. Hughes and McCollum emphasized that parents of hospitalized infants are not just dealing with an acute health care issue, but are also trying to deal with other parts of their lives. Stress was reported in finding child care for other children in the family that prevented them from visiting the hospitalized child, or their interactions with family and friends who did not know what they were going through. Parents were anxious about the forced separation between them and their infant due to the intensive care hospitalization, and reported the anxiety produced by the roller coaster ride of the child doing better one day and struggling the next. Perceptions of stress were individualized and influenced by the meaning of the situation for each of the parents.

In a study of parents of infants who are deaf, Meadow-Orlans (1994) found that the parents did not score significantly higher on measures of parenting stress or general life stress when compared to parents of infants with normal hearing. Fathers, in this study, reported parenting stress at a level similar to mothers. High levels of stress did not accompany the diagnosis of deafness, and social support was associated with lower levels of parenting stress. Krauss (1993) reported that mothers of infants and toddlers with various disabilities did not demonstrate overall depression or feelings of incompetence. Positive adaptation was related to adequate family income, a lack of significant negative life events not related to the child, helpfulness of the support

ACTION STEPS 7.1: *HELPING PARENTS COPE WHEN THEIR CHILD IS DIAGNOSED WITH A DISABILITY*

Smith (in NICHCY, 1994b) has the following recommendations for parents upon the diagnosis of disability in their infant or toddler:

- ❑ Seek the assistance of another parent.
- ❑ Talk with spouse, family, and significant others.
- ❑ Rely on positive sources in your life.
- ❑ Take one day at a time.
- ❑ Learn the language and terminology.
- ❑ Seek information.
- ❑ Do not be intimidated by the presence of people from the medical or educational professions.
- ❑ Do not be afraid to show emotion.
- ❑ Learn to deal with the natural feelings of bitterness and anger.
- ❑ Maintain a positive outlook.
- ❑ Keep in touch with reality.
- ❑ Remember time is on your side.
- ❑ Seek out programs.
- ❑ Take care of yourself.
- ❑ Avoid pity.
- ❑ Decide how to deal with others.
- ❑ Keep daily routines as normal as possible.
- ❑ Remember that this is your child.
- ❑ Recognize that you are not alone.

received by the mother, extent to which the mother viewed her family as a cohesive supportive unit, and the child's behavior. The single most influential factor related to positive adaptation was the child's behavior.

Turnbull and Turnbull (1997) urged parents to utilize parent-to-parent programs and to take care of themselves. Other suggestions to help families are presented in Action Steps 7.1. Family involvement programs have, in the past, focused on mothers. Yet fathers may have their own needs and priorities, and have different strengths and resources that they can use to meet those needs (Darling & Baxter, 1996). Siblings also experience change.

Siblings

With the birth of a child with a disability, the other children in the family must adjust to a brother or sister who, because of the disability, may require a large portion of time, attention, money, and psychological support (National Information Center for Children and Youth with Disabilities [NICHCY], 1994a). Sibling relationships are the child's first social network, and may serve as the basis for interactions with people outside the family (Powell & Gallagher, 1993). The younger the child, the more difficult it is for him or her to understand the situation. Younger children may mimic the child with a disability, or regress to less mature behavior. Elementary school-aged children may feel embarrassed or ashamed. Young adults, on the other hand, may have future-oriented concerns, wondering how the people with whom they socialize will accept the brother or sister with a disability.

Because of the stress that may result with the addition of a baby with disabilities to the family, siblings need an explanation of the tensions within the family and the cause of the tensions (NICHCY, 1994a). Siblings may experience stress as individuals, and as family members. They may become frustrated, angry, develop low self-esteem, withdraw, or become irritated (Powell & Gallagher, 1993). Yet, unlike their parents, siblings have little knowledge of life without a brother or sister with a disability (Featherstone, 1980).

Parents of children with disabilities should be urged to engage all of their children in future plans. Families should develop specific financial plans for future care, grounded in the state's laws regarding guardianship and independence. Siblings of children with disabilities should know where to access the records of the sibling with disabilities. Families should document medical care and financial arrangements, while gaining an understanding of the legal and eligibility requirements of programs.

EARLY INTERVENTION SERVICES

My child was enrolled in a home-based early intervention program at the age of four months. A teacher trained in early intervention came to our house for two hours every other week. Speech therapy was initiated when my daughter was six months old on a monthly basis with the same agency. During these visits the team members were always very positive. They were able to identify new skills during each session and give home program suggestions. At times I did not look foreword to the visits, but I was often left with a good feeling after they took place. Because the early intervention program provided therapeutic services on a consultative basis, we elected to have our daughter receive direct occupational therapy beginning at four months and physical therapy at eight months on alternating weeks. She later began receiving individual speech therapy every other week. Instead of continuing home-based early intervention, at eighteen months my child began attending a center-based early intervention program twice a week. Each session was two hours and continued the focus on parent-child interactions and home program suggestions. The staff was helpful with developmental suggestions; however, it was the contact with other parents that offered me the emotional support I needed at times. Again when my daughter had a 'good' day at school or therapy it made a difference in my day. (Gantz, 1999)

In terms of other special education services, programs for infants and toddlers with disabilities are relatively new. Congress established the programs for infants and toddlers in 1986 in response to the need to (a) enhance the development of infants and toddlers with disabilities; (b) reduce costs by minimizing the need for special education through early intervention; (c) maximize independent living; and (d) enhance the ability of families to meet their child's needs.

According to IDEA 97 regulations, infants and toddlers with disabilities are young children, from birth through age 2, who are experiencing measurable developmental delays in cognitive development, physical development (including vision and hearing), communication development, social or emotional development, and adaptive behavior. Infants and toddlers with disabilities may also have a diagnosed physical or mental condition that has a high probability of resulting in developmental delay. A condition that has a high probability of resulting in developmental delay may include chromosomal, genetic, or congenital disorders; hearing and vision disabilities; metabolic disorders; disorders that reflect central nervous system problems; congenital infections; fetal alcohol syndrome and other disorders that occur due to prenatal exposure to substances; and severe attachment disorders. States may identify infants and toddlers who are at risk due to factors such as low birth weight, anoxia, infection, or a history of abuse or neglect (U.S.C. 34 CFR Part 303, Sec. 303.16).

Early intervention services are those that:

1. Are designed to meet the developmental needs of each child eligible . . . and the needs of the family related to enhancing the child's development;
2. Are selected in collaboration with the parents;
3. Are provided (a) under public supervision; (b) by qualified personnel; (c) in conformity with an individualized family service plan; and (d) at no cost unless ... federal or state law provides for a system of payments by families, including a schedule of sliding fees;
4. Meet the standards of the state (U.S.C. 34 CFR 303.12).

The service providers, according to Federal regulation, are responsible for consulting with parents and other professionals to ensure that services are effective. In addition, the service providers work with parents to provide those services, and participate in the assessment of the child and family. Through assessment, integrated goals and outcomes for the individualized family service plan are developed. A wide array of services may be provided through early intervention. These services are presented in Table 7.1.

There are objectives for early intervention services in addition to those in the Federal regulations. Bromwich (1997) suggested that for infants and toddlers who are at risk for disabilities, early intervention services should do the following:

1. Support and encourage pleasurable interaction between infants and parents;
2. Enable parents and primary caregivers to gain a sense of competence as parents;
3. Interest parents in observing their infants and being more sensitive to their cures;
4. Find ways of helping parents reduce stress on themselves and other family members;
5. Provide information and facilitate parents' use of community services.

In their study of how early intervention services are used, Kochenek and Buka (1998) reviewed the extent to which services made available to children and their families are actually fully utilized. They found that the assignment of the service coordinator is a critical event in utilization of early intervention services. Sixty-nine percent of the families used the majority of the services made available to them. Kochenek and Buka found that when their service providers were younger and closer in age to the mother, there were significantly higher utilization rates. Mothers who relied on

Table 7.1   Early intervention services described in the IDEA 97 regulations.

Assistive technology	Includes evaluation; purchasing, leasing, or acquiring the assistive technology device; selecting, modifying, or replacing the device; coordinating therapy related to the device; and training and technical assistance for child, family, and professionals
Audiology	Identification; referral for medical services; auditory training, prevention, amplification
Family training	Counseling and home visits, to understand special needs of the child and child's development
Medical services and health services	For diagnosis or evaluation
Nursing services	Assessment of health status; providing nursing care; administering medication or treatment
Nutrition	Assessing history, organic variables, feeding skills and problems, developing plans, making referrals
Occupational therapy	Addresses functional needs including identification and assessment, adaptation, prevention, or minimization of impact of initial disability
Physical therapy	Promotion of sensorimotor function, screening, prevention, individual and group services
Psychological services	Testing, interpreting results, interpreting information, planning and managing a program
Service coordination	Services provided by service coordinator
Social work	Home visits; social/emotional assessment; individual or family counseling; working with problems in living situation; working with community resources
Special instruction	Design of learning environments, curriculum planning, providing families with support, working with child
Speech-language pathology	Identification, referral for medical or other professional services; provision of direct services
Transportation	Travel and related costs to enable a child to participate
Vision	Evaluation, assessment, referral, and training

professionals for service decisions used services more than those who were more independent in decision-making.

Families are generally satisfied with early intervention services. McWilliam, Lang, Vandiviere, Angell, Collins, and Underdown (1995), using family surveys and interviews, reported that parents expressed overwhelming satisfaction with most services. Families ascribed most of their positive experiences to positive relationships with individual professionals. Their negative experiences were most often related to difficulties in finding out about, receiving, and monitoring services. Families spent a great deal of time and energy securing services, particularly specific therapies for their children. McWilliam et al. concluded that early intervention services are meeting most families' expectations. However, there may be some shortage of specialists relative to families' expectations.

THEORETICAL FOUNDATIONS OF FAMILY INVOLVEMENT IN EARLY INTERVENTION SERVICES

My child was enrolled in a home-based early intervention program at the age of four months. A teacher trained in early intervention came to our house every other week for one hour. At times I did not look forward to the visits, but I was often left with a good feeling after they took place.

The family-centered philosophy is the basis of family involvement in early intervention. In a family-centered approach, professionals support the child's family to determine and meet its needs in relation to the child (Dunst, Trivette, & Deal, 1988). The term "family-centered" refers to both a philosophy of care to a set of practices (Bruder, 2000). The basis of family-centered involvement is empowerment. For the professional, empowering families "works you out of the job," whereas doing things "for" families can build in paternalism and dependency (Dunst, Trivette, & Deal, 1988).

Turnbull and Turnbull (1997) defined empowerment as the ability to get what you want. The goal of empowering parents is to help them make decisions and take action serving their self-selected needs (Dunst et al., 1988). Dunst et al. proposed three criteria for empowering parents. First, the professional should take a proactive stance, assuming that parents are either competent or capable of becoming competent. Second, professionals should create opportunities for families to display their strengths in order to gain new competencies. Third, professionals should enable families to acquire a sense of personal control over their lives and the affairs of their families. The satisfaction of families with family-centered programs has been documented.

Brotherson and Goldstein (1992) reported that parents believed that they knew their children best and that professionals should use parents' information about their child and family as data for intervention decisions. Parents asked that professionals provide sufficient time in their work to develop and maintain a relationship with the parents and family. In contrast, parents identified four issues that constrained their effectiveness and used their time ineffectively: (a) a lack of coordination between professionals; (b) being overwhelmed with what they were asked to do; (c) the distances to and between services; and (d) a lack of flexibility in scheduling. Parents should be recognized as competent, contributing members of their child's team, with knowledge to share. When family service coordinators implemented a family-centered model, families reported a high degree of satisfaction and a low degree of dissatisfaction. When they did not implement the family-centered model adequately, parents reported little satisfaction and a high degree of dissatisfaction (Romer & Umbreit, 1998).

In early intervention, family members and professionals form a team. Three team models have emerged for early intervention services (Howard, Williams, Port, & Lepper, 1997): multidisciplinary, interdisciplinary, and transdisciplinary. In the traditional multidisciplinary team model, members work independently to provide assessment and direct services to children. In this model the child and family move from professional to professional to receive assessment and treatment service. In the interdisciplinary team model, professionals conduct their assessments and plan goals together, but continue to provide direct services independently. In the transdisciplinary model, the emerging model in early intervention, professionals share roles and may combine their assessment and treatment tasks. The teacher may be implementing a plan written by the physical therapist, or the parent may be implementing a feeding program designed by the occupational therapist (Howard et al.). The transdisciplinary team model addresses the need for unified plans of intervention, and does away with turfism and inflexibility on the part of professionals.

Transdisciplinary teams view child development as an integrated, interactive process (McGonigel, Woodruff, & Roszmann-Millican, 1994). In this model, the team develops the individualized family service plan (IFSP) by designing outcomes and strategies, activities, and services to meet the identified needs of the child and the priorities of the family. Transdisciplinary teams recognize that planning services for children and their families is too complex to be completed at a single meeting. During implementation, transdisciplinary teams depend on role release, i.e., the primary service provider uses the information and skills offered by other team members as well as his or her own discipline-based expertise during treatment.

Effective teamwork can only occur through mutual trust, respect, practice, and hard work (Howard et al., 1997). Howard et al. proposed three fundamental guidelines: consensus, flexibility, and process collaboration. The first is the use of consensus building rather than authoritarian structures. Consensus is the extent to which individuals agree on issues such as goals, activities, and priorities (Beckman, Robinson, Rosenberg, & Filer, 1994). Setting priorities with families is difficult unless the negotiation and compromise inherent in consensus building are in place. In addition, flexibility is essential. Professionals, as members of a transdisciplinary team, must be willing to share roles as well as information. Finally, the process that the group uses to function must be attended to with care. All participants should be comfortable in sharing their concern, listening, and valuing input. Parents should be greeted as team members and put at ease.

Relationships are key in early intervention. In their survey of parents' and service coordinators' descriptions of variables that influence collaborative relationships, Dinnebeil, Hale, and Rule (1996) reported that interpersonal skills are the most critical. Judge (1997) found that parents desired some control over needed services, resources, and supports.

LEGAL ASPECTS OF EARLY INTERVENTION SERVICES

As parents we value honesty and sincere compassion. Although I had been involved in many IFSP's the experience of having others share their observations and assumptions, in the area of their expertise, about my own child is somewhat daunting. At times a statement may be made based more on the generalizations the person knows about Down syndrome rather than the reality of my daughter. Each professional is trained to see the deficits in my child and share them with me. At the same time they are asking me to see the beautiful things she is accomplishing. This contradiction is felt during each IFSP meeting and at times during individual sessions.

My periodic frustration with professionals relates to the view of normal development. In normal development, there is a range in the ages given for the acquisition of motor, cognitive, social, language and adaptive behaviors. One view has broadened the range of skill mastery to include the slightest emergence of a skill. Another view is only seeing the abnormal in my daughters' development. Sometimes at eighteen months of age, the throwing of a toy is simply that and not a precursor for future abnormal behaviors.

The development of the IFSP is being driven by our concerns. It is difficult to always be confident in the strategies used to help my daughter to develop to her potential. If another parent is trying a different approach to a similar need, it can easily make us second-guess what we are doing. As a parent you begin to know when the professionals in your life are offering honest and non-judgmental input, regardless of how non-traditional the approach might be. I have learned that you really will explore many options if there is a chance that it will help your child. I am not looking for permission from the professionals on the team, just honesty and open mindedness. At times professionals shy away from being as candid with parents as they encourage parents to be with them. Truly enabling parents to ask questions and advocate for their child is essential, however it can be a threat to professionals who feel they must and do know more than the parent.

As a parent and professional I now see the issue of confidentiality in a new light. I have found that professionals share a fair amount of information about the children or families they work with. When my daughter was born I was amazed how many people knew quite early, because a professional had told them about her birth. I know I had a heightened degree of sensitivity and still do on some days, however it made me wonder what else was being shared. During team meetings as a professional it is important to share with other members information, but additional co-workers do not need to know about specific issues during casual conversations. (Gantz, 1999)

The basis for early intervention services is the IFSP. The IFSP is developed collaboratively by a team that includes the parent or parents of the child; other family members if the parent requests; an advocate or outside persons if the parent requests; a services coordinator who has been working with the family since the initial referral of the child or who has been designated as responsible for implementing the IFSP; individuals who were directly involved in assessing the child; and, as appropriate, the individuals who will be providing services. The regulations indicate that if any of these team members is unable to attend, they may participate through a telephone conference call, having a knowledgeable authorized representative at the meeting, or by reviewing records of the meeting. The meeting should be conducted in settings and times convenient to families and in the native language of the family or other mode of communication used by the family. Meeting arrangements should be made early enough to ensure the participation of everyone invited. All aspects of the IFSP must be fully explained to parents and informed written consent must be obtained from parents before any services are provided (U.S. C. 34 CFR Part 303, Sec. 303.342–343).

The IFSP must be developed within 45 days of referral. In addition, every 6 months, or more frequently if warranted or at the family's request, the IFSP must be reviewed. During this review, progress towards outcomes and the need for modification of services or outcomes are considered. This periodic review can be accomplished through a meeting or by another means acceptable to the parents, such as telephone communication. A meeting must be conducted at least annually to review the IFSP and determine what services are needed and will be provided (U.S. C. 34 CFR Park 303, Sec. 303.342).

The IFSP is both a process and a document. It must include the following:

- Information about the child's present levels of physical development (including vision, hearing, and health status), cognitive development, communication development, social or emotional development, and adaptative behavior, based on professionally acceptable objective criteria;
- A statement of the family's resources, priorities, and concerns related to enhancing the child's development;
- Major outcomes expected to be achieved for the child and family, and the criteria, procedures, and timelines used to determine progress and whether revisions are necessary;
- A statement of the early intervention services, including the frequency, intensity, and method of delivery of services, the extent to which services are provided in the natural environment, location of services, and payment arrangements, if any;
- A description of medical and other services that are not required by IDEA, and the funding sources used;
- Dates for initiation and duration of services;
- Name of the service coordinator from the profession most immediately relevant to the child's or family's needs who will be responsible for the implementation of the IFSP and coordination with other agencies;
- Steps to be taken to support transition of the child to preschool or other services (U.S. C. 34 C.F.R. Part 303, Sec. 303.344).

The Beach Center on Families and Disability (1996a) suggested three separate meetings for writing a "family friendly" IFSP. The first meeting involves listening. Prior to this session, parents are asked if they would like to visit various programs and gather any evaluation and assessment information that they have available to them. During the first meeting, the family should discuss (a) what the family wants, (b) family priorities and concerns, (c) family plans, and (d) how the family will decide whether the plans are working. The second meeting usually involves assessing the child. This information is discussed during the third meeting or the "official" IFSP meeting. During this meeting the family, with other team members, determines what should be in the written plan and which professionals will work with the child and family. The Beach Center urges professionals to make family members as comfortable as possible throughout the IFSP process, respect the family's view or perspective, and acknowledge their strengths.

A significant part of the IFSP process is to discuss and document family strengths. Family strengths include the ability to (a) enhance its own sense of well being, (b) increase each others' opportunities to interact with others, (c) balance individual needs with those of the rest of the family, (d) discuss concerns openly, and (e) get the services and support they need from other people (Beach Center on Families and Disability, 1996b).

The 1997 Amendments to the Individuals with Disabilities Act emphasized that early intervention services for infants and toddlers must occur in a natural environment (U.S.C. 34 CFR 303.12).The Connecticut Birth to Three Natural Environments Task Force (1997) indicated that the natural environment means:

- The family's sense of isolation is decreased by connecting families to natural sources of support such as friends, neighbors, or others in the community;
- Supporting the family in their effort to identify the child's strengths and gifts;
- Helping the family build relationships that focus on the child, not the disability;
- Increasing the child's language and communication skills;
- Providing services that are stimulating and responsive to their needs;
- Providing typically developing children for opportunities for positive interactions with children with disabilities.

The issue of the natural environment has an impact on the family goals and priorities documented in the IFSP. The Connecticut Birth to Three Natural Environments Task Force (1997) suggested that professionals ask (a) what will happen in the family's daily routines to support the proposed outcome of the IFSP and (b) by whom and where in the various settings in which the child and family live could the outcome be practiced. They suggest that family supports should help the family use and strengthen their social networks and natural sources of support. In addition, family supports should promote the integration and inclusion of children with disabilities into all aspects of community life.

SPECIAL CONSIDERATIONS FOR INVOLVING PARENTS IN EARLY INTERVENTION SERVICES

As my daughter continues to grow and develop her wonderful and unique personality we see how similar she is to other children without Down syndrome. She is slightly delayed in her fine motor skills, as well as language and cognitive abilities. Her gross motor skills have always been an area of strength. She engages in typical toddler antics; playing with the toilet paper roll, looking at books, kicking a soccer ball and dancing to music she plays on the piano. As a parent you begin to see beyond the Down syndrome and see the child. As a professional it is important to move beyond the label and discover the person. (Gantz, 1999)

The Service Coordinator

An essential person in early intervention is the service coordinator. Service coordination includes "the activities carried out by a service coordinator to assist and enable a child eligible … to receive the rights, procedural safeguards, and services that are authorized to be provided…" (34 CFR Sec. 303.22). According to the IDEA regulations, the service coordinator is responsible for coordinating all services across agency lines and serving as a single point of contact for helping parents obtain the needed services. Service coordination is described as an active process that assists parents in gaining access to services, coordinates those services, facilitates the timely delivery

of services, and continuously seeks the appropriate services for each child. The activities of the service coordinator include:

- Coordinating evaluations and assessments;
- Facilitating and participating in the IFSP;
- Assisting families in identifying available service providers;
- Coordinating and monitoring the delivery of available services;
- Informing families of the availability of advocacy services;
- Coordinating with medical and health providers;
- Facilitating the development of transition plans to preschool services (34 CFR 303.22).

Hurth (1998) described several quality assurance indicators for service coordination. First, she suggests that caseloads must be low enough to allow a service coordinator to build relationships with families and understand their concerns, priorities, needs, and abilities. In addition, caseloads should be flexible, because family needs may range from intensive support to occasional visits. Hurth suggests that families be provided a choice in selecting a service coordinator who can accommodate their needs and preferences. Though training will be necessary, family members can be successful service coordinators. Finally, system evaluation, monitoring, and oversight are essential to maximize the early intervention system's strengths and correct for problems or inequities.

Working with parents of infants and toddlers who are at risk presents several considerations for service coordinators. Bromwich (1997) contended that the role of the service coordinator is to enable parents to remain in control of services, and avoid the authority-layman gap that can occur. Parents' priorities and concerns should be dealt with first. Respecting parents' goals for the infant and involving parents in planning is essential to effectiveness. Services should build on parents' strengths, and respect for individual styles of parent-infant interactions. Bromwich argues that parents should be provided a rationale and information regarding recommendations, and should be "given an out" so that a sense of failure is not experienced if the suggestion doesn't work. Empathy is also important, and the service coordinator should be able share the parents' feelings when an infant is not responsive to a particular intervention.

Dinnebeil and Rule (1994), in interviews with three groups: "experts," parents, and service coordinators, reported the attitudes, interpersonal skills, and type of knowledge that may be helpful in working with families. Parents and service coordinators described productive qualities that were grounded in building rapport. Parents preferred service coordinators who provided information relevant to their family's needs, demonstrating a concern for the family's children, and maintaining a positive attitude towards the family. Professionals, "experts," suggested that parents' productive behaviors could be judged by the ability of the parents to follow through on activities discussed, communicate needs clearly, have a positive attitude towards the child, and hold positive beliefs about themselves as parents.

Drug and Alcohol Exposure

Working with families in which drug and alcohol use has played a role in the infant or toddler's disability raises unique issues for the early intervention professionals. Though qualitative differences between babies who have been prenatally exposed to drugs and alcohol and their families and babies for whom drug and alcohol exposure is not an issue have been identified in the literature, care must be taken to avoid stereotyping families and falling into a deficit-model trap. Gottwald and Thurman (1994) reported that infants prenatally exposed to cocaine, for example, were asleep or distressed for significantly longer periods of time than drug-free infants. In addition, mothers who used cocaine spent significantly more time disengaged from, or passively looking at, their infants than mothers who were not using cocaine.

Unfortunately, findings of studies such as that presented by Gottwald and Thurman (1994) may have contributed to presumptions by professionals. Thurman, Brobeil, Ducette, and Hurt (1994), for example, showed videotape segments of two 24-month-old children to teachers. One of the children had been prenatally exposed to cocaine, and the other had not. Children were judged less favorably when professionals were told that the children were exposed to cocaine. Policy recommendations to address the needs of infants and young children affected by substances emphasize that labels such as "crack babies" or "drug kids" should not be used (Poulsen, 1994).

In addition, Poulsen recommended that comprehensive developmental assessment should be used with all at-risk children where substance abuse is suspected, and developmental services for at-risk children should begin at birth. These services should be comprehensive and family centered.

Poulsen (1994) contended that treatment addressing drug recovery should take place in the context of total family needs, rather than in isolation. Including children in the treatment, however, brings new challenges as well as benefits (Van Bremen & Chasnoff, 1994). Treatment programs must establish priorities for both time and content of interventions related to parenting. Van Bremen and Chasnoff suggested that all professionals must understand that what happens in the hallways and cafeteria when clients, children, and staff interact may have even more of an impact on parenting than what happens in carefully planned lessons.

Engaging Fathers

Due to a variety of logistics and social reasons, mothers more often attend school meetings than fathers (Cripe & Stroup, 1998). May (in Cripe & Stroup) suggested that agency, programs, brochures, and newsletters be made as attractive and engaging to fathers as mothers. When calling home, he suggests asking for the father rather than the mother, requesting his presence and personally asking his perceptions regarding the child, the program, and so on. Other suggestions for engaging fathers are presented in Figure 7.1.

Generally, young fathers present unique needs. Schwartz (1999) stated that programs for young fathers may have a goal of helping young fathers develop the behaviors and assume the responsibilities of parenthood by providing them with emotional support and useful services, recognizing the limitations of adolescent attitudes and economic realities. Schwartz argues that it is essential to give fathers practical help at the outset, and to arrange attractive, structured father-child activities. In addition, young fathers may need legal support regarding paternity issues, as well as information about the birth process and meeting infant needs. Specific skills in mediation for successful co-parenting may be helpful for young fathers.

Parents with Mental Retardation

There are a number of myths about parents with mental retardation, i.e., that their children will also have mental retardation, that they will have many children, that they are inherently inadequate parents, or that they are unable to learn (Espe-Sherwindt & Crable, 1993). However, there is no evidence that a parent having mental retardation will have an adverse effect on the child (Ingram, 1993). Though parental rights have been terminated upon the determination that a parent has mental retardation without regard to the parents' actual abilities, most parents who have mental retardation are capable of raising their children (Hayman, 1990).

As with any parents, various factors can influence how the child develops physically and emotionally. Ingram (1993) said that people who have mental retardation may need temporary or ongoing help in learning how to care for their children's needs.

Engage fathers by

- having specific programs for fathers only, on topics important to them such as financial matters, education, vocational options;
- sponsoring meetings organized and chaired by fathers, with male professionals as speakers;
- sponsoring social events such as barbecues, a trip to the zoo or swimming pool, or an evening of Monday Night Football;
- designing evening or weekend classes specifically aimed at fathers;
- strategically involving men in recruiting other men;
- appealing to the practical, pragmatic side of men by completing a project (e.g., building blocks, starting a garden, etc.);
- making sure fathers are part of a well-thought-out program for all family members;
- encouraging mom to encourage dad;
- offering activities for both parents;
- scheduling activities on weekends or evenings;
- sponsoring activities that teach fathers how to help their children learn;
- displaying pictures of fathers and children around the school or center;
- telling fathers that their contribution is important.

Figure 7.1   *Engaging fathers.* (*Beach Center, 1996c; Cripe & Stroup, 1998*)

Espe-Sherwindt and Crable (1993) suggest that a responsible early intervention program for parents with mental retardation begins with and emphasizes the relationship between the parent and the service coordinator. In addition, parents with mental retardation should be provided an opportunity for input and decision-making at each step of service delivery, recognizing that making decisions may be difficult for them. Programs should be designed to promote competence, and recognize the parents as adult learners. Early intervention programs involving parents with mental retardation should emphasize the development of informal, ongoing supports, and define successful outcomes for the family.

Ethnic, Cultural, or Linguistic Diversity

When working with parents, teachers must recognize the impact of ethnic, cultural, or linguistic diversity on parent-child interactions. For example, in a study of "spoiling" an infant, using the definition of spoiling as excessive self-centered and immature behavior resulting from the failure of parents to enforce consistent age-appropriate limits, 75% of the sample agreed that you could indeed spoil an infant. However, there were cultural differences. Caucasian parents tended to report that you cannot spoil an infant, and said that they would attend to cries by holding, picking up, and rocking the child. African American parents, however, tended to indicate that you can and shouldn't spoil an infant. They believed that holding the baby a great deal and responding quickly to a baby's cry would be indulgent (Solomon, Martin, & Cottington, 1993).

PARENT INVOLVEMENT ACTIVITIES

Collaboration in Hospitals

One site for parent collaboration unique to early intervention is the hospital. Long, Artis, and Dobbins (1993) suggested that using an "infant educator" in the hospital is useful to provide early intervention services. Families indicated that they desired support groups, information on child development, and information on how to play with their child. Even in hospital settings, the IFSP enables parents to communicate their concerns and priorities while empowering them during a period of family crisis. To aid in developing relationships with their infant, parents are encouraged to "live-in" with their child. Several issues became apparent in their work:

- Effective communication is vital to a collaborative partnership;
- Families of children hospitalized for longer periods of time are increasingly interested in information to enhance their child's development;
- Parents find support through meeting other parents of children with similar needs;
- A single hospital contact improves cooperation between community-based early intervention services and hospital staff;
- Training for staff in family-centered care practices must be ongoing.

Parents Supporting Parents

Parent-to-parent programs are those programs that help parents who have children with disabilities or chronic illnesses find each other and provide consistent support for each other. Parent-to-parent programs have traditionally been grassroots efforts. Santelli, Turnbull, Marquis, and Lerner (1997) reported that both veteran and new parents reported that they received support from parent-to-parent programs.

Though many parent-to-parent programs run with little or no funding, Santelli et al. (1997) suggested that you seek some funding before beginning such a program. Veteran parents should be recruited and trained. These training activities typically include an orientation, discussion of a positive philosophy about persons with disabilities, and self-awareness activities. In addition, information about community resources and the referral process, and communication and listening skills are often presented. Key to a parent-to-parent program is establishing a referral and matching system. Referrals may come from a variety of sources, but in established programs they are most often from doctors and hospitals. Parent-to-parent matches are made carefully and generally based on similar disability and family issues. An additional strategy, parents sharing their stories, is described in Action Steps 7.2.

Parents on Advisory Committees or Boards

Parents are often involved in state and regional interagency coordinating councils. Some parents may require support when they serve on such advisory councils, committees, or boards. Parents have indicated that, though willing to contribute time and

ACTION STEPS 7.2: *PARENTS SHARING THEIR STORIES*

Gabbard (1998) stated that parents can use their stories to connect with other parents. Parents can shape their stories so that key themes emerge and improvements are made within a program or system. Parents may tell their story to

- provide a constructive outlet for grief and anger;
- help service providers by sharing stories for effective networks-to-programs;
- support the family in their commitment to themselves and their children;
- influence public opinion by illustrating how policies affect families;
- help parents feel less alone in their change efforts;
- communicate the need and strengths of early intervention programs to legislators or policy makers;
- entertain others;
- share information that cannot be easily presented by charts or graphs with others who do not directly experience the problem of parenting a child with a disability;
- raise awareness and promote sensitivity to the experience and knowledge that grows from experiences.

Gabbard (1998) suggested three steps for families to "tell their story." First, parents must prepare the story by studying the audience, and making sure the story flows from beginning, to middle, to end. In presenting the story, parents should try to relax, project, and monitor their pace. Giving eye contact is important, and, if appropriate, humor can provide some emotional release. It is important to give the audience time to ask questions. Props or audio visuals may be used to enhance a story. Crying is perfectly acceptable, but pausing and collecting yourself is necessary before continuing. In following up, parents should seek feedback so that they can develop the story and emphasize effective features.

---

energy, they are not always able to absorb the costs of participation (Popper, 1997). Some agencies fund the cost of gas, tolls, parking, child care and meals. Some agencies provide stipends rather than actual costs.

Another issue that emerges as parents assume advisory roles is the issue of accountability. Popper reported that parents hoped that policies would encourage involvement of more parents so that the load can be shared broadly rather than having one or two parents being asked repeatedly to participate or to serve as speakers. Possible roles for parents in these activities are presented in Figure 7.2. Care should be taken, however, to avoid parent burnout; any one parent should not be required to assume too much responsibility for too long (Circle of Inclusion, 1998).

Parents as Staff Members

Parents have begun to move from the volunteer level to paid positions as parent consultants or parent advisors. Parents may be hired for positions in which their expertise as parents is necessary, or in positions such as clerical staff or van drivers, often the first contact a parent has with a program. Clarity of role and function is essential in these positions. Parents may need formal training. Evaluation of their work may

```
┌─────────────────────────────────────────────────────────┐
│                                                           │
│  Parents may                                              │
│                                                           │
│    • review grants;                                       │
│    • act as members of task forces;                       │
│    • serve on advisory boards;                            │
│    • act as co-trainers for preservice or inservice activities; │
│    • act as paid program staff or consultants;            │
│    • serve as mentors for other families;                 │
│    • participate in a needs assessment process;           │
│    • serve as advocates;                                  │
│    • participate in focus groups;                         │
│    • serve as members of committees to hire new staff;    │
│    • participate at conferences and working meetings;     │
│    • participate in quality improvement initiatives.      │
│                                                           │
└─────────────────────────────────────────────────────────┘
```

Figure 7.2   *Roles for Parents.* (*Cripe & Stroup,* 1998)

prove to be an essential challenge. At times when a parent becomes an employee, other parents' attitudes toward them changes. Professionals may view the parent consultant as a fellow worker, while others might consider the parent an outsider without real credentials. Some parents may view the parent consultant as a professional rather than a parent (Popper, 1997).

Written Communication

Written materials for parents should be presented in standard language rather than in professional jargon. Examples and personal experiences are helpful (Circle of Inclusion, 1998).

THE TRANSITION TO PRESCHOOL

Ninety days before the child's third birthday, a meeting is convened, with the permission of the family, to begin formal transition procedures. Though all of the child's IFSPs have addressed issues of transition, this meeting begins the formal work and documentation. In fact, some professionals recommend starting the transition "out" process when the child enters the early intervention program. The service coordinator contacts all members of the child's team, and shares relevant information including timelines for completion of the activities to be developed during the meeting. The family identifies their interests and concerns, receives information about their rights, and reviews and signs consent forms for the release of records from the early intervention program to the local education agency or school district. In addition, the family must review and sign the consent for evaluation to determine whether the child is eligible for special education services. Family members can be helped to prepare for their roles in the transition by visiting with other parents who have experienced the transition process, viewing videos, or preparing questions to ask at the meeting (Cripe & Stroup, 1998).

About 6 months before the child is 3 years old, the team writes transition outcomes that identify the strategies and activities for the child's transition. The outcome includes the notification of the 90-day meeting. The family may visit local programs, or ask the family service coordinator for a recommendation of quality programs in the area.

Once the placement of the child is determined, a plan for making the transition a positive experience must be included in the decision-making process. Some factors to consider include moving the child into the program gradually (for example, starting out only 2 days a week rather than 5), placement in the program at the beginning of the school year, visiting the program with the family, or having the family service coordinator visit the program a few times once the child is attending and have them evaluate how the child is doing (Cripe & Stroup, 1998).

Personal future planning may be helpful in designing transitions. In future planning, parents and/or family members, friends of the family, special service providers, preschool staff, and friends of the child participate. In this way, input is obtained from a variety of people who know the child. Using this process, the group begins by documenting on flip charts or large sheets of paper questions such as "What are this child's strengths? Givens? Needs? Ideal day?" From such questions, goals are developed and prioritized, and objectives are created (Cripe & Stroup, 1998).

The logistics of a successful transition must also be clarified at this meeting. The "Circle of inclusion" staff helps the parents to engage in discussion and training. The specific procedures needed to prepare the child to function in the next environment should be delineated, ensuring that planning occurs in a systematic, individualized, timely, and collaborative way. The structure and transmission of information among team members should be included, as well as the necessary services to promote and support the placement.

SUMMARY

- Families of young children with disabilities may be challenged by requiring services, addressing financial concerns, and future planning that they may not have previously considered.
- In early intervention services, the role of the service coordinator is crucial.
- Family-centered programming, the basis of family involvement in early intervention, supports the child's family to determine and meet needs in relation to the child.
- Relationships are key in early intervention.
- The IFSP is the basis for services in early intervention.
- The transition to preschool services is a period of stress and changes for the child and family.

REFERENCES

Beach Center on Families and Disability (1996a). *How to get a family-friendly IFSP. Fact sheet.* Lawrence, KS: Beach Center on Families and Disabilities.

Beach Center on Families and Disability (1996b) *Recognize and acknowledge family strengths. Fact sheet.* Lawrence, KS: Beach Center on Families and Disabilities.

Beach Center on Families and Disability (1996c). *How to maximize fathers' involvement with their children who have disabilities. Fact sheet.* Lawrence, KS: Beach Center on Families and Disabilities.

Beckman, P. J., Robinson, C. C., Rosenberg, S., & Filer, J. (1994). Family involvement in early intervention: The evolution of family-centered service. In L. Johnson, R. J. Gallagher, & M. J. LaMontagne (Eds.), *Meeting early intervention challenges: Issues from birth to three* (2nd ed.), pp. 13–32. Baltimore: P. H. Brookes.

Blacher, J. (1989). Sequential stages of parental adaptation to the birth of a child with handicaps: Fact or artifact? In B. E. Hanft (Ed.). *Family Centered Care* (pp. 31–47). Rockville, MD: American Occupational Therapy Association.

Bragg, R. M., Brown, R. L., & Berninger, V. W. (1992). The impact of congenital and acquired disabilities on the family system: Implications for school counseling. *The School Counselor*, 39, 292–299.

Bromwich, R. (1997). *Working with families and their infants at risk.* Austin, TX: Pro-Ed.

Brotherson, M. J., & Goldstein, B. L. (1992), Time as a resource and constraint for parents of young children with disabilities. *Topics in Early Childhood Special Education*, 12, 508–527.

Bruder, M. B. (2000). Family-centered early intervention: Clarifying our values for the new millennium. *Topics in Early Childhood Special Education*, 20(2), 105–115, 122.

Circle of Inclusion (1998). *Preschool inclusion manual.* Washington, DC: Author.

Connecticut Birth to Three Natural Environments Task Force (1997). *Service Guidelines No. 2: Natural environments.* Hartford, CT: Department of Mental Retardation.

Cripe, J., & Stroup, V. (1998). *Preschool inclusion manual.* Lawrence, KS: Circles of Inclusion.

Darling, R. B., & Baxter, C. (1996). *Families in focus: Sociological methods in early intervention.* Austin, TX: Pro-Ed.

Dinnebeil, L. A., & Rule, S. (1994). Variables that influence collaboration between parents and service coordinators. *Journal of Early Intervention*, 18(4), 349–361.

Dinnebeil, L. A., Hale, L. M., & Rule, S. (1996). A qualitative analysis of parents' and service coordinators' descriptions of variables that influence collaborative relationships. *Topics in Early Childhood Special Education*, 16(3), 322–347.

Dunst, C. J., Trivette, C. M., & Deal, A. G. (1988). *Enabling and empowering families: Principles and guidelines for practice.* Cambridge, MA: Brookline Books.

Espe-Sherwindt, M., & Crable, S. (1993). Parents with mental retardation: Moving beyond the myth. *Topics in Early Childhood Special Education*, 13(2), 154–174.

Featherstone, H. (1980). A *difference in the family: Life with a disabled child.* NY: Basic Books.

Gabbard, G. (1998). Family experiences: Ways to lead change through telling your story. NEC*TAS *Early Childhood Bulletin*, Spring, 1998, 1–6.

Gallimore, R., Bernheimer, L. P., & Weisner, T. S. (1999). Family life is more than managing crisis: Broadening the agenda of research on families adapting to childhood disability. In R. Gallimore, L. P. Bernheimer, D. L. MacMillan, D. L. Speece, & S. Vaught (Eds)., *Development perspectives on students with high-incidence disabilities* (pp. 55–80). Mahway, NJ: Lawrence Erlbaum.

Gantz, S. (1999). Personal communication.

Gottwald, S. R., & Thurman, S. K. (1994). The effects of prenatal cocaine exposure on mother-infant interaction and infant arousal in the newborn period. *Topics in Early Childhood Special Education*, 14(2), 217–231.

Harry, B. (1992). Making sense of disability: Low-income, Puerto Rican parents' theories of the problem. *Exceptional Children*, 59, 27–40.

Hayman, R. L. (1990). Presumptions of justice: Law, politics, and the mentally retarded parent. *Harvard Law Review*, Vol. 103.

Helm, D. T., Miranda, S., & Chedd, N. A. (1998). Prenatal diagnosis of Down syndrome: Mothers' reflections on supports needed from diagnosis to birth. *Mental Retardation*, 36(1), 55–61.

Hodapp, R. M., & Zigler, E. (1993). Comparison of families of children with mental retardation and families of children without mental retardation. *Mental Retardation*, 31(2), 75–87.

Howard, V. F., Williams, B. F., Port, P. D., & Lepper, C. (1997). *Very young children with special needs: A formative approach for the 21st century*. Columbus, OH: Merrill.

Hughes, M., & McCollum, J. (1994). Neonatal intensive care: Mothers' and fathers' perceptions of what is stressful. *Journal of Early Intervention*, 18(3), 258–268.

Hurth, J. (1998). Service coordination caseloads in state early intervention systems. NEC*TAS *Notes* No. 8, p. 1–6.

Ingram, D. (1993). *Parents who have mental retardation*. Washington, DC: The Arc.

Judge, S. L. (1997). Parental perceptions of help-giving practices and control appraisals in early intervention programs. *Topics in Early Childhood Special Education*, 17(4), 457–476.

Kochenek, T. T., & Buka, S. L. (1998). Influential factors in the utilization of early intervention services. *Journal of Early Intervention*, 21(4), 323–338.

Krahl R. (1989). *Rebuilding your life dream: Family life with a disabled child*. Iowa City, IA: University of Iowa.

Krauss, M. W. (1993). *Stability and change in the adaptation of families of children with disabilities*. Paper presented at the Annual Meeting of the Society for Research in Child Development, New Orleans, LA, March 25–28, 1993.

Long, C. E., Artis, N. E., & Dobbins, N. J. (1993). The hospital: An important site for family-centered early intervention. *Topics in Early Childhood Special Education*, 13(1), 106–119.

McGill-Smith, P. (1992). Can't get on the train without a ticket. *Teaching Exceptional Children*, 25, 49.

McGonigel, M. J., Woodruff, G., & Roszmann-Millican, M. (1994). The transdisciplinary team: A model for family-centered early intervention. In L. Johnson, R. J. Gallagher, & M. J. LaMontagne (Eds.), *Meeting early intervention challenges: Issues from birth to three* (2nd ed.), pp. 55–132. Baltimore: P. H. Brookes.

McWilliam, R. A., Lang, L., Vandiviere, P., Angell, R., Collins, L., & Underdown, G. (1995). Satisfaction and struggles: Family perceptions of early intervention services. *Journal of Early Intervention*, 19(1), 3–60.

Meadow-Orlans, K. P. (1994). Stress, support, and deafness: Perceptions of infants' mothers and fathers. *Journal of Early Intervention*, 18(1), 91–102.

National Early Childhood Technical Assistance System (NEC*TAS, 1999). *Overview to the Part C Program under IDEA*. Chapel Hill, NC: Author.

National Information Center for Children and Youth with Disabilities (1994a). *Children with disabilities: Understanding sibling issues*. Washington, DC: Author.

National Information Center for Children and Youth with Disabilities (1994b). *A parents' guide to accessing programs for infants, toddlers, and preschoolers with disabilities*. Washington, DC: Author.

Popper, B. K. (1997). Enhancing family roles in EI programs. *Early Childhood Bulletin*, October, 1997. NEC*TAS.

Poulsen, M. K. (1994). The development of policy recommendations to address individual and family needs of infants and young children affected by substance use. *Topics in Early Childhood Special Education*, 14(2), 275–291.

Powell, T. H., & Gallagher, P. (1993). *Brothers & Sisters: A special part of exceptional families* (2nd ed.), Baltimore: Paul H. Brookes Publishing.

Romer, E. F., & Umbreit, J. (1998). The effects of family-centered service coordination: A social validation study. *Journal of Early Intervention* 21(2), 95–110.

Santelli, B., Turnbull, A., Marquis, J., & Lerner, E. (1997). Parent-to-parent programs: A resource for parents and professionals. *Journal of Early Intervention*, 21(1), 73–83.

Schwartz, W. (1999). *Young fathers: New support strategies.* (ERIC Digest No. DOUD 99-1). New York: Clearinghouse on Urban Education, Columbia University.

Seligman, M., & Darling, R. B. (1992). *Ordinary families, special children* (2nd ed.). NY: Guilford.

Skinner, D., Bailey, D. B., Correa, V., & Rodriguez, P. (1999). Narrating self and disability: Latino mothers' construction of identities vis-a-vis their child with special needs. *Exceptional Children*, 65(4), 481–495.

Solomon, R., Martin, K., & Cottington, E. (1993). Spoiling an infant: Further support for the construct. *Topics in Early Childhood Special Education*, 13(2), 175–183.

Thurman, S. K., Brobeil, R. A., Ducette, J. P., & Hurt, H. (1994). Prenatally exposed to cocaine: Does the label matter? *Journal of Early Intervention*, 18(2), 119–130.

U. S. C. 34 CFR 303 Sec. 303 et seq.

Turnbull, A. & Turnbull, R. (1997). *Families, Professionals, and Exceptionality: A special Partnership*. Columbus, OH: Merrill.

Van Bremen, J. R., & Chasnoff, I. J. (1994). Policy issues for integrating parenting intervention and addition treatment for women. *Topics in Early Childhood Special Education*, 14(2), 254–274

Wesley, P., Dennis, B., & Tyndall, S. (1997). *Quicknotes: Inclusion resources for early childhood professionals*. Chapel Hill: University of North Carolina, Frank Porter Graham Child Development Center.

CHAPTER 8

Engaging Families of Preschoolers and Kindergarten Students with Disabilities

Mef and Jonathan

The most important decision any parent must make regarding their children, with or without disabilities, is their child's education. Most parents, or parents of children who are typically developing, aren't faced with the issue of formal education until their children are of preschool or kindergarten age. A parent of a child with a disability must face that issue as early as possible in order to maximize their child's potential. And, parents of children with disabilities are faced with more complex issues and options.

As the transition to preschool approached I was faced with three options: place him in a specialized environment much like early intervention in which all the children have special needs, place him in a mainstreaming environment with only a few typically developing children, or place him in a fully inclusive environment with the majority of children being typically developing. There were many factors to consider. First, there were his education rights as stated in IDEA. Also, I wanted Jonathan to be as much like other children as possible. Jonathan had spent three years in the segregated environment of his Early Intervention group and had benefitted from the direct teaching style. But, Jonathan had little opportunity to learn from his peers. His language skills were progressing while others in the class were non-verbal. I felt he could benefit more from increased interactions with children who would model appropriate communication.

Jonathan's preschool setting proved to be a most supportive environment for both of us. Again trained professionals were working with my son. Again I was learning a great deal. There was much to know about how to help my son achieve success and thrive in a heterogeneous community. As the school year progressed I saw that inclusion could be successfully implemented. I felt Jonathan was being successfully included in a "regular" learning environment.

After experiencing such success at the preschool level I thought the transition to elementary school would be equally successful. I had become a true believer in full inclusion and thought things could only get better from this point on. I wanted Jonathan to attend the Montessori school where my other children had gone and been successful. I had an established relationship with the school and was an active participant in school activities. The initial reaction to accepting Jonathan into the school was as welcoming as his preschool. However, challenges and obstacles began to surface within the first month of school, and I began to question my decision to continue inclusive education for my son.

Learning Objectives

After completing this chapter, you will be able to discuss these topics:

1. Preschoolers and kindergartners with disabilities
2. The theoretical foundation of family involvement in preschool and kindergarten special education services
3. Special considerations for involving families in preschool and kindergarten programs
4. Activities that may involve parents in preschool and kindergarten programs
5. Helping families with the transition to kindergarten and first grade

PRESCHOOLERS AND KINDERGARTNERS WITH DISABILITIES

Within the first few months of Jonathan's life, I came to realize his development was indeed very delayed, and that to maximize his potential, I would need to seek additional support. It was difficult to face the fact that alone I was unable to provide the necessary stimulation for my son to develop his skills.

There is a strong contrast between early intervention and preschool programs. In early intervention programs, parents are usually updated on their child's progress on a weekly basis, and the family may see the service provider each time he or she visits the child. Early childhood special education services for preschool children generally do not offer such frequent communication between parent and service provider. Many young children ride a bus or van to or from the preschool, so families may not have face-to-face contact with providers. Even when children are brought to the center by their families, the opportunity for conversation is limited by the hectic atmosphere of many children arriving and departing at the same time (Hadden & Fowler, 1997).

In a study of risk factors effecting preschoolers who are approaching kindergarten, Zill, Collins, West, and Hausken (1995) reported that half of today's preschoolers are affected by at least one risk factor, and 15% are affected by three or more factors. The risk factors they studied include the following:

- Mother has less than a high school education;
- Family is below the official poverty line;
- Mother speaks a language other than English as her primary language;
- Mother was unmarried at the time of the child's birth;
- Only one parent is present in the home.

Attending a Head Start, prekindergarten, or other center-based preschool program was linked to greater competence in literacy skills in 4-year-olds. This finding remained significant even when other child and family characteristics were taken into account.

Though "preschool" has traditionally not been an option for most children, a number of federal programs now fund schools to provide preschool programs. Preschool programs may be funded through the Individuals with Disabilities Education Act (IDEA). In addition, school systems are often Head Start grantees and delegate agencies, offering Head Start programs in school facilities. Additional preschool programs are funded through Title I of the Elementary and Secondary Education Act, and are based in high-poverty-area schools, serving children who are at risk of later failing in school (Clifford, Early, & Hills, 1999).

States also provide funding for preschool programs. In a recent study, 39 states reported that they provide funding for some preschool programming (Mitchell, Ripple, & Chanana, 1998) and 34 states provide statewide, comprehensive initiatives for preschoolers (Knitzer & Page, 1998). Public school systems are a major source of services to preschool children (Clifford, Early, & Hills, 1999).

Though IDEA 97 regulations use the term "developmental delay," 45 states and territories (including American Samoa, the District of Columbia, and Guam) utilize the traditional IDEA disability categories for children. Only five states use an early childhood disability category for early childhood, and two states are noncategorical for all ages. Three states and three jurisdictions use only separate disability determination for children ages 3 through 5 years (deFosset, 1999).

The Division for Early Childhood of the Council for Exceptional Children (1996) presented a concept paper on the use of developmental delay as an eligibility category. Rather than using the traditional disability categories such as mental retardation or learning disabilities, the Council stated that a developmental delay category of eligibility should be available for children from birth through age 8. The Division recommended that the same developmental delay category be used for 3 to 5-year-olds as is in place for birth through 2-year-olds. Developmental delay was defined as a significant delay in the process of development, which is an indication that development is significantly affected and that without special intervention, it is likely that educational performance at school age will be effected (DEC, 1991). The use of developmental delay solves some of the transition problems between infant/toddler and preschool services.

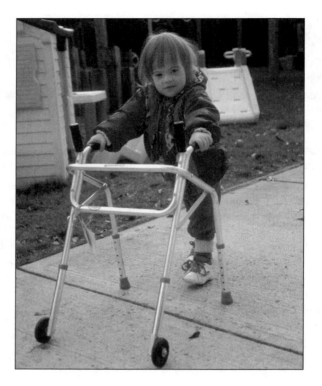

Kindergarten

The modern kindergarten was designed by Froebel in 1840, as a place for children of all classes. Though the teaching profession in Germany was essentially male, Froebel called upon women to staff kindergartens. In that he believed that women had a natural maternal instinct towards working with children, he developed an institute to train women kindergarten teachers in the early 1840s. In the United States, the first public school kindergartens were provided in St. Louis in 1873. They were founded and staffed by women (Allen, 1988).

Kindergarten programs may be either half-day (either three hours in the morning or three hours in the afternoon, with no lunch served) or full-day. Because of changes in society and education, all-day/everyday kindergartens are most popular (Gullo, 1990). Changes in the number of single parent and dual employment households have increased the need for a seamless day for children of kindergarten age. Families who have difficulty coordinating kindergarten and child care during the day find the full-day programs attractive (Housden & Kam, 1992). States often fund full-day kindergarten programs in high poverty area schools using funds designated for students at-risk (Fromberg, 1992). However, full-day kindergarten is also popular in rural areas because it eliminates the need for buses at mid-day (Heaviside, Farris, & Carpenter, 1993).

Rothenberg (1995) contended, however, that the actual issue is the creation of developmentally and individually appropriate learning environments for all kindergarten children, regardless of the length of the school day. She suggests that full-day kindergartens allow for greater depth of study, reduce transitions for the children, and provide greater continuity. Full-day kindergarten programs should integrate learning through project work in an unhurried setting, involving children in hands-on experiences.

One difficulty with developmentally appropriate kindergarten programs is parents' and administrators' desire to "see" teaching occurring. To some parents and administrators, active children look as if they are enjoying themselves too much, and there may be concerns that children are just playing (Fromberg, 1992). However, through careful communication, the "look of learning" in developmentally appropriate kindergartens can be explained.

THEORETICAL FOUNDATION OF FAMILY INVOLVEMENT IN PRESCHOOL AND KINDERGARTEN

The professionals involved demonstrated a collaborative effort in assisting in Jonathan's attainment of his goals. There was consistent communication, on both a daily basis and more formally through IEP conferences. Modifications and adaptations were readily made as needed to help assure my son's success. In addition, there was always a positive and welcoming attitude toward my son, the challenges he presented, and me.

Teachers and parents both have critical roles in effective partnerships. Meaningful participation for parents and children is an important and necessary part of inclusive education (Soodak & Erwin, 2000). Swick (1992) emphasized that viable partnerships can be created by engaging in joint learning activities, supporting each other in their respective roles, carrying out classroom and school improvement activities, conducting collaborative curriculum projects, and participating together in various decision-making activities. In the family-school structure, parents must carry out learning, doing, supporting, and decision-making roles. Teacher roles include nurturing, supporting, guiding, and decision-making. Swick suggested that an action-oriented philosophy of family-school support and nurturance is a powerful support for children's learning. Such a family action-oriented program responds to the varying needs and interests of children and families. A family-centered focus becomes part of the school's fabric.

Naturalistic Intervention

One of the bases of working with children with disabilities in preschools is natural environments and naturalistic intervention. Naturalistic intervention provides promising intervention alternatives based on the realities of settings (Barnett, Carey, & Hall, 1993). Barnett et al. indicated that naturalistic intervention defines problem situations rather than problem children. These strategies are based on efforts to understand situations prior to intervening. In addition, a series of decision strategies allows for continued reframing and refinement of target behaviors and interventions rather than diagnostic decision-making. Naturalistic intervention is grounded in naturally-occurring parent efforts that are likely to be successfully implemented, and interventions that can be adapted to the parents' style in the context of functional analysis of real situations. Naturalistic interventions use interviews to scan problem behaviors and circumstances and to analyze problems in depth. Observations are used to determine important decisions and behaviors to integrate with interview results. The dominant focus in naturalistic intervention is to assist caregivers within the settings.

Naturalistic intervention design emphasizes and capitalizes on the natural interactions of the child and persons in closest contact with him or her. Effective intervention requires that professionals not only analyze child behaviors within the problem context, to identify family or school variables that influence performance, but also specify current levels of performance for well-selected and meaningful behaviors, as well as goals or expectations for performance. The plans that are developed refer to the ways in which the adults organize their behavior. Naturalistic intervention has been documented to deal with family issues such as being limited in their ability to move about in the community due to their children's dangerous behavior in cars or community settings; having lost friends or social support for reasons related to embarrassment over their child's behavior, or having missed considerable sleep due to their child's sleep patterns. Families represent the most powerful and pervasive influence in which a child will ever participate, and support for all family members should be provided depending on age and inclination (Fox, Dunlap, & Philbrick, 1997).

An additional issue that emerges for preschool children is that of positive behavioral support. Positive behavioral support is grounded in functional communication and skill development, social inclusion and participation, and family support (Fox, Dunlap & Philbrick, 1997). Positive behavioral support begins with a collaborative relationship. The first activity in working with families is to gain an understanding of the family, including its lifestyle, completing a functional assessment of problem behavior, then using person-centered planning to bring together the important persons in the child's life to focus on the child's capacities and develop a vision for the child's future. A comprehensive support plan is then written, including hypotheses about the function of the child's problem behavior, long-term supports for the child and family, short-term prevention strategies to assist the child in negotiating environments and interactions without using the problem behavior, communication skill instruction, and strategies for presenting a consequence for the child's behavior (Fox, Dunlap, & Philbrick, 1997). Family support is developed from a parent needs assessment conducted to gather information about the parents' need for information and assistance in understanding and responding to the disability, gaining access to services, managing the child's behavior, teaching the child skills, and communicating with others about the child. The assessment also is concerned with the family's social support, and financial needs.

SPECIAL CONSIDERATIONS FOR INVOLVEMENT

[Kindergarten] was an important transition in my child's life. Home-school communication was at a minimum, especially during those crucial first weeks of school. And, since Jonathan rode the bus, there was no opportunity for a personal exchange of information regarding his

transition. In addition, it was school policy that parents of kindergarten children were denied access to the classrooms during the first months of school. Although Jonathan's language skills were good, he was unable to recall information and express to me the events of his school day. When contact with the teacher finally occurred it was presented negatively. It was in reference to his behavior, and I remember the teacher commenting that she didn't know what to do. She was supposed to be a trained professional with whom I am entrusting the care and education of my son.

Families moving from early intervention to preschool and kindergarten programs are facing a transition to a different way of doing business. Hadden, Wischnowski, and Fowler (1997) reported that in their sample, most of the families moving from early intervention programs experienced a reduction in communication, and were dismayed that they didn't have more frequent communication with the school. Whereas early intervention often allows families to see the teacher every day, preschool programs decrease face-to-face conversations. Many children are on a bus; even those transported by families have few opportunities for conversation with the teacher because of the hectic nature of arrival and departure times. Even greater distancing between parents and teachers occurs at kindergarten.

The link between family and school changes at preschool (Coleman, 1991). Coleman suggested that participation should begin with careful planning. He suggested that a good place to begin is to document potential barriers to parent involvement, including factors such as family structures (dual employment, single parent, teenage parent) and family work schedules. Documentation of these potential barriers can be used to develop policies that work, such as providing options as to when or where parent conferences are held.

Coleman also stated that parent participation should consider the resources and expertise of parents. Parents should be offered a range of support, partnership, or leadership roles. He argued that teachers should include topics that relate to both classroom and family environments when they develop newsletters, information materials, and conduct parent meetings. Parents should be given a list of possible questions they can ask teachers throughout the year.

Involving Fathers of Preschool Children

Typically, mothers continue to oversee their children's education in preschool; whereas fathers are seen as less involved. By looking at specific information about fathers, however, activities may be designed that will engage them in their preschooler's education. The Beach Center on Families and Disability (1998) presented five points to consider when working with fathers. First, the interactions of fathers with their children with disabilities or without disabilities varies. Fathers of children without disabilities spend more time with their children out of the home, such as going to church or shopping; whereas fathers of children with disabilities tend to interact with their children at home. Second, fathers tend not to follow activities suggested by educators; to engage fathers, teachers need to find out the father's present activities and build on them. Third, fathers report that they spend a great deal of time watching television with their children; teachers can collaborate with fathers to identify ways to increase child interaction during television watching. Fourth, fathers like to problem-solve, therefore suggested activities should incorporate a logical, problem-solving process. Finally, fathers tend to engage in fewer verbal activities with their children than do mothers; consequently, fathers need information on understanding their preschooler with a disability.

Levine (1993) identified four potential barriers to fathers' participation in Head Start or other state funded preschool programs. First, fathers may be afraid of exposing their inadequacies. Second, staff program members, often female, may be ambivalent about the involvement of fathers. Third, mothers may also prevent some fathers' involvement. Fourth, programs may be designed and delivered in such a way as to discourage fathers from participating. McBride, Obuchowski, and Rane (1996) suggested that programs should be specific in their reasons for developing parent involvement activities for men, making sure it is a continuing commitment rather than a "hot" issue that will fade. In addition, teachers should recognize that there may be some resistance to involving men, who may be considered poor models or as not playing a role in the child's life. The key for educators is to identify the men who are in the lives of young children and engage them, recognizing that they may not be the biological fathers of the children. Staff members, typically women, may need training and support to encourage male involvement and accept male involvement. While programs to encourage fathers are being designed and implemented, mothers should not be ignored. McBride et al. suggested that program staff go slowly and explore which parts of their parent involvement program that is presently in place may be applied to men rather than "reinventing the wheel."

Interagency Collaboration

Working with families who are engaged with social service agencies is a challenge for teachers. The social services system tends to divide problems of children and families into rigid and distinct categories that fail to reflect the interrelated causes and solutions of the problems (Kunesch & Farley, 1993). In working with families, Kunesch and Farley found that families expressed the concern that the services they really needed weren't available and that other services were unacceptable. They stated that, in order to be profamily, social service systems must be comprehensive, meet a wide range of needs, and address the issues of prevention. Services should be family-centered, family-driven and integrated with each other and the community. Services should be developmental, and flexible enough to be sensitive to individual needs as well as cultural, gender, and racial concerns. In addition, services should be outcomes-oriented.

Kunesch and Farley (1993) offered several guidelines for effective collaboration. All key participants should be involved so that decisions and activities will receive widespread support and recognition. A shared vision should be established, and ownership in the plans should be built at all levels. Services should establish communication and decision-making processes that recognize disagreements among collaborators as part of the process.

Families from Diverse Cultural, Ethnic, or Linguistic Groups

Low-income, minority parents who are involved in their children's education see themselves as the primary educators of their children (White, 1995). They take on the role of home tutor. These home environments are places where learning and teaching occur. Parents supply their children with an assortment of education materials. Parents who are involved place a strong value on education, and see learning as the key to future success and a better life. Parents who are involved have high aspirations for their children.

Hispanic families have historically been reluctant to turn their young children over to nonfamily members for care. About half of Hispanic mothers stay at home with their children, and those who need child care often prefer using relatives rather than a preschool (Fuller, Eggers-Pierola, Holloway, Liang, & Rambaud, 1994). Hispanic families often decided, however, to enroll their children when there is active, persuasive, and culturally appropriate recruitment. Recruiters in the Hispanic community are often not linked to a particular school, but may be church leaders, members of community-based organizations, social service providers, or pediatricians who share the goal of ensuring that young children receive early education (Lewis, 1993).

McCollum and Russo (1993) suggested that providing English language or other skill development classes for adults can bolster parents' belief in the value of the entire program. Offering comprehensive services, including case management, can also

ACTION STEPS 8.1: *ENGAGING HISPANIC PARENTS IN THEIR CHILDRENS' PRESCHOOL EDUCATION*

Espinosa (1995) suggested the following strategies to engage Hispanic parents in the preschool education of their children:

- ❏ face-to-face communication in the Hispanic parents' primary language;
- ❏ nonjudgmental communication, supporting the strengths of the parents;
- ❏ perseverance in maintaining an environment that provides activities that respond to a real need or concern of the parents;
- ❏ bilingual support, in which all communication is in Spanish and English;
- ❏ strong leadership and administrative support, with flexible policies, a welcoming environment, and a collegial atmosphere;
- ❏ staff development focused on Hispanic culture;
- ❏ community outreach, including family literacy programs, vocational training, English as a Second Language programs, improved medical and dental services, and other social services.

increase parents' likelihood to enroll their children. If Hispanic parents feel coerced and not listened to, they do not necessarily benefit from increased contact with the school (Espinosa, 1995). Several strategies to engage Hispanic parents in the preschool education of their children are presented in Action Steps 8.1.

Coleman (1991) said that teachers seek advice and assistance from parents when introducing young children to various cultures through materials, stories, art, or other events. In addition, he contends that teachers should avoid making generalizations about children from various backgrounds. Suggestions specific to individual cultures are not meant to hold for all children representing that specific ethnic, cultural, or linguistic group. General cultural differences must be balanced with an assessment of the individual child, the child's family, and the community. In addition, teachers should be careful to ensure that children are not segregated during classroom activities.

PARENT INVOLVEMENT ACTIVITIES

The two years Jonathan spent in kindergarten had become a learning process for the school and me. I worked hard toward developing an effective method of communication, assisted in giving information about available outside resources, advocated for a personal aide, and assisted in appropriate modifications and adaptations in curriculum and routines.

Keating (1998) argued that not only are family members an integral part of the child's team, they ultimately make the key decisions about the child's preschool program. In order to engage families, she suggests making the preschool program a family-guided program. Developing a family-guided program has an impact on every decision made about the program, generally, and the child, specifically. Keating presents a process to review the ways in which families can be actively engaged in the program.

Table 8.1   Parent choice and decision matrix.

Activity	Roles for Family Members	Choices and Decisions
Intake	Observer	Parents may choose to:
	Mentor	Visit alone
	Parent-consultant	Bring child to visit
	Visitor	Meet with parent-partner
		Meet with parent-consultant
		Come to parent meeting
		Meet with director/teacher
		Receive written information

The first step of the process is to identify the specific program aspects in which the family and child participate. These components may include referral, eligibility evaluation, IEP development, program implementation, annual review, and the transition to kindergarten. For each of the program components, the typical activities that occur for the family and the team are identified. For example, during the referral or intake process, the family is engaged in completing a series of forms, visiting the program, and having the child make a visit. After the routine activities in each program component have been identified, the preschool staff can begin to discuss the roles and options provided for families within each activity, and the decisions the family needs to make regarding the activity. For example, the family may decide the treatment format, or combination of treatment formats, which is most appropriate for them. After completing this process for each program component, a matrix such as the one in Table 8.1 is provided. This matrix assists in communicating with each family about choices and decisions, implementing family-guided practices, and evaluating the program.

Families may also be involved in activities that go beyond their child's program. These roles are similar to those described for parents in early intervention programs, including advisory board members, co-trainers, paid program staff, paid consultants, mentors, participants in the needs assessment process, group facilitators, and advocates. Keating (1998) also recommended several activities to receive information from families. These activities are presented in Figure 8.1.

Initial Parent-Teacher Contact

Preschools are a new environment for parents as well as their children. Spinelli (1999) said that an initial parent letter should include an introduction, and an explanation of class schedules, goals, and objectives. Parents should be invited to share information. This level of interaction should continue with an ongoing class newsletter.

Hadden and Fowler (1997) suggested that teachers use a written questionnaire for families of new students, but it may be better to gather the information in a telephone

- Focus groups on specific issues
- Family-staff coffee hour
- Professional-in-training dinner
- Community and program needs assessments
- On-site visits to other programs
- Brainstorming sessions before developing educational materials
- Reviewing drafts of all written materials
- Parent panel during orientation for new staff
- Follow-up phone calls for families in transition
- Developing transition materials
- Developing parent-satisfaction survey
- Breakfast (or lunch) with the director
- Suggestion book

Figure 8.1 *Informal family activities.*

or face-to-face interview with the parents before the child enters the programs. Possible questions for this survey are provided in Figure 8.2.

Parent Conferences

Though parents may have had frequent formal interactions with professionals while their child was receiving early intervention services, the formal "parent-teacher conference" usually does not emerge until the child enters preschool. Because this style of home-school collaboration may be new to the parent, the teacher should focus, initially, on building rapport, and attending to issues that effect the child both at home and school (Spinelli, 1999). Before the conference, the teacher should provide enough notice so that the parent can prepare. The conference should be scheduled at a mutually convenient time. (Jordan, Reyes-Blanes, Peel, Peel & Lane, 1998),

Prior to the conference, teachers should tell parents what they hope to accomplish during the conference. Parents should be asked what they want the teacher to discuss during the session. Before the conference, the teacher should also send a letter that includes the conference date, beginning and concluding time, location, purpose, agenda, and a list of the persons to be present with some indication of their role. The parents should be invited to bring a support person, a relative or friend, if they wish. Parents and teachers should confer in a private, comfortable location. Sufficient time should be allowed for the conference, and the allotted time should be made clear to the parent before the conference begins (Jordan et al., 1998). At the beginning of the conference, parents and teachers should list the key points to be addressed, and review them at the end of the session (Spinelli, 1999).

Coleman (1991) characterized the comfortable conference environment for parents. Parents should be assisted by the following:

- Ensuring enough time so that the parent does not feel rushed;
- Pointing out projects and work samples in the classroom that involved his or her child;

Communication:
    How does your child communicate with you? With others?
    How does your child use gestures? Words?
    How do you communicate "no"? How does your child communicate discomfort? The
    need for help? Pleasure?

Mealtime:
    What are your child's favorite and least favorite foods?
    Are there any food textures your child will avoid?
    Will your child try new foods without coaxing?

Rest time:
    Does your child have a special item he or she can bring to school to help at rest time?
    Does your child like to be hugged or touched, or have his or her back rubbed?
    Does you child usually nap? How long?

Learning and participation:
    What are your child's strengths?
    Does you child have any health needs?
    Does your child take any medication?
    How does your child indicate the need to use the bathroom?
    What directions does your child follow easily?
    What other information would be of help?

Figure 8.2 *Topics for information-gathering before the child enters the preschool.*

- Beginning and ending the conference by noting something positive about the child;
- Asking open-ended questions;
- Communicating in a way that matches and respects the parent's background;
- Sending nonverbal messages of respect and interest;
- Facing the parent and maintaining eye-contact;
- Asking the parent to share feelings and suggestions for addressing issues.

Written Communication

Fromberg (1992) suggested the use of one-line daily notes to support parent involvement in preschools and kindergarten. By just writing a single line, such as "Lucy enjoyed working with clay today" parents are given a way to converse with their child about the school day. Class newsletters are an additional way to support parents through written communication.

Home Learning Activities

Teachers may design activities that engage their children in home learning with their parents. Fromberg (1992) described the use of mathematics "homework" that goes home in a zip lock bag each week. For example, there may be a note describing the work the class is currently doing with tallies, and a request that the child tally the number of brothers, sisters, or pets who live in the home. Another activity may be a request that students measure objects using a foot-long piece of yarn, and list some objects that are as long as the yarn and others that are shorter and longer.

Backpack activities are also used. Backpacks may go home for a week at a time and include activities for the parent and child to do together (Fromberg, 1992). Cohen (1997) described the use of book backpacks. In each backpack there are five to seven books centered on a theme or author. Themes included folktales, fairy tales, grandparents, ecology, birthdays, and travel. In addition to the children's books, Cohen included a book for parents on child development, play, organizing birthday parties, or traveling with kids, in an effort to encourage the parents to use reading materials that correspond to the backpack themes. In addition, each backpack included a composition book, in which children and parents are encouraged to write or draw pictures about their readings. An inventory card is included to help parents return the entire contents of the backpack. Cohen suggests using parent volunteers to keep track of who has which backpack and to check inventory cards against the returned contents.

HELPING FAMILIES WITH THE TRANSITION TO KINDERGARTEN AND FIRST GRADE

The transition to elementary school was all very different from the previous experiences in early intervention and preschool.

Many children have difficulties with the transition between kindergarten and preschool, because of the differences in philosophy, teaching style, and structure that sometimes occur between preschool and public school programs. Transition efforts should be designed to help ease the entry into school by preparing children and families for the differences they will encounter (Lombardi, 1992). In addition to dealing with the specifics of transition, however, there are three characteristics of programs that will lead to continuity between the early childhood program the child is receiving and the new program. These three characteristics include the following:

- Developmentally appropriate practice, which whether in a preschool or kindergarten classroom, responds to the natural curiosity of young children, reaffirms a sense of self, promotes positive feelings towards learning, and helps build skills in language, problem-solving, and cooperation;
- Parent involvement, which is responsive to the diversity among families;
- Supportive services, which respond to the comprehensive needs of children and families.

Traditionally schools have not played a role in ensuring these services, as have preschools.

The transition to kindergarten is stressful for all parents. Leaving the safety of preschool for public school is a milestone for the child and the family (remember all those crying moms as the school bus pulled away?). Conn-Powers, Ross-Allen, and

Holburn (1990) recognized this milestone, and proposed the following goals for successful transitions:

1. Promoting rapid adjustment of the child and family;
2. Enhancing the child's independent, successful participation;
3. Promoting collaboration among all participants;
4. Supporting and empowering the family;
5. Ensuring continuity of services;
6. Increasing satisfaction of all participators with the outcomes of the transition as well as the process;
7. Increasing the likelihood that the child is successful in the general education kindergarten and the elementary school mainstream.

The most common practices used by teachers with parents of children entering kindergarten are (a) a talk with parents after school starts, (b) a letter to parents after the beginning of the school year, and (c) an open house after school starts. The least common practice was making a home visit (Little, 1998). Unfortunately, teachers in schools with the greatest needs (such as poverty areas, minority students, and inner urban settings) relied more heavily on group-oriented practices after the beginning of school, though families in these settings needed a more intense experience to connect with school. Teachers described several barriers to a transition into kindergarten, including late class lists, a lack of a transition plan, working during the summer without a salary, and the transition process taking too much time (Little).

Keating (1998) described several strategies to support families in transition. She suggests that families be provided with information about what the next placement for their child entails, including site visits, resource packets, group discussions, or fact sheets. Using this information as a base, the teacher can then discuss the transition process steps, outcomes, and responsibilities with the family. Forming a support group of families experiencing the transition process may be helpful, as well as distributing resources to parents about parent rights, individualized education plan development, and decision-making. Working with parents to determine communication strategies to be used for conveying student activities and information, such as daily notebooks, phone calls, or periodic meetings, could be helpful. In addition, Keating suggested providing a resource list for siblings and a strategy to respond to situations that they might encounter during the school year regarding their sibling with a disability.

An initial meeting regarding the transition process can be extremely helpful. During this meeting, the steps that will be followed in the transition can be openly discussed and identified. These steps provide a way of involving the family. The specific procedures to prepare the child to function in the next school environment are described. By following specific steps, planning can occur in a systematic, individualized, timely, and collaborative fashion. Designated steps will also provide structure and guidelines for the transmission of information among team members, and clarify the necessary services for the placement. Finally, having carefully delineated the steps, various supports can be implemented to increase satisfaction for all participants (Keating, 1998).

Pianta and Kraft-Sayure (1999), in their research on parent concerns, reported that about two thirds of the parents indicated that the transition to kindergarten was generally smooth, with the children excited and communicative rather than anxious. Nearly 35% of the families, however, indicated that kindergarten produced a disruption in family life, forcing adjustments in schedules. Parents reported that the following activities were helpful in their child's transition to kindergarten:

- Ongoing communication between the school and family about the child's needs, meetings to engage in solving problems and reporting successes, and written correspondence;
- Child and parent familiarity with the school prior to the start of kindergarten, including formal and informal visits and prior experiences by parents and siblings;
- Child participation in preschool or child care;
- Mutually agreed upon standards for child performance and behavior.

Parents stated several reasons for negative experiences related to the transition to kindergarten. The child may demonstrate behavioral and emotional concerns, or demonstrate reluctance to go to school. In addition, there may be significant family adjustment difficulties because of the interruption of the family schedule and the cumulative stress of a child's change in routines. Parents also reported problems when the teachers had unrealistic expectations about the child, or when there were difficulties in engaging in ongoing communication.

Kindergarten teachers, on the whole, are more concerned about social, functional, and behavioral skills than academics (Hains, 1992). Rous and Hallan (1998) suggested looking at five areas of skills for children in transition from preschool to kindergarten. These include (a) classroom rules, (b) work skills, (c) communication, (d) social/behavioral, and (e) self-management. Careful assessment of skills in these areas can be incorporated into objectives for transition in the child's IEP.

The transition to kindergarten may have an impact on the goals and objectives in a child's IEP; remember, however, that the IEP goals and objectives are written in response to the child's and not the program's needs. Teachers may integrate methods for teaching general transition skills into whole class activities and the class-wide curriculum. For example, imitation can be supported by playing games such as "Simon Says" and "Follow the Leader." In some situations, children may need to be familiarized with expectations specific to a program into which they are being transitioned (Chandler, 1993).

Meier and Schafran (1999) advocated the use of community collaboration in order to ease the transition to kindergarten. They invited elementary schools to hold orientation to kindergarten meetings at the early childhood sites. During these orientation meetings, elementary school principals and teachers provide information on kindergarten issues such as curriculum, parent involvement, schedules, before- and after-school care, busing, food programs, and language programs.

A fall outreach program for parents is helpful. It offers information about school choices, special education services, and magnet schools. It is followed by kindergarten registration during the winter. In the spring, small groups of children visit their designated kindergarten classrooms and schools accompanied by a teacher or instructional assistant from their preschools. In addition, the elementary school conducts outreach about parent involvement, before- and after-school care, busing, meal programs, and school schedules.

Additional issues emerge in the transition to first grade. Ninety-eight percent of all children attend kindergarten prior to entering first grade (Zill et al., 1995). Though kindergarten has become a nearly universal experience, the population of children entering kindergarten is becoming more and more diverse. Over half of the kindergarten teachers in a recent study report having regular meetings with first-grade teachers to discuss continuity in the curriculum between kindergarten and first grade. Over half the teachers report arranging for their kindergarten class to visit a first-grade class. However, less than 25 percent of the teachers say they attend transition meetings, send parents information on how placements in the first grade are made, attend meetings to plan transitions for individual children, or plan transition activities for students with disabilities. A lack of connection between home and school remains problematic (Little, 1998).

SUMMARY

- There is a strong contrast between the nature of parent-teacher contact between early intervention and preschool programs.
- Young children with disabilities may be identified as "developmentally delayed" or as having one of the traditional IDEA disability categories.
- Creating a developmentally and individually appropriate kindergarten program is a challenge for teachers.
- Family involvement in preschool and kindergarten is grounded in nurturing and shared decision-making.
- When working with families, naturalistic interventions and positive behavioral support is emphasized.
- Special efforts may be needed to engage fathers and families from diverse ethnic, cultural, or linguistic groups.
- Parent involvement activities must be derived from parent interests and needs.
- The initial parent-teacher contact is critical, and should be carefully planned.
- The transition from preschool to kindergarten is stressful for all parents, and additional strategies should be employed when the child has a disability.
- Though often less well-structured, specific transition activities for the move from kindergarten to first grade are needed.

REFERENCES

Allen, A. (1988). Let us live for our children: Kindergarten movements in Germany and the United States, 1840–1914. *History of Education Quarterly*, 2, 23–48.

Barnett, D., Carey, K. T., & Hall, J. D. (1993). Naturalistic intervention design for young children: Foundations, rationales, and strategies. *Topics in Early Childhood Special Education*, 13(4), 430–444.

Beach Center on Families and Disability (1998). *How to maximize fathers' involvement with their children who have disabilities: Fact*

Sheet. Lawrence, KS: University of Kansas.

Chandler, L. K. (1993). Steps in preparing for transition: Preschool to kindergarten. *Teaching Exceptional Children*, 25(4), 53–55.

Clifford, R. M., Early, D. M., & Hills, T. W. (1999). Almost a million children in school before kindergarten: Who is responsible for early childhood services? *Young Children*, 54(5), 48–51.

Cohen, L. E. (1997). How I developed my kindergarten book backpack program. *Young Children*, 51(2), 69–71.

Coleman, M. (1991). Planning for the changing nature of family life in schools for young children. *Young Children*, 46(4), 15–20.

Conn-Powers, M. C., Ross-Allen, J., & Holburn, S. (1990). Transition of young children into the elementary education mainstream. *Topics in Early Childhood Special Education*, 9, 91–105

deFosset, S. (1999). *Section 619 Profile* (9th ed.). Washington, DC: NEC*TAS.

Division for Early Childhood (1991). *Statement to the U. S. Senate Subcommittee on Disability Policy with respect to reauthorization of Part H and amendments to Part B of the Individuals with Disabilities Education Act, regarding services to children from birth to age six and their families.* Pittsburgh, PA: Division for Early Childhood.

Division for Early Childhood (1996). *Developmental delay as an eligibility category: A concept paper of the Division for Early Childhood of the Council for Exceptional Children* (Adopted: September 10, 1996). Reston, VA: Council for Exceptional Children.

Espinosa, L. M. (1995). *Hispanic parent involvement in early childhood programs.* ERIC Digest No. ED382412. Urbana, IL: ERIC Clearinghouse on Elementary and Early Childhood Education.

Fox, L., Dunlap, G., & Philbrick, L. A. (1997). Providing individual supports to young children with autism and their families. *Journal of Early Intervention*, 21(1), 1–14.

Fromberg, D. P. (1992). *The full-day kindergarten: Planning and practicing a dynamic themes curriculum.* New York: Teachers College Press.

Fuller, B., Eggers-Pierola, C., Holloway, S. D., Liang, X., & Rambaud, M. (1994). *Rich culture, poor markets: Why do Latino parents choose to forego preschooling?* Washington, DC: American Educational Research Association and National Science Foundations (ED371–855).

Gullo, D. (1990). The changing family context: Implications for the development of all day kindergartens. *Young Children*, 45(4, May), 35–39.

Hadden, S., & Fowler, S. A. (1997). Preschool-a new beginning for children and parents. *Teaching Exceptional Children*, 30(1), 36–39.

Hadden, S., Wischnowski, M., & Fowler, S. (1997). Transitions from Part H to Part B: A family perspective. Unpublished manuscript: University of Illinois, Urbana-Champaign.

Hains, A. H. (1992). Strategies for preparing preschool children with special needs for the kindergarten mainstream. *Journal of Early Intervention*, 16(4), 1–12.

Heaviside, S.E., Farris, E., & Carpenter, J. (1993). *Public school kindergarten: Teachers' views on children's readiness for school.* Washington, DC: National Center for Educational Statistics.

Housden, T. & Kam, R. (1992). *Full day kindergarten: A summary of the research.* Carmichael, CA: San Juan Unified School District.

Jordan, L., Reyes-Blanes, M. E., Peel, B. B., Peel, H. A., & Lane, H. B. (1998). Developing teacher-parent partnerships across cultures: Effective parent conferences. *Intervention in School and Clinic*(13), 141–147.

Keating, J. (1998). Chapter Eight: Transition Steps. In *Preschool Inclusion Manual*,

Circles of Inclusion. Lawrence, KS: Circles of Inclusion.

Knitzer, J., & Page, S. (1998). *Map and track: State initiatives for young children and families.* New York: National Center for Children in Poverty, Columbia University.

Kunesch, L. G., & Farley, J. (1993). *Collaboration: The prerequisite for school readiness and success.* ERIC *Digest* No. EDOPS93-8. Champaign, IL: Clearinghouse on Elementary and Early Childhood Education.

Levine, J. A. (1993). Involving fathers in Head Start. A framework for public policy and program development. *Families in Society,* 7(1), 4–19.

Lewis, M. C. (1993). *Beyond barriers: Involving Hispanic families in the education process.* Washington, DC: National Committee for Citizens in Education.

Little, L. (1998). Nearly half of nation's teachers have concerns about many children entering kindergarten: Press Release from the National Center for Early Development and Learning. Chapel Hill, NC: Frank Porter Graham Child Development Center.

Lombardi, J. (1992). *Beyond transition: ensuring continuity in early childhood programs.* ERIC Digest ED345867. Urbana, IL: ERIC Clearinghouse on Elementary and Early Childhood.

McBride, B., Obuchowski, M., & Rane, T. (1996). *Father/male involvement in Prekindergarten at-risk programs: Research building practice.* Workshop presented at the Family Resource Coalition Biennial Conference, Chicago, IL.

McCollum, H., & Russo, A..W. (1993). *Model strategies in bilingual education: Family literacy and parent involvement.* Washington, DC: U. S. Department of Education, Office of the Under Secretary (ED365168).

Meier, D., & Schafran, A. (1999). Strengthening the preschool-to-kindergarten transition: A community collaborates. *Young Children,* 54(3), 40–46.

Mitchell, A., Ripple, C., & Chanana, N. (1998). *Prekindergarten programs funded by the states: Essential elements for policy makers.* New York: Families and Work Institute.

Pianta, R. C., & Kraft-Sayure, M. (1999). Parents' observations about their children's transitions to kindergarten. *Young Children,* 54(3), 47–52.

Rothenberg, D. (1995). *Full-day kindergarten programs.* ERIC Digest No. ED382410. Urbana-Champaign, IL: Clearinghouse for Elementary and Early Childhood Education.

Rous, B., & Hallan, R. A. (1998). Easing the transition to kindergarten: Assessment of social, behavioral, and functional skills in young children with disabilities. *Young Exceptional Children,* 1(4), 17–26.

Soodak, L. C., & Erwin, E. J. (2000). Valued member or tolerated participant: Parents' experiences in inclusive early childhood settings. *Journal of the Association for Persons with Severe Handicaps,* 25(1), 29–41.

Spinelli, C. G. (1999). Home-school collaboration at the early childhood level: Making it work. *Young Exceptional Children,* 2(2), 20–23.

Swick, K. J. (1992). *Teacher-parent partnerships.* ERIC Digest No. ED351149. Urbana, ILL: ERIC Clearinghouse on Elementary and Early Childhood Education.

White, R. M. (1995). *Factors explaining the involvement of African-American and Hispanic parents in an urban Head Start program.* Dissertation Abstracts International.

Zill, N., Collins, M., West, J., & Hausken, E. G. (1995). Approaching kindergarten: A look at preschoolers in the United States. *Young Children,* 51(1), 35–38.

CHAPTER 9

Engaging Families During the Primary Years

Franky and Elizabeth

The birth of a baby is one of the most memorable events in one's life. Elizabeth was our third child in four years. Knowing that our home would soon be filled with three preschoolers was an exciting thought and yet an overwhelming thought in terms of managing three children under four years of age. The pregnancy went smoothly, and the delivery was the easiest of the three thus far. It was thrilling to know that on Christmas Eve, we would be bringing this new baby home to celebrate Christmas with her siblings. My organizational skills had kicked in early and the presents were wrapped and the cards signed and addressed, but waiting for that one last name to be added. However, that day and the days to follow, didn't adhere to the schedules as planned.

My early suspicions that something was wrong were confirmed five or six hours after Elizabeth's birth when our obstetrician came in and discussed the possibility of Down syndrome. The pediatrician followed giving us medical information as well. And, in a matter of minutes the world, as we had known it, was changed forever. The news was devastating and shocking. For me, my mind raced back and forth, from the here and now, to the future. Questions loomed in front of me: How will our preschoolers handle this? How will we handle this? How will others handle this? How will we tell our parents and family? What effect will this have on our family? Who will protect her from harm? And, what do I put on the Christmas cards or do I send them?

These questions and many more took a backseat one hour later when the pediatrician told us that they were preparing Elizabeth to be transferred by ambulance to a children's hospital in St. Louis because she had stopped breathing several times and the doctors suspected a heart defect. They wanted her to be seen by a cardiologist and wanted to run tests. All the questions, thoughts, and worries about Down syndrome thus far were pushed to the back of our minds, and the only thought at that point was praying that she would live through the night. My husband accompanied Elizabeth and the ambulance to the hospital in the city.

I was left alone in a hospital room with a mother whose baby was being brought to her and her family and friends were arriving. The feelings of sadness and grief at that moment were almost more than I could bear. At my request, I was given a private room to be alone with my thoughts. I began the task of calling family and friends and I don't even remember any of those conversations. One of the friends that I called was Tom Shea, my college professor and friend of many years. He asked if I was alone and when I said yes, he simply showed up in twenty minutes. He sat with me that night and talked. I mentioned the Christmas cards and he said, "You add Elizabeth's name and send the cards." He was one of the first supports that I had. Our parents and other family members followed with this support and love and somehow we knew we would get through this.

Kindergarten is still perceived by many as a preparation for school. Unfortunately, beginning with first grade, there is a decrease in flexibility in the general education course of study, and an increase in expectations regarding behavior. Families are challenged by children with disabilities who excelled in an inclusive preschool, and "made it through" kindergarten, perhaps after two years, only to be stymied by first grade. Parent-teacher communication throughout this time is vital.

Learning Objectives

After completing this chapter, you will be able to discuss these topics:

1. Parenting children during the primary years
2. Engaging families during the primary years
3. Family-involvement programs that have been demonstrated to be effective during the primary years
4. The transition to middle school

PARENTING CHILDREN DURING THE PRIMARY YEARS

We have a typical family life where Elizabeth contributes as much as any other member of our family. She has taught all of us more than we have taught her over the years. Our family takes trips, vacations, and attends church and family gatherings like any other families. Elizabeth adds to our family. I can't imagine our family without her. She inspires all of us to work harder and to complain less.

Alper, Schloss, and Schloss (1995) report that during the elementary years, the needs of children with disabilities center on acquiring appropriate academic, social, community access, and self-management skills. Individual family members serve as advocates for their children. They describe two important features related to families. First, the entire family, not just the person with disability, needs services and supports to meet their needs and avoid loss of control and responsibility. Second, the roles and needs of children with disabilities and their family members evolve and change over

time. As children grow and mature, parents develop additional needs for communi-cation, support for their children in extracurricular activities, economic support, respite care, and information about the future. All members of the family of a child with disabilities play multiple roles, including nurturing caregiver, observer, team members, decision maker, tutor, learner, counselor, and advocate. In addition, each family member has the right to be a "normal" person and live a "normal" life.

Though parents' expectations remain fairly stable over time, their developmental expectations for their children begin to decline by the time the children are 7 years old. However, when children are 3 years old, parents' developmental expectations are less likely to be related to the children's characteristics. The decline or shift in par-ents' expectations may actually be related to their recognition of their children's strengths and struggles, and an adjustment to more realistic expectations. The child's characteristics, rather than early parent expectations, are the best predictors of par-ents' developmental expectations and child outcomes by the time the child is 11 years old (Clare, Garnier, & Gallimore, 1998).

Specific research has been conducted regarding children with learning disabil-ities. Parents have reported significant challenges in parenting their child. Dyson (1996) suggested that parents are challenged by the length of time taken for the recognition, identification, and assessment of children with disabilities. In addi-tion, the child's own problems (skipping classes, suspension from school, not get-ting along with peers, low self-esteem, and minor behavior problems) can be stressful for families. Families reported concerns about their children's academic experiences, such as negative report cards and inflexible policies. In addition, par-ents were concerned about future educational programs, and the increased chal-lenges of young children who are gifted, creative, and talented and have learning disabilities.

When dissatisfaction is great enough, parents may choose to remove their child from the school. In their report of parents who took advantage of school choice, Lange, Ysseldyke, and Lehr (1997) reported that the primary reason parents chose different schools was that the child's needs were better met, followed closely with the potential of greater teacher attention and information. The parents' responses indicated that they wanted to be informed early-on if there were any problems developing, and wanted to work with teachers in their child's education program, having their knowledge and opinions valued. Lange and associates recommend that when parents choose to remove a child from your program, you should determine the reasons, and communicate those reasons to all involved personnel. Schools should examine the communication system between the school and home, as well as reviewing the school's policies and practices.

ENGAGING FAMILIES

You will provide services for my child for one school year. I will be advocating for my child for the rest of her life. I want you to look at the "big picture."

In regards to primary schools, Petit (1989) described various dimensions of family involvement: (a) monitoring, (b) informing, and (c) participation. In monitoring, schools make parents aware of the school situation. These activities include informational conversations (such as at open houses or school programs), weekly bulletins, or public invitations to special school programs and activities. In informing, communication is specifically between a classroom teacher and parents, and includes activities such as parent-teacher conferences, class newsletters, bulletin boards, reports, phone calls, and take-home packets. In the final level, participation, teachers use parents in the school or classroom. Parents might act as aides, help with bulletin boards, or make games and activities.

Parent participation is contingent on a wide range of variables. Coleman (1991) said that a good place to begin developing activities for parents is by attending to the barriers to family involvement. Factors such as family structures (dual careers, single parent, teenager parent) and work schedules (full-time, job sharing, flextime, third shifts) can have a significant impact on how parents can participate. More options may be needed as to when parent conferences, for example, are held (before, during, and after school), how they are held (face-to-face, by telephone, by computer, in small groups), or where they are held (at school, in the home, in a community center, or at the parent's workplace). The resources and expertise of parents should be considered, offering parents a range of support, partnership, and leadership roles. Teachers can include topics that relate to both the classroom and family environments when they develop informational newsletters and parent meetings.

Homework

Homework is a major issue in elementary school. In working with parents to support their children in doing homework, Pierangelo and Jacoby (1996) suggested setting up a homework schedule and helping the student prioritize assignments. Though it's

ACTION STEPS 9.1: *EVALUATING YOUR HOMEWORK PRACTICES*

Bryan and Sullivan-Burstein (1997) argued the importance of teacher examination of homework practices. When you make a homework assignment, try

- ❏ noting how long you feel an assignment should take students to complete and then having the students write down how long it actually took them to complete it;
- ❏ putting smiling, frowning, and neutral faces on the corner of assignments and have the students circle the one that describes their feeling about the assignment;
- ❏ discussing length and frequency of assignments with other teachers at your grade level;
- ❏ working with other teachers to adopt similar practices regarding homework;
- ❏ using games and fun activities as homework activities;
- ❏ making assignments relevant to the students' lives outside the classroom;
- ❏ rewarding homework completion;
- ❏ using a planner to help students acquire organizational skills and communicate with parents;
- ❏ working with parents to communicate how much homework you plan to assign and the approximate length of time it should take;
- ❏ suggesting activities that parents can do with their children;
- ❏ asking parents to sign completed homework;
- ❏ encouraging parents to talk with the child about what happened during the school day.

tempting, they said that parents avoid sitting next to the child while he or she does homework. Parents should set reasonable homework time periods for their child. When checking homework, check small groups of problems at a time, and check correct problems first. It is best to discuss homework questions before the student plunges into the assignment.

In any single classroom, children vary in reports of the amount of homework they receive, their parents' involvement in helping them do homework, teachers' individualization of assignments, and feedback (Bryan, Nelson, & Mathur, 1995). Bryan and Sullivan-Burstein (1997) quoted parents as saying that homework had dominated and ruined their lives, and teachers as indicating that homework is at times their worst nightmare. Yet both teachers and parents assume that homework will develop responsibility, character, and personal management skills. A self-evaluation for teachers regarding their homework practices is provided in Action Steps 9.1.

Jayanthi, Bursuck, Epstein, and Polloway (1997) used focus groups to identify communication problems between schools and families, factors that contribute to the problems, and recommendations for teachers and parents with regard to homework. Problems in communication occur when parents and teacher do not initiate communication, waiting for the other to provide desired information. In addition, families and teachers reportedly do not communicate often enough, early enough, or regularly enough. Problems with follow-through and clarity of communication were also noted. Several factors were identified as contributing to these problems. Teachers and parents may lack time, knowledge, or understanding and awareness of ways to communicate. Parents, teachers, and students may have negative attitudes about communication, and may have different expectations. Jayanthi et al. suggest that teachers provide to parents computer generated progress reports on student homework, and use written modes of communication. At the beginning of a semester, teachers can provide parents with information about course assignments for the semester, homework adaptations, and policies on missed assignments and extra credit homework. Teachers should also understand that homework may be a low priority for families when compared with other home issues. In addition, teachers should initiate procedures and help students complete and submit homework on time.

Recommendations with regard to homework were also made for parents. To facilitate communication, parents were urged to call teachers early in the morning so that they can return the call later in the day. Parents should communicate expectations to both teachers and their children with regard to homework and communication, and make every attempt to attend parent-teacher meetings. Parents should check with their children about homework each night, and establish consequences when children do not complete their homework and follow through with those consequences. Parents should also provide teachers with phone numbers, and keep them informed as to when and where they can be reached.

Parent-Teacher Conferences

Parent-teacher conferences are the primary way for teachers to communicate with parents of children with disabilities during the elementary and middle school years. Rose (1998) gave several common sense suggestions regarding the conference. She urged that teachers communicate their concerns early and keep a log of the child's behavior, grades, and missing assignments. At the conference, the teacher should welcome the parents warmly. Any concerns should be put in writing, with careful consideration to the words used. Parents may be angry, and the teacher should allow for the anger and seek parents' suggestions on ways to overcome the problem or issue. Concrete solutions are essential, and emphasizing the student's greatest strengths can be helpful. At times, it may be useful to partner with the principal during a potentially difficult conference. Following the conference, communication should continue.

Positive interpersonal relationship-building is an essential part of successful parent-teacher conferencing. Perl (1995) suggested that the "problem" conference can be seen as an opportunity of improving relationships. She contends that teachers should communicate genuine caring and build rapport during the conference. As previously suggested, it is essential that teachers engage in active listening during the conference. Teachers must attend to the parents' words, body language, and emotions and feelings. During the conference, the teacher should assume the parent's point of view, and try to put into his or her own words the "affect" behind the parent's words. Perl urges teachers to take an empowerment perspective, assuming that all people have strengths and ability as well as the capacity to become more competent, and that failure to display competence is actually a failure of the social system to create opportunities for the competencies required. Parents who are empowered attribute change as resulting from their own behaviors or actions.

ACTION STEPS 9.2: *HELPING FAMILIES PREPARE FOR CONFERENCES*

Clark's (1999) questions should help parents identify topics for discussion. It may be helpful to send families this list of potential questions before the conference. Questions may include:

- ❏ What are some of the specific problems occurring in the classroom? When do they occur? What happens after these problems occur?
- ❏ What is the teacher doing to address these problems?
- ❏ What is the plan to deal with these problems?
- ❏ What can be done to help at home?
- ❏ When should we meet again?

If there are no specific problems, questions may include:

- ❏ What does my child do that surprises you?
- ❏ What is my child reluctant to do?
- ❏ What is a goal you would like to see my child achieve?
- ❏ What can I do at home to support what is being done at school?

Parents may not have a clear sense of what is expected of them during a conference. By communicating with the family, teachers can increase the relevance and potential of the discussion. Action Steps 9.2 provide some questions that may be helpful when preparing families for conferences.

Concerns with Natural Supports

Natural supports are those that occur in the regular interaction pattern of the classroom, rather than those that are "special" or imposed (Forest & Pearpoint, 1992). Though parents may be pleased with inclusive practices, some parents expressed concerns about inadequate support and insufficient teacher education (Yasutake & Lerner, 1997). Grove and Fisher (1999) discussed the existing tension between the belief in inclusive practices, which is embraced by parents, and the actual practice of not receiving "special help." Insufficient resources for support are a significant concern of parents (York & Tunidor, 1995). The stakes in the primary grades are higher than they have been in preschool and kindergarten; there are grades, students who are retained are easily identified, and the content is more academic. Natural supports, however, are the first choice in including students. How can you address parents' concerns?

Giangreco, Cloniger, and Iverson (1993) argued that the family is the cornerstone of relevant and longitudinal educational planning. Families know certain aspects of their children better than anyone else, and families have the greatest vested interest in seeing their children learn and succeed. Families are engaged throughout the child's school career, and the family has to live with the outcomes of educational decisions. Teachers, Giangreco et al. contended, should communicate to parents that special education is a service, not a place. By describing what is happening in the classroom in terms of valued life outcomes, teachers can help parents understand the supports provided to their children.

Teachers can also help parents understand the role of natural supports by approaching accommodations for children with disabilities in the same way they would approach students without disabilities. Peers can be used to support students and help students with disabilities make connections. Teachers should work with parents to help them understand that extra personnel can be an unknowing barrier to a student's successful integration (Grigal, 1998).

Another way to work with parents is to help them focus on their child as a member of the class. In that way, the student "belongs" to the classroom teacher, not the special education support personnel. The general education teacher treats the child with a disability as one of the group as much as possible, but provides selected supports such as maintaining proximity, assigning peer helpers, or providing extra cues. Parents need to be assured that teachers plan for their students with disabilities much in the same way that they plan for other students, beginning with content and moving to the modifications and accommodations (Janney & Snell, 1997).

Curriculum

Parents and teachers usually agree that children should learn whatever will ultimately enable them to become healthy, competent, productive, and contributing members of their communities. Agreement regarding the specifics of what should be learned in the primary grades, however, is difficult to achieve. Katz (1999a) described part of this tension as a "push down" effect on education, with the intense interest in standards, competencies, and promotion policies. Parents, desiring that their children achieve, may push for early academic instruction. However, Snow, Burns, and Griffin (1998) reported that the amount of drill and practice required for successful reading at an early age may undermine children's disposition toward reading. In addition, comprehension is most likely to be dependent on actual reading and not just on skill-based reading instruction. Students who are unable to be successful at formal academic work are likely to feel incompetent (Katz, 1999a).

Katz (1999b) described two approaches to the curriculum: the academic or instructivist perspective, where children are seen as dependent on adult interaction for the learning of academic knowledge and skills, and the constructivist approach, which sees young children as active constructors of knowledge. The tension between "instructivists" and "constructivists" is seen among parents who desire that their children not "waste time" on projects or play (instructivists) and those who prefer developmentally appropriate, open-ended materials (constructivists). These parents need help to see the usefulness of projects in which students apply the academic skills they are taught during the "instructive" part of the curriculum. Parents, also, may need help to understand the issues of readiness and child development.

Parents' concerns about drill and practice are exacerbated by the current emphasis on standardized testing in the primary grades. Perrone (1991) argued that if tests play a significant role in grade advances or are the primary basis for a school's ac-

countability, the test becomes the curriculum. Students in the primary grades may not be able to come to a natural understanding of mathematics concepts, for example, but on drilling addition and subtraction facts in isolation. It is important to help parents understand the role of standardized tests, and the challenges of using such tests with children in the primary grades. For children with disabilities, the role of alternative assessment must be clarified.

PARENT INVOLVEMENT ACTIVITIES

Our children with disabilities bring a gift to the classroom because instructional strategies that are good for children with disabilities are good for all children.

As you engage parents in the education of their primary school children, it is important to remember that school practices encouraging parents to participate in their children's education are more important than family characteristics such as parental education, family size, marital status, socioeconomic level, or student grade in determining the level of parent involvement (Dauber & Epstein, 1993). Beliefs and attitudes about school participation have been related to the amount of parent engagement, rather than socioeconomic status or the child's disability (Coots, 1998).

Parents prefer involvement activities that center around the curriculum needs of their children. Parents are interested in meetings and workshops that show them how to help their children. In addition, parents feel a need for ongoing dialogue with teachers, administrators, and other parents and want to be included in classroom activities (Meyers, 1989). One example of a curriculum-based project was described by Simic (1991). This is a language arts program that encourages participation in the classroom for those parents who are able to volunteer their time, but it also emphasized participation at home.

In the language arts involvement model, the teacher informed parents through a letter that students would be integrating reading and writing into the language arts and that they would be involved in a variety of literature experiences. Parents and students were encouraged to share reading at home, and strategies for sharing books were explained and sent home for parent reference. As students became more excited about the literature-based program, a letter was sent home recounting some of the students' positive experiences, and asking for parent volunteers to help with small group discussions and book projects. As the year continued, the writing process was explained and activities in which the students were engaged were described so that parents could assist the children at home. In the same letter, parents were invited to volunteer to come to the classroom to help small groups of students with the authoring cycle, edit final drafts, type student stories, and assist with bookmaking. Parents were also given opportunities to help in book selection for new literature groups. Teachers sent home book club orders and suggestions and recommendations for book selection. Periodically, parent letters were sent home telling of the progress students were making with literature and authoring cycles. An invitation to observe these activities was extended.

Sussell, Carr, and Hartman (1996) described a multifaceted approach to providing support for families. The family support services program provides a wide range of supports, including:

- A parent advisory committee newsletter;
- Listings of community resources;
- Listings of state and national organizations of interest to families with children with disabilities;
- Information folders on various disabilities for distribution to both parents and teachers;
- Files containing articles of special interest to parents;
- An instructional materials center, from which parents could borrow materials for their use and to use with their child;
- Parent education activities, including parent support groups, a bilingual parent advisory committee, and general parent education programs;
- Workshops and training activities for current and future teachers;
- Educational activities for children without disabilities.

Williams and Cartledge (1997) used a daily notebook to send daily notes to parents. In their letter to parents to invite them to use the notebook, teachers emphasized the importance attached to parents' involvement in their children's education, and their expectations for classroom behavior. The teachers then solicited parents' partnership in the process through regular communication. The letter ended with a description of the daily notebook and what the teacher, parents, and students could do to make it work.

Parent Group Meetings

One format for a parent group meeting is an information session based on parent feedback within a family-focused framework. McDonald, Kysela, Martin, and Wheaton (1996) reported that parents presented important ideas for engaging parents in their children's education and treatment. They suggested using parent-friendly materials that are enjoyable to read, free from jargon, and informative. Meetings should be scheduled for family convenience, at times when parents can attend. The atmosphere should be informal and flexible, with parents learning as much from each other as from the materials presented by the facilitators.

Cheney, Manning, and Upham (1997) suggested meeting families face to face, and asking them what they want to learn at these meetings. Their plan consisted of 18 group meetings during the school year and one weekend retreat. The parents with whom they worked identified the topics they wished to learn about as (a) strategies for setting realistic child and family goals; (b) learning and using effective communicating skills in the home and community; (c) problem-solving skills for application with school staff, and (d) skills to enhance their self-esteem and personal empowerment.

THE TRANSITION TO MIDDLE SCHOOL

If you treat Elizabeth as a responsible person, she will act responsibly. See her strengths, not just her weaknesses. Encourage her independence. Allow her to make choices (even if you feel they aren't the correct ones). Facilitate exchanges with peers and interactions with them.

The curriculum is modified correctly if the student can complete most of the assignments independently. I want educators to know that Elizabeth will grow up to become a responsible taxpaying citizen who will contribute to her family and community in many ways.

Though IDEA 97 does not require specific transition activities to middle school, such activities are necessary for students with disabilities and their parents. Typical children, moving to middle school, reported concerns about (a) changing classes; (b) reduced parent involvement; (c) interacting and working with more teachers; (d) having no recess or free time; (e) how the teachers would grade them; (f) peer pressure; (g) developmental differences between boys and girls; (h) cliques; (i) fears of a new, larger, impersonal school, in which they need to interact with older children; (j) lack of experience joining and functioning in extracurricular activities; (k) coping with student lockers and following the school schedule; and l) longer-range assignments (Weldy, 1991). Students' perceptions of the quality of their school life declines during the transition to middle school.

- Teachers from sending and receiving schools should meet to discuss curriculum and instructional practices.
- Teachers from receiving schools can visit sending schools to initiate personal contacts.
- Letter should be sent home welcoming students and families, and inviting them to school activities.
- Special education and related services personnel should meet to "staff" students.
- "Pen pals" may be set up between the sending and receiving schools.
- Prior to the first day of school, an unstructured school visitation day should be scheduled, so that students can walk through the building and informally meet teachers. A more structured open house can be held after a week or two of school.
- Handbooks, with phone numbers, school mission, schedules, teachers identified by grade, team and/or subject, schedule of periods, lunch procedures, and other practical information, should be provided.

Figure 9.1 *Transition activities.*

Schumacher (1998) said that students making the transition into middle level schools need to receive support before, during, and after the move. Efforts should be made to help the students build a sense of community, respond to individual needs, and facilitate the transition. Weldy (1991) suggested that plans for transition programs should include several activities that involve students, parents, teachers, and staff from both the sending and receiving schools. A time line for the transition process should be established, with scheduled meetings for discussion. The financial and human resources available to support the transition process should be assessed, and efforts should be made to evaluate any transition programs. Schumacher's examples of transition activities are presented in Figure 9.1.

SUMMARY

- During the primary school years, the whole family needs support. In addition, the needs of children and their families evolve as the child matures.
- Developmental expectations of parents of children with disabilities begin to decline by the time the children are 7 years old.
- Parent engagement in the primary grades includes monitoring, informing, and participating.
- Homework emerges as an issue during the primary grades.
- Parent-teacher conferences emerge as a primary means of communication in the primary grades.
- A wide range of activities may be employed to engage parents of primary age children.
- The transition to the middle grades is a challenging one for children and families, and requires support.

REFERENCES

Alper, S., Schloss, P. J., & Schloss, C. N. (1995). Families of children with disabilities in elementary and middle school: Advocacy models and strategies. *Exceptional Children, 62*(3), 261–270.

Bryan, T., Nelson, C., & Mathur, S. (1995). Homework: A survey of primary students in regular, resource, and self-contained special education classrooms. *Learning Disabilities Research and Practice, 10*(2), 85–90.

Bryan, T., & Sullivan-Burstein, K. (1997). Homework how-to's. *Teaching Exceptional Children, 29*(6), 32–37.

Cheney, D., Manning, B., & Upham, D. (1997). Project DESTINY: Engaging families of students with emotional and behavioral disabilities. *Teaching Exceptional Children, 30*(1), 24–29.

Clare, L., Garnier, H., & Gallimore, R. (1998). Parents' developmental expectations and child characteristics: Longitudinal study of children with developmental delays and their families. *American Journal on Mental Retardation, 103*(2), 117–129.

Clark, A. (1999). *Parent-teacher conferences: Suggestions for parents.* ERIC Digest No. EDOPS9912. Champaign, IL: ERIC Clearinghouse on Elementary and Early Childhood Education.

Coleman, E. (1991). *Planning for parent participation in schools for young children.* ERIC Digest No. ED342463. Urbana, IL: ERIC Clearinghouse on Elementary and Early Childhood Education.

Coots, J. J. (1998). Family resources and parent participation in schooling activities for their children with developmental delays. *The Journal of Special Education, 31*(4), 498–520.

Dauber, S. L., & Epstein, J. L. (1993). Parents' attitudes and practices of involvement in inner-city elementary and middle schools. In N. Chavkin (Ed.), *Families and schools in a pluralistic society* (pp. 53–72). Albany, NY: State University of New York Press.

Dyson, L. L. (1996). The experiences of families of children with learning disabilities: Parental stress, family functioning, and sibling self-concept. *Journal of Learning Disabilities, 29*(3), 280–286.

Forest, M., & Pearpoint, J. (1992). Families, friends, and circles. In J. Nispet, (Ed.), *Natural supports in school, work, and in the community for people with severe disabilities* (pp. 65–86). Baltimore: Paul H. Brookes.

Giangreco, M. F., Cloniger, C., & Iverson, V. (1993). *Choosing options and accommodations for children.* Baltimore: Paul H. Brookes.

Grigal, M. (1998). The time-space continuum. Using natural supports in inclusive classrooms. *Teaching Exceptional Children, 30*(6), 44–51.

Grove, K. A., & Fisher, D. (1999). Entrepreneurs of meaning: Parents and the process of inclusive education. *Remedial and Special Education, 29*(4), 208–215.

Janney, R. E., & Snell, M. E. (1997). How teachers include students with moderate and severe disabilities in elementary classes: The means and meaning of inclusion. *Journal of the Association for Persons with Severe Handicaps, 22,* 159–169.

Jayanthi, M., Bursuck, W., Epstein, M. H., & Polloway, E. A. (1997). Strategies for successful homework. *Teaching Exceptional Children, 30*(1), 4–7.

Katz, L. G. (1999a). *Another look at what young children should be learning.* ERIC Digest No. EDOPS995. Champaign, IL: ERIC Clearinghouse on Elementary and Early Childhood Education.

Katz, L. G. (1999b). *Curriculum disputes in early childhood education.* ERIC Digest No. EDOPS9913. Champaign, IL: ERIC Clearinghouse on Elementary and Early Childhood Education.

Lange, C. M., Ysseldyke, J. E., & Lehr, C. A. (1997). Parents' perspectives on school choice. *Teaching Exceptional Children*, 30(1), 14–19.

McDonald, L., Kysela, G., Martin, C., & Wheaton, S. (1996). The Hazeldean Project: Strategies for improving parent information sessions. *Teaching Exceptional Children*, 29(2), 28–32.

Meyers, E. (1989). *Teacher/parent handbook*. NY: Impact II.

Perl, J. (1995). Improving relationship skills for parent conferences. *Teaching Exceptional Children*, 28(1), 29–31.

Perrone, V. (1991). *On standardized testing*. ERIC Digest No. ED338445. Urbana, IL: ERIC Clearinghouse on Elementary and Early Childhood Education.

Petit, D. (1989). *Opening up schools*. Harmondsworth, England: Penguin.

Pierangelo, R., & Jacoby, R. (1996). *Parents' complete special education guide*. West Nyack, NY: Center for Applied Research in Education.

Rose, M. C. (1998). Handle with care: The difficult parent-teacher conference. *Instructor*, 108(3), 92–93, 101.

Schumacher, D. (1998). *The transition to middle school*. ERIC Digest No. EDOPS986. Champaign, IL: ERIC Clearinghouse on Elementary and Early Childhood Education.

Simic, M. (1991). *Parent involvement in elementary language arts: A program model*. ERIC Digest No. ED326901. Bloomington, IN: ERIC Clearinghouse on Reading, English, and Communication.

Snow, C. E., Burns, M. S., & Griffin, P. (1998). *Preventing reading difficulties in young children*. Washington, D.C.: National Academy Press.

Sussell, A., Carr. S., & Hartman, A. (1996). Families R Us: Building a parent-school partnership. *Teaching Exceptional Children*, 28(4), 53–57.

Weldy, G. R. (1991). *Stronger school transitions improve student achievement: A final report on a three-year demonstration project "Strengthening School Transitions for Student K-12."* Reston, VA: National Association of Secondary School Principals.

Williams, V. I., & Cartledge, G. (1997). Passing notes—to parents. *Teaching Exceptional Children*, 30(1), 30–35.

Yasutake, D., & Lerner, J. (1997). Parents' perceptions of inclusion: A survey of parents of special education and non-special education students. *Learning Disabilities: A Multidisciplinary Journal*, 8(3), 117–120.

York, J., & Tunidor, M. (1995). Issues raised in the name of inclusion: Perspectives of educators, parents, and students. *Journal of the Association for Persons with Severe Handicaps*, 20(1), 31–44.

CHAPTER 10

Engaging Families in Middle School and Junior High School

Annie, Riley, and Sarah

Sarah has always had what her preschool teacher called "a strong personal agenda." At ballet class, for example, when the other students were practicing their positions in the mirror, and Sarah was "being beautiful" in her own way, the teacher asked if she would like to do what the rest of them were doing. Sarah said no.

Sarah also has learning disabilities. School has been a challenge since the day she came home for kindergarten asking for pencils that wrote words. Sarah's thoughts about school weren't that she wasn't somehow doing what the other students were doing, but that she was working with faulty equipment. Unlike our other children who just seemed to figure out reading, Sarah struggled, reading very little until she repeated first grade, and suddenly went directly into chapter books. She persisted in occasionally writing whole pages completely reversed through fourth grade. Her verbal skills always saved her. Until she reached late middle school/junior high.

As school became more difficult, Sarah kept up her effort and made C's, and at times, D's. Then Sarah, who spent her preschool years arranging intricate scenarios with doll houses and "little people" again found herself. She discovered Broadway shows. She discovered the Internet fanfiction culture around Broadway shows. She started a web page. She wrote stories with coauthors around the world. The spell-checker which she was loath to use in school became her friend. Word processing was her key into a world of communication with individuals who shared her interests. Her computer acumen astounds us, as we watch her animated web page, complete with music. We are daily confronted with the contrast of a capable, confident young techie and the struggling schoolgirl. How can someone so competent and confident continue to slip behind her peers at school, and scamper beyond them in front of the computer?

As students with disabilities enter the middle grades, parents are confronted with new impressions of what their lives will be. As other students become more independent in their schoolwork, the added complexity of the middle and junior high grades often forces students with disabilities to need more support. The role of parent sometimes becomes that of the "homework police." Parent conferences may be litanies of what the child is not doing. Emphasis is often on the "can't," which is at times interpreted as "won't."

In this chapter we'll explore parent-teacher relationships and activities in the middle and junior high grades.

Learning Objectives

After completing this chapter, you will be able to discuss these topics:

1. Parenting children during middle childhood and early adolescence
2. Challenges to engaging the families of middle childhood and early adolescent children
3. Activities and programs that have been used to engage the families of middle childhood and early adolescent children
4. The transition to high school

PARENTING CHILDREN DURING MIDDLE CHILDHOOD AND EARLY ADOLESCENCE

The transition to the middle grades was difficult. Whereas the other students had achieved mastery of the basic conventions for writing, Sarah was still using unconventional spelling and limited use of the mechanics of writing to communicate creative, complex stories. She also became aware that she tackled assignments differently than her peers. She argued that it didn't bother her, yet she would make statements such as "I'm not stupid, you know" which made us think her academic skills issues were closer to the surface than she wanted to project. Her interactions with us at twelve and thirteen weren't really that much different from our interactions with her three older siblings had been, but they were more intense.

Developmentally, children in middle schools are entering preadolescence. De-Bord (2000) stated that during this time, children often feel disorganized, with rapid and uneven growth. They are not quite adolescents because they are not sexually mature, and are struggling to meet the expectations of both parents and friends. The number of dangerous situations to which children are exposed grows significantly during this period. Early adolescents (years 10 through 15) are characterized by seven developmental needs:

- Positive social interaction with adults and peers;
- Explicit structure and clear limits on physical activity;
- Creative expression;
- Competence and achievement;

- Meaningful participation in families and school;
- Participation as a member of a community, with opportunities for self-definition (Scales, 1991).

These students need to believe that they are successful, well-liked, and have the freedom to live in a just world (Stevenson, 1992). Though most children in middle childhood do not experience a stressful adolescence, there is a growing number of young adolescents at risk for school failure (Scales, 1991).

As students approach the transition from an elementary, self-contained classroom to departmentalized settings, they demonstrate a decline in self-esteem, values toward school subjects, and belief in their own ability to achieve (Wigfield & Eccles, 1994). Wigfield and Eccles have explained these declines as at least partially attributed to school settings failing to meet the developmental needs of young adolescents. Though young adolescents want to be autonomous, are increasing oriented to their peers, and are concerned about social acceptance, they are placed in large, less personable schools, with fewer strong teacher-student relationships, and more competitive and controlled environments. At this time girls begin to score lower on measures of self-esteem than do boys. Girls begin to discover the disparity in power and prestige associated with life options for males and females (Orenstein, 1994).

If declines in values and self-esteem occur, at least in part, due to school settings, what should be happening in educational settings for these students? Urdan, Midgley, and Wood (1995) suggested that focusing on tasks diverts attention from social and ability comparison to task completion and achievement. Interdisciplinary teams foster feelings of belonging. They urge the use of authentic assessment based on personal goals, progress, and improvement, using challenging intellectual material to focus on relevant problems and issues. Using real tasks in these assessments helps students see the relevance of the material. Opportunities for exploration, noncompetitive intramurals, and hands-on activities incorporate the need for physical activity and movement (Beane, 1990). The use of service projects and project-based learning strategies capitalize on the need for creative expression and meaningful participation and experimentation in terms of identity within a community, and the need for ethnic expressions of identity.

For girls, middle school can be a time of decreasing self-esteem and academic achievement. Orenstein (1994) reported that many girls think well of themselves in the primary grades but begin to decline in self-confidence and acceptance of their body image by the age of 12. From kindergarten through the fifth grade, boys and girls tend to perform at the same level in science. By junior high school, girls' self-reported confidence and interest in science classes begin to drop lower than boys', with girls blaming their failures in the classrooms on themselves as their male peers blame "unfair teachers" or "tests that are too hard" (Coffman, Onstad, & Wurster, 1998).

A general decline in school performance may correspond with this decline in self-esteem (Rothenberg, 1995). The decline in self-esteem and accompanying decline in academic achievement has been related to (a) teachers giving boys preferential treatment in school (AAUW, 1992), (b) girls realizing through their observations of women's roles that women hold positions of less societal status (Rothenberg, 1995);

or (c) parents' socialization (Rothenberg), Girls are twice as likely to be depressed, and attempt suicide four or five times as often as boys (although boys are more likely to be successful) (Debold, 1995). By the age of 10, girls have often internalized the messages that they are to be pretty, kind, obedient, and absent of bad thoughts or feelings (McDonald & Rogers, 1995). Many African American and Latino girls demonstrate evidence of a decline of self-esteem by becoming disaffected with schooling in general (AAUW, 1992). Latinos leave school at a greater rate than any other cultural group (Orenstein, 1994).

Rothenberg (1995) presented several recommendations for middle schools. Curricula should be gender-fair, and girls should be encouraged to participate in all academic courses, especially science, math, and advanced courses. Issues of equity, fairness, power, gender, race and politics should be dealt with directly and age appropriately. Girls should be supported to resist pressures to conform to outdated stereotypes that limit their achievement (Debold, 1995). Textbooks, popular media, and literature can be reviewed critically to examine the ways in which women and girls are presented.

ENGAGING THE FAMILIES OF MIDDLE CHILDHOOD AND EARLY ADOLESCENT CHILDREN

> By the time Sarah hit the middle grades we were getting pretty tired of dealing with schools. We'd receive a report card and think, "Why don't we just home school?" Sarah was baffling everyone. Here was this obviously bright, creative individual who read everything she could put her hands on, yet who couldn't write a simple paragraph. I know it's hard for teachers, but we got pretty tired of hearing what she couldn't do. First, we lived with her and knew what she couldn't do. Second, there was this whole other person, the "out-of-school Sarah" who was so competent at so many things.

Parent involvement dramatically declines as students enter the middle grades. In their analysis of the National Longitudinal Study of 1988, Catsambis and Garland (1997) reported that most parents are trying to supervise and guide their children during the middle grades, but with limited assistance from schools. Families are more likely to supervise and set rules about activities that families traditionally control (such as doing family chores) than about activities for which they lack information (such as improving report card grades). A significant number of middle school parents and their families report that they are isolated from or unconnected with their schools and are uninformed about students' progress and their school's programs. Even when compared with high school, a higher proportion of parents report that the school contacts them about their teen's academic programs and doing volunteer work in the 12th grade than in the 8th grade. Parent initiated contacts about academic programs and volunteering are also higher in high school than in the middle grades.

Catsambis and Garland (1997) also reported significant differences among parents related to race and ethnicity. African American and Latino parents provide the highest level of parental supervision. White parents, however, were the lowest in maintaining specific rules about grades and homework, yet the highest in reporting regular discussions about school. African American parents experience the sharpest drop in

school-initiated contacts regarding student progress. Asian American parents report a drop in their initiating contacts with the school concerning academic programs.

Nearly all parents reported that they expected their eighth grader to continue schooling beyond high school. A slightly higher percentage of African American and Latino than White or Asian parents stated that they started saving for college by the eighth grade. However, Asian Americans save a larger amount of money. Eighth grade mean comparisons show that Asian American parents are most likely to have the highest educational expectations, the highest student enrollment in academic private lessons, and the most student museum visits. Asian Americans also reported the lowest level of communication with their children, schools, and communities. Latinos tend to have relatively low levels of parental involvement in the eighth grade, and have the lowest averages for school-initiated academic contacts, with the least participation in social activities at the school. African American parents reported the highest level of teen supervision and the strictest rules, whereas white parents continue to report the most social contact with the school (Catsambis & Garland, 1997).

When working with families of children with disabilities in the middle grades, it is important to remember that the entire family, not just the person with disability, needs services and supports to meet their needs and avoid loss of control and responsibility (Alper, Schloss, & Schloss, 1995). The demands of parenting a teenager may increase parents' needs for information and respite. The roles and needs of children with disabilities and their family members evolve and change. In the middle grades, there is an increased emphasis on student needs in the areas of academic skills, community access, social skills and friendship, and the skills necessary for the child to appropriately manage sexual development and maturity (Alper, Schloss & Schloss). This is very different from earlier needs to develop basic academic and self-care skills.

Alper, Schloss, and Schloss (1995) said that as children with disabilities enter middle childhood, there are additional communication needs between the school and family. Families need increased support in extracurricular activities for the child, and, perhaps, respite care. With the emerging importance of the peer group, students need outlets for interaction with their peers without the direct supervision of parents. A support similar to an instructional assistant may be necessary so that students are able to actively participate in clubs and sports. Economic support may become an issue, and family members may need information about the future and ways to continue to help their child to independence.

Alper et al. (1995) suggest that teachers remember that all members of the family of a child with disabilities have multiple roles: nurturing caregiver, observer, team member, decision-maker, tutor, learner, counselor, and advocate. Some of these roles may become overwhelming. Exhaustion in filling all of these roles may contribute to the decrease in family involvement around this age. Each family member has a right to be a "normal person" and to have interests and activities of his or her own.

Desimone (1999) formed several conclusions related to family involvement and middle childhood students. First, when there is active communication between the family and the school, grades are higher. Grades are also higher when family members are active volunteers in the school. Though active communication can be a challenge and may even be seen as an intrusion by some young adolescents, volunteering is even more difficult for many families.

After completing an analysis of family-school relationships across nine schools, Rutherford and Billig (1995) presented the following recommendations for parent involvement in the middle grades:

- The stakes are high and immediate, so family involvement is of great importance. Active participation of families is strongly related to the successful middle school experience, so family involvement is worth the effort.
- The challenges of involving families can in themselves become opportunities. Through the involvement of families programs improve, sensitivity to diversity may increase, and teacher efforts are supported.
- Relationships are key in family and community involvement. If family members don't feel valued and equal participants, they are unlikely to participate.
- Responsibility and decision-making must be shared by a broad array of players, including the child. Through increasing participation in decision-making, family members and the child increase their sense of ownership of the program.
- Sustained parent/family involvement and community involvement depends on active advocacy by leaders. If principals and community leaders don't support family involvement, it is unlikely to continue.
- A system of supports for teachers is critical to parent and family involvement. Ways to provide teachers with the time and materials necessary to engage families must be identified and implemented.

- Families need connections to the curriculum. If what happens in school is completely foreign to what happens at home, families are unable to relate and participate.
- Schools need connections to the community. Through using the community, opportunities for adult models and real tasks are increased.

Homework (Again!)

Homework, often already an issue in the primary grades, increases in importance during middle school. An increased issue in the middle grades is the parents' ability to help children with their homework. Callahan, Rademacher, and Hildreth (1998) described a parent involvement program for sixth- and seventh-grade students who are at risk. Parents were provided strategies for increasing self-management and reinforcement. Students participated in parallel groups. Without exception, parents who received instruction in helping their child with self-management and utilized the reinforcement strategies described improved in both their homework completion and quality. However, parents who participated in the training, yet did not implement the program, did not experience increased success.

Epstein (1992) argued that teachers' use of homework plays a critical role in family involvement. She describes a program in which homework assignments require students to talk with someone at home about something interesting that they are learning in class. Parents are not asked to help students successfully complete their assignments, but are engaged as supports. Letters describing the program, including objectives of each activity, when it is due, and the materials needed to complete it allow parents to be informed partners with the teacher concerning the students' homework.

Friendships

An important challenge and concern for parents of children with disabilities is friendships for their children. In a study of parents' perception of the friendships of their middle-childhood children, Wiener and Sunohara (1998) reported that about half of the children self-reported at least one close, stable, and mutual friend of about the same age who either was in his or her class at school or lived in the neighborhood. Two of the children had idiosyncratic relationships, with children considerably different from them in terms of interests, temperaments, and academic skills, and the remainder had unstable, not mutual or limited-companionship friends, often with much younger children. The children's mothers sometimes disagreed with the child that the child-nominated friends were truly friends, claiming that there was insufficient contact or that other children exploited their sons or daughters. Several mothers attributed their children's problems with making and sustaining friendships with children of the same age to their children's social immaturity or social-skills deficits. The parents of children who had friends frequently facilitated the child's social relationships in nonintrusive ways, creating a context in which the child could develop mutual friends in spite of severe social skills deficits.

PROGRAMS FOR FAMILIES OF MIDDLE CHILDHOOD AND EARLY ADOLESCENT CHILDREN

*Being engaged at school is more difficult with Sarah than our other children. She is very con-
scious of her abilities and disabilities, and wants little additional attention drawn to her. I can
work in the library, as long as it isn't when her class comes. I can send in snacks, but I really
shouldn't appear at the door with them. Her autonomy is so important to her self-image! Since
middle school it's become apparent that we have to consider her feelings in terms of our engagement with the school.*

When middle schools develop comprehensive programs of school, family, and
community partnerships, parents become involved and students profit (Sanders & Simon, 1999). By the middle grades, students with disabilities can begin to become self-
advocates as well. Battle and Murphy (1996) suggested that teachers use a
communication system that places the student at the center of the communication
process. In that the transition to adult life is more complex for students with disabilities than their peers, Battle and Murphy suggested the use of portfolios to monitor
student growth and progress, and to build a strong description of the student's abilities and skills. In addition, they advocated helping students learn assessment and
conference skills through practicing in the classroom, and conducting conferences at
which students present their portfolios to parents. Students can be supported in becoming active participants in their own IEP meetings, and assisted in verbalizing what
they feel they need to be successful.

Conferences

Parent teacher conferences have traditionally excluded the student. Hackman
(1997) however, said that student-led conferences may be effective in facilitating dialogue between parent, teacher, and child. He argued that student-led conferences
meet the goals of (a) encouraging students to accept personal responsibility for
their academic performance; (b) teaching students the process of self-evaluation;
(c) facilitating the development of students' organizational and oral communication skills; (d) encouraging students, parents, and teachers to engage in open and
honest dialogue; and (e) increasing parent attendance at conferences (Hackmann,
1996; 1997).

Student-led conferences involve three phases: preparation, conferencing, and
evaluation (Countryman & Schroeder, 1996). In the preparation phase, teachers must
work with students to provide them with an appropriate conference structure. In the
weeks before the conference, students are taught how to lead the conference, and are
assisted with collecting and preparing information to be shared with parents. Students are assisted in recognizing that excuses will not work, and that they should
present artifacts to their parents that depict their progress. Students are also engaged
in role-playing various conference scenarios with student partners. Teachers should
also communicate the conference format to parents, so that parents are encouraged
to support their child as the teacher serves as facilitator.

ACTION STEPS 10.1: *PROCEDURES FOR STUDENT-LED CONFERENCES*

Hayden (1998), a seventh-grade teacher, describes several practical ways to prepare for student-led conferences:

- ❏ Prepare from the beginning of the year, asking students to keep binders with their graded work.
- ❏ About 3 days before the conferences, students glean from their binders examples for a conference portfolio. Students select a special project, a quiz, a homework assignment, and one assignment from which they feel they learned the most. Students then write a 9-week reflection on their grades and their study habits. After completing these reflections, students set goals for the next 9 weeks.
- ❏ Students write invitations to parents several days before the conferences.
- ❏ Students role-play how the student can manage the conference. "Cases" involve handling a poor grade and questions parents may ask.
- ❏ Students are provided a checklist of the information the teacher wishes to cover.
- ❏ Students open the conference by introducing the teacher to his or her parents. Several conferences may be held at the same time, with the teacher moving from table to table.
- ❏ If parents can't come to the conference, the student can take the portfolio and checklist home and hold the conference there. Parents can write a brief response.
- ❏ At the end of the conferences, students write a postconference reflection.

During the conference, the focus is typically on academic grades. However, with the increased use of portfolios, the student-led format provides an opportunity for students to share the contents of their portfolios and explain why each artifact was selected. The teacher can help family and student develop a plan of action that recognizes the student's accountability for academic progress while permitting parents to support the child. Because the conference may include more content, they may take more time, and at least 20 to 30 minutes should be scheduled. Either immediately following the conference or shortly thereafter, students, parents, and teachers should provide their feedback concerning the format. In Hackman's earlier work (1996), more than 90 % of the parents and students preferred the student-led conferences, and parent attendance increased.

The student-led format may be challenging for some parents and students. In those cases, Hackman (1997) recommended allowing students the option of a traditional conference, reserving 5 minutes at the end of the conference for a private conversation between parent and teacher or, permitting the parent to schedule a follow-up conferences with the teacher. When a parent is unable to attend at school, student-led conferences could take place in the home independently. However, the student at home does not have the teacher's support, and the integrity of the format may not be maintained without the teacher's presence. Additional information about student led conferences is provided in Action Steps 10.1.

Parent Groups

Parent groups seem to be utilized often with parents of middle school students. Goodman, Sutton, and Harkavy (1995) evaluated the effectiveness of workshops in their middle school setting. In presenting family workshops related to children's development, parents indicated that they were relieved to find out they were not alone in experiencing adolescent challenges. The workshops were successful, they suggested, because school "authorities" acknowledged and listened to parents, parents learned that other families had lives and problems like their own, and the ideas presented were genuinely helpful. Cheney, Manning, and Upham (1997) utilizing biweekly meetings with a weekend retreat, also presented workshops that were well received. These workshops emphasized strategies for setting realistic child and family goals, learning and using effective communication skills, problem solving, and skills to increase self-esteem and personal empowerment.

THE TRANSITION TO HIGH SCHOOL

Even typical students leaving middle school for high school report concerns about being picked on by older students, having harder work, making lower grades, and getting lost (Phelan, Yu, & Davidson, 1994). The move to high school may involve a decline in grades and attendance (Barone, Aguirre-Deandreis, & Trickett, 1991). High school transition programs, however, may have a positive impact on the move (MacIver, 1990). Mizelle (1999) suggests that providing students with a challenging, supportive middle school experience is an equally important factor in their making a successful transition to high school.

MacIver (1990) recommended a variety of activities that (a) provide students and parents with information about the new school; (b) provide students with social support during the transition; and (c) bring middle school and high school teachers and staff together to learn about one another's curricula and requirements. In terms of providing information to students and parents, activities such as "shadowing" a high school student or attending a presentation by high school students may be helpful. Activities that provide social supports may be a "big sister big brother" program, a spring social event for current and incoming high school students, and writing programs where eighth-grade students correspond with high schools students. Activities that create a mutual understanding of the curriculum requirements at both levels may also be helpful. Middle school and high school administrators, counselors, and teachers can work together to learn about the programs, courses, curricula, and requirements of their respective schools (Vars, 1998).

Mizelle (1999) felt that parent involvement in the high school transition process may be encouraged through a variety of activities. Parents may have a conference with their child and the high school counselor to discuss course work and schedules, visit the high school with their child in the spring or in the fall, or spend a day at the child's school. Parents may also be involved in the design of the transition activities for students. Parents of students who are already in high school are a good source for other parents and may help encourage new parents to be involved.

SUMMARY

- In early adolescence, all children often feel disorganized and experience rapid and uneven growth.
- As students transition to middle school, they often demonstrate a decline in self-esteem, values toward school subjects, and a belief in their own ability to achieve. Girls begin to score lower on measures of self-esteem than boys.
- Middle schools may be restructured to be more responsive to students in preadolescence.
- Parent involvement dramatically declines as students enter the middle grades and the roles and needs of students with disabilities and their families evolve and change.
- Friendships emerge as a significant issue for families of children with disabilities in the middle grades.
- Students with disabilities, needing to develop self-advocacy skills, should begin to increase their participation in conferences and decision-making. Parents may need support with this changing role.

REFERENCES

Alper, S., Schloss, P. J., & Schloss, C. N. (1995). Families of children with disabilities in elementary and middle school: Advocacy models and strategies. *Exceptional Children*, 62(3), 261–270.

American Association of University Women (AAUW). 1992. *How schools shortchange girls: A study of major findings on girls and education*. Washington, D.C.: AAUW.

Barone, C., Aguirre-Deandreis, A. I., & Trickett, E. J. (1991). Mean-ends problem-solving skills, life stress, and social supports as mediators of adjustment in the normative transition to high school. *American Journal of Community Psychology*, 19(92), 207–225.

Battle, D. A., & Murphy, S. C. (1996). *Communication: Teaching middle grades exceptional students to become self-advocates*. San Antonio, TX: National Rural Education Association.

Beane, J. (1990). *A middle school curriculum: From rhetoric to reality*. Columbus, OH: National Middle School Association.

Callahan, K., Rademacher, J. A., & Hildreth, B. L. (1998). The effects of parent participation in strategies to improve the homework performance of students who are at risk. *Remedial and Special Education*, 19(3), 131–141.

Catsambis, S., & Garland, J. E. (1997). *Parental involvement in students' education during middle school and high school*. Baltimore, OH: Center for Research on the Education of Students Placed at risk.

Cheney, D., Manning, B., & Upham, D. (1997). Project DESTINY: Engaging families of students with emotional and behavioral disabilities. *Teaching Exceptional Children*, 30(1), 24–29.

Coffman, S. F., Onstad, M., & Wurster, S. E. (1998). *Closing the gender gap in science*. Champaign, IL: University of Illinois Department of Human and Community Development.

Countryman , L. L., & Schroeder, M. (1996). When students lead parent-teacher conferences. *Educational Leadership*, 53(7), 64–68.

Debold, E. (1995). Helping girls survive the middle grades. *Principal*, 74(3), 22–24.

DeBord, K. (2000). *Parenting teens*. Raleigh, NC: North Carolina Cooperative Extension.

Desimone, L. (1999). Linking parent involvement with student achievement: do race and income matter? *The Journal of Educational Research*, 93(1), 11–30.

Epstein, J. L. (1992). TIPS: *Teachers involve parents in schoolwork, language arts, and science/health: Interactive homework for the middle grades*. Baltimore:Johns Hopkins University, Center on Families, Communities, Schools, and Children's Learning.

Goodman, J. F., Sutton, V., & Harkavy, J. (1995). The effectiveness of family workshops in a middle school setting: Respect and caring make the difference. *Phi Delta Kappan*, 76(9), 694–700.

Hackman, D. G. (1997). *Student led conferences at the middle level*. ERIC Digest No. ED407171. Champaign, IL: ERIC Clearinghouse on Elementary and Early Childhood Education.

Hackman, D. G. (1996). Student-led conferences at the middle level: Promoting student responsibility. NAASSP *Bulletin*, 80(578), 31–36.

Hayden, L. (1998). *Letting students lead parent conferences*. Middle Matters, National Association of Elementary School Principals, fall, 1998. Available at www.naesp.org/comm/mmf98b.htm.

MacIver, D. J. (1990). Meeting the needs of young adolescents: Advisory groups, interdiscplinrary teaching teams, and school transition programs. *Phi Delta Kappan*, 71(6), 458–464.

McDonald, L., & Rogers, L. (1995). *Who waits for the white knight? Training in nice*. Paper presented at the American Educational Research Association, San Francisco, CA. ED385380.

Mizelle, N. B. (1999). *Helping middle school students make the transition into high school.* ERIC *Digest No.* EDOPS9911. Champaign, IL: ERIC Clearinghouse on Elementary and Early Childhood Education.

Orenstein, P. (1994). *Schoolgirls: Young women, self-esteem, and the confidence gap.* New York: Doubleday.

Phelan, P., Yu, H. C., & Davidson, A. L. (1994). Navigating the psychosocial pressures of adolescence: The voices and experiences of high school youth. *American Educational Research Journal, 31*(2), 250–267.

Rothenberg, D. (1995). *Supporting girls in early adolescence.* ERIC Digest. No. EDOPS954. Champaign, IL: ERIC Clearinghouse on Elementary and Early Childhood Education.

Rutherford, B., & Billig, S. H. (1995). Eight lessons of parent, family, and community involvement in the middle grades. *Phi Delta Kappan, 77*(1), 64–66, 68.

Sanders, M. G. & Simon, B. S. (1999). A *comparison of school, family, and community partnership programs at elementary, middle and high schools.* Paper presented at the an-

nual meeting of the American Educational Research Association, Montreal, Canada.

Scales, P. C. (1991). A *portrait of young adolescents in the 1990s: Implications for promoting healthy growth and development.* Minneapolis, MN: Search Institute and Center for Early Adolescence.

Stevenson, C. (1992). *Teaching ten to fourteen year olds.* White Plains, NY: Longman.

Urdan, T., Midgley, C., & Wood, S. (1995). Special issues in reforming middle level schools. *Journal of Early Adolescence, 5*(1), 9–37.

Vars, G. F. (1998). You've come a long way, baby! In R. David (Ed.), *Moving forward from the past: Early writings and current reflections of middle school founders* (pp. 222–233). Columbus, OH: National Middle School Association.

Wiener, J., & Sunohara, G. (1998). Parents' perceptions of the quality of friendship of their children with learning disabilities. *Learning Disabilities Research and Practice* 13(4), 242–257.

Wigfield, A., & Eccles, J. (1994). Children's competence beliefs, achievement values, and general self-esteem: change across elementary and middle school. *Journal of Early Adolescence, 14*(2), 107–138.

CHAPTER 11

Secondary Students and the Transition to the Community

Paul and Linda

Linda came to live with us as a foster child when she was six years old. She had been living in a residential facility for children with behavior disorders and developmental disabilities. We knew that she had several disabilities—she was overactive, didn't speak, had really thick glasses, and nobody really knew what her cognitive level was.

We adopted Linda when she was seven. I can't even begin to imagine how it must feel to be the biological parent of a child with severe disabilities because we knew from the start that Linda did, but I do know a bit how it must feel. As her father, I went through many of the same feelings as other parents of kids with disabilities, hoping that maybe with a loving home and good schools and lots of counseling she could be "fixed." At the same time, I was never at peace until I finally admitted to myself that it would never happen. That Linda would always have mental retardation and need medication to manage her behavior and use thick glasses and be difficult to understand. I loved and enjoyed Linda from the beginning, but once I owned the knowledge that she would never be "normal," I could accept her as she was and feel OK with realistic expectations for her.

From the time we adopted her, we had lots of crazy experiences with professionals in education and other fields. The first was a well-meaning person who ran a program for kids with learning disabilities. Her attempt to support us was to say that if we worked with Linda we could probably get her to test out as having learning disabilities rather than mental retardation.

There were a lot of little things also, like the well-meaning older woman next door (whom Linda got to know and really like) who introduced herself to Linda as *her "next door grandma." The only problem was that Linda had just come to live with us and wasn't really sure of whom everybody in the family was. Needless to say, there was a little resulting confusion.*

Several others followed. First there was the dentist, a professor at a dental school, who said she was autistic because she didn't talk and tried to strap her to a papoose board while he examined her mouth. Needless to say, Linda threw a fit when he tried to strap her down. The appointment ended with Pat, Linda's mom and my wife, taking her out before the dentist did anything else. Then there was the psychiatrist who tried to use psychoanalysis and get Linda, who didn't talk, to describe her feelings about her parents.

At school, we once had an IEP conference which her special education teacher's supervisor attended because Linda was showing some "disruptive behaviors" and we were "problem parents" because we asked her teacher what approaches she used. Unfortunately, the supervisor was too concerned about the manicured fingernail she broke during the meeting to be of much help to anyone.

The transition from school to work and the community is not going well for students with disabilities. The Harris Survey on the current status of persons with disabilities in American life (1998) reported significant gaps between the employment rates of individuals with and without disabilities. Only 29% of individuals with disabilities of working age (18–64) work full or part-time, compared to 79% of individuals without disabilities. About a third (34%) of adults with disabilities live in households with total incomes of $15,000 or less, compared with 12% of those without disabilities. One in 5 individuals fails to complete high school, compared with 1 in 10 of individuals without disabilities. Among adults with disabilities who work full-time, fewer than half (46%) say that their work requires them to use their full talents or abilities, and 47% indicate that the jobs they can get don't pay enough. Only about 1 in 3 (33%) adults with disabilities is very satisfied with quality of life, as compared to 6 of 10 (61%) of adults without disabilities. This gap has widened over the past four years.

Learning Objectives

After completing this chapter, you will be able to discuss these topics:

1. Issues related to parenting adolescents with disabilities
2. The roles of families in transition
3. Transition services used by students and their families
4. Issues related to parents and the behavior of the adolescent
5. Tensions that may emerge in the transition process

PARENTING ADOLESCENTS WITH DISABILITIES

Linda is a great swimmer (she can do real somersaults off the diving board), is a hard worker, and is a real pleasure to be around. She loves CD's, clothes, and riding her bike. Her room at her house is decorated with posters of N'Sync, Leonardo DiCaprio, and Rickey Martin. She adores her younger sister, Madeline (who is ten) and her brother Will (who is five) and loves her grandmas, aunts, uncles, and cousins.

Parenting any adolescent is a challenge. The task of the adolescent, becoming one's own person, puts a teenager at odds with his or her parents. Klimek and Anderson (1987) suggested that adolescents move through manic phases of elevated mood, hyperactivity, excitability, poor judgment, the desire to get away from home, and depressive phases of doubt, caution, fear, and vulnerability. During adolescence, students replace their relationships with parents with relationships with peers and reality. Klimek and Anderson contend that, to facilitate the transition from adolescence to adulthood, parents and other significant adults need to (a) achieve and maintain emotional neutrality; (b) develop the capacity for relating to and enjoying the uniqueness of each child, and (c) adhere to the larger developmental perspective.

Family influence, however, is an important force in a student's preparation for his or her role as a worker (Lankard, 1995). Mortimer (1992) reported that the variable that had the most effect on students' educational plans and occupational aspirations was parental education. Parents with postsecondary education passed its importance to their children. Family income is also a strong contributor, especially for girls (Mortimer). The self-efficacy of girls with respect to career opportunities is linked to the financial support they can expect to receive from their parents. Family attitudes about school, work, education, and career goals and aspirations have a long-term impact on the adolescent's career choices, decisions, and plans (Lankard).

Lankard (1995) contrasted research related to two cultural groups, Mexican Americans and Korean Americans, to describe the influence of parent culture on educational and occupational aspirations and decisions. Clayton (1993) reported that though Mexican American parents often verbalized their desire for more education for their children, continuing education was often out of reach for financial reasons. Mexican American parents focused on continuing education in the career development process. Korean families, on the other hand, focused on career selection (Kim, 1993). Parents begin placing pressure on their children to select a professional career from the time the child is very young. College students confirmed that their career choices reflected the cultural model of success of their parents.

Middleton and Loughead (1993) presented three categories of parental involvement in their children's career development. First, parents may be positively involved. They may also be uninvolved. Most destructive, however, is negative involvement. In negative involvement, parents are often controlling and domineering. Students feel frustration and guilt when they do not meet their parents' expectations. Students may select careers to please their parents rather than meet their personal goals.

FAMILIES AND TRANSITION

Linda attends a site-based vocational training program through her school district and will graduate, hopefully having a full-time job through the state's vocational rehabilitation program. She loves working in retail—shelving items, removing items from shipping boxes, etc.—

and gets great performance evaluations both at school and at part-time jobs she gets through a job-training program.

One of the primary purposes of IDEA is to ". . . ensure that all children with disabilities have available to them a free appropriate public education that emphasizes special education and related services designed to meet their unique needs and prepare them for employment and independent living" (IDEA 97, 20 USC 1401 300.1 (a)). Section 300.347 (b) requires that, beginning no later than age 14, each student's IEP include specific transition related content, and beginning no later than age 16, a statement of needed transition services. Unfortunately, this attention is not given to many students without identified disabilities. High schools often direct most of their efforts toward the 25% of students who will graduate from college (Peters, 1994). Students who do not plan to pursue a four-year degree after high school are often placed in a "general track" and expectations for their academic achievement tend to be low. Though concerns may emerge about students who are not college-bound, even successful students are sometimes stymied by changes when they leave high school (Paris, 1995).

There are legal mandates for students with identified disabilities. IDEA 97 (20 USC 1401 (30) Sec. 300.29) defines transition services as "a set of coordinated activities that is

- Outcome oriented, promoting movement from school to postschool activities, including postsecondary education, vocational training, integrated employment (including supported employment), continuing and adult education, adult services, independent living, or community participation;
- Based on individual student needs;
- Includes instruction, related services, community experiences, and the development of employment and other post-school adult living objectives;
- Inclusive of daily living skills and functional evaluation if appropriate."

Special education may be a transition service if it is provided as specially designed instruction or related services required to assist a student with a disability to benefit from special education.

Transition plans become an issue for students when they reach the age of 14, and services are to be in place when the student becomes 16. Transition services may not all be designed and implemented by the school; public agencies may participate, and the plan should include each participating agency's responsibilities or linkages, before the student leaves the school setting. The annual goals (including benchmarks or short-term objectives) and services for a student must include the instruction and educational experiences that will assist the student to prepare for transition from secondary education to postsecondary life (NICHCY, 1999).

Engaging families, however, goes beyond mandated meetings. Johnson and Rusch (1993) in their survey of 200 families of students with disabilities, found that parents were significantly less involved in their child's transition than they desired. Almost three-fourths desired involvements, whereas slightly more than one-third reported that they were actively involved. Significantly more parents desired to have an equal part in decision-making than were given the opportunity. In addition, parents reported that they wanted to be involved in finding job placements and community living arrangements for their young adult child more often than they had the opportunity to do so.

Izzo and Shumate (1991) argued that parents should be actively involved in the transition process because they know their children better than anyone else, and thus are critical resources. Parents are effective in maintaining continuity of training and of purpose, and can help with changes professionals desire but are unable to accomplish. Parents can act as role models for their adolescent children, making job success more likely, and can act as community supporters. Parents are experienced as service coordinators for their children, and can provide support and encouragement that complement professional efforts.

TRANSITION

Linda has grown up to be a successful, independent young lady. She is now twenty years old and lives in a two-bedroom house about five minutes from our home. Working with a private agency, she and her roommate lease their home, pay their bills, and do everything else that a young person living on her own would do. The agency provides a live-in staff member and other staff members during waking hours to help Linda and her roommate do and learn what they need to live independently. Her staff team leader, Tracy, is almost like family to Linda—Linda plays with her young children, goes out to eat and to the mall with Tracy and her mother, and goes to her house. We're very proud of her—the only down side is that, like other twenty-year-olds, she is often "too busy" to come home for a visit.

Borgen and Amundson (1995) suggested that supportive family and friends are one of the factors related to successful transition from high school to the community. Recognizing the developmental needs of young people, they suggest a competence model with eight main areas. These areas include:

1. Developing multiple plans, rather than a single plan, which is abandoned when barriers arise;
2. Self-advocacy and marketing, helping students with communication skills, self-confidence, organization, and adaptability;
3. Managing changing relationships, recognizing that parents need to allow young people sufficient room to develop their own sense of identity;
4. Meeting basic needs, including a sense of meaning in life, physical and emotional security, and basic structure in relationships and living;
5. Coping with stress, helping students develop organizational ability, problem solving, self-confidence, and relaxation techniques;
6. Coping with loss, including death in the family, parental separation and divorce;
7. Bridging programs, so that students have "hands-on" experiences and are geared toward postsecondary services;
8. Information and information access, providing up-to-date information on careers, education programs, and market trends.

School-to-Work Opportunities

School-to-work opportunities are becoming more and more available for individuals with disabilities. As a result of the School to Work Opportunities Act, a wide range of initiatives for transition are now in place. "School-to-work" recognizes that of the students who complete secondary school, three-quarters enter the work force directly, and may lack academic and occupational skills (Lewis, 1997). Rather than a single model, school-to-work initiatives are identified by (a) being a part of the secondary curriculum, (b) involving participation of employers, and (c) involving actual or simulated on-the-job experience, resulting in formal or informal certification of skills (Hollenbeck, 1996).

There are several school-to-work practices that have been reported to have a significant effect on students and the classroom (Cicmanec & Boston, 1996). Teachers structure classroom activities to integrate academic skills with skills required for successful employment. In addition, teachers form partnerships with business people, technical workers, and others in the public sector to provide resources and enhance classroom experiences. In school-to-work, students are provided job-related experiences which connect them to the work environment, such as job shadowing and mentoring. Working with teachers and families, teachers broaden their knowledge of various vocations, collaborating with employers to provide contextual learning activities and to set achievable goals.

Transition Services

In their study of transitions for students who completed and who did not complete high school, Milam and Love (1998) reported that most of the parents stated that their sons and daughters did not receive needed transition services. The majority of parents of both groups reported that their sons and daughters needed job training and placement services. Teachers indicated that community-based services made a significant difference between the two groups of students, and that more students who completed high school than those who left actually received special vocational instruction. Inclusion also was a factor in students remaining in school; a greater percentage of students who completed school spent a greater percentage of their day in the general education classroom. As a result of this extensive study, Milam and Love concluded that:

- Students may have a better sense of their daily instructional process and job experiences than their parents;
- Parents of students who left high school special education held idealistic expectations in the areas of academic and social skills;
- Parents may be more futuristic in their orientation to skills for their sons and daughters;
- Parents may be reporting student needs from the perspective of independence or how their sons or daughters can survive on their own;

- Students' reports of substance abuse may represent overstatements or even boasting.

In their study comparing mothers of adolescents with and without identified disabilities, Lehmann and Baker (1995) found that both groups of mothers expect independence for their children. Mothers of adolescents with disabilities, however, reported the need of their children for support in order to achieve independence from their families. In a later study, Lehmann (1998) compared mothers of adolescents with disabilities and mothers of adolescents in vocational education. The two groups of mothers did many of the same child-rearing activities, but there were differences in the amount of support adolescents with disabilities needed. Mothers of adolescents with disabilities spent a great deal of time acting as advocates and protectors of their children as well as assisting with their children's community integration. Lehmann cautions that the perceptions and involvement of mothers may be at odds with the current movement to student self-determination. When compared to parents of vocational education students, mothers of adolescents with disabilities were more positive in describing their children, but were more concerned about social relationships and adult services (Lehmann & Roberto, 1996). Masino and Hodapp (1996) using the National Educational Longitudinal study, also found that parent expectations for students with and without disabilities were similar. However, students with disabilities are underrepresented in colleges and universities.

Family involvement in the transition to work is essential. Whitney-Thomas and Hanley Maxwell (1996) found that parents of students with disabilities, as the transition approaches, feel greater discomfort and pessimism than do parents of students without disabilities. They have a less positive vision, and the transition may be as problematic for parents as it is for the students. Students themselves, however, report that family involvement in their transition is important to them (Morningstar, Turnbull, & Turnbull, 1995). Morningstar et al. found that students reported that parents and extended family members influence career vision. Students expressed a desire to live close to their families, and a need to use their families as role models rather than professionals. A critical theme that emerges was a lack of systematic attention to the process of planning for the future, with the majority of students identifying family members as their support during the transition process. Students reported that they are seeking autonomy in making certain kinds of decisions, but also desire ongoing support from their families. Devlieger and Trach (1999) found similar results that parents and the focus persons for their study are more involved in transition than agency personnel. When school and agency efforts were employed, placement often resulted in sheltered employment, whereas personal or parent efforts resulted more often in self-employment and continuing education.

Parent involvement for children who are placed in residential facilities also remains high. Blacher, Baker, and Feinfeld (1999) interviewed parents 1, 2, and 3½ years following placement. Visitations remained high with some sort of visit reported at least monthly by more than 80% of the families. The parents reported that they thought and talked about their child frequently. Though still concerned and attached to their children, virtually all parents reported family life to be better following placement, especially in recreation, social life, and relationships with their other children.

In recognition of the need to engage individuals with disabilities and their families in the transition process, personal futures planning has emerged. Personal futures planning recognizes that the individual with a disability and his or her family should be engaged in determining the services and supports needed and wanted (Mount, 1992). The McGill Action Planning System (MAPS) (Vandercook, York, Forest, 1989) is a personal futures planning process in which the primary emphasis is on the involvement of students with disabilities in the school community. MAPS is structured around seven key questions. These questions include:

- What is the student's history?
- What is the dream or vision for the student?
- What is the nightmare—the least desirable outcome—for the student?
- Who is the student?
- What are the student's strengths, gifts, and abilities?
- What are the student's needs?
- What would be the student's ideal day, and what must be done to make this happen?

Rather than based on the curriculum or the special education program, MAPS bases educational planning on a vision for the student. This personal futures planning becomes a lifestyle planning process (O'Brien & Lyle, 1997) in which the student's desirable future, necessary activities and supports, and developing resources are needed. The

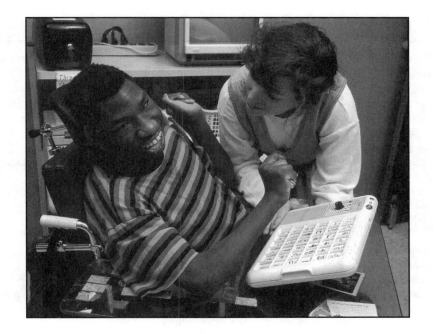

quality of life for the student is measured through (a) the student's presence in the community, (b) the amount of choice given the student, (c) the student's competence, (d) respect given the student, and (e) student participation in the process and community.

Hutchins and Renzaglia (1998) suggested the use of interviews to explore concerns and issues related to current and future vocational instruction and experiences. The interview contains six sets of questions focusing on: parental expectations, experience and preference, personal needs, family support, transportation, and wage benefits. The first set of questions, parental expectations, helps identify family members' attitudes and goals for future employment for their child. Specific questions involve the student's current responsibilities at home, interest in student employment, where the child will live after graduation, resources available, and the amount of time the family wishes the child to spend on a job. The second set of questions, experiences and preference, focuses on work experiences and family perceptions of the student's satisfaction and success in those experiences. Personal needs questions include gathering information about the personal care or communication needs of the child. In terms of family support, the family's role, such as parents' assuming responsibility for reporting absences or monitoring personal appearance, is explored. Transportation issues, discussed next, often appear to be a primary barrier for accessing and maintaining long-term employment. Parents are asked to indicate where they live and where they anticipate the child will live after graduation. The last questions of the interview focus on an explanation of the wages and benefits available during vocational education. The use of this interview prevents professionals from

ACTION STEPS 11.1: *INTERVIEWING PARENTS*

Hutchins and Renzaglia (1998) proposed a format for interviewing parents about current and future vocational instruction. Specific questions can be used in each area:

Ask the parents about their expectations for their child:

- What are your goals for your child's future employment?
- Do you feel these are realistic goals or dreams?
- How do you feel about these goals?
- Does your child have responsibilities at home that will help him or her reach these goals?
- Where will your child live after graduation?
- What resources does your family have to support your child?
- How many hours each week do you want your child to work?

Ask the parents about their child's experiences and preferences:

- What work experiences has your child had?
- How satisfied do you think your child was in those jobs?
- How successful do you think your child was in those jobs?
- How much support did you provide your child? Specifically, did you report your child's absences? Monitor personal appearance?
- How well did your child communicate in the work setting?
- How much support did your child need in personal care?

Review with the parents how their child will be transported:

- How do you see your child getting to work?
- If your child will not live at home, will he or she have access to public transportation? Is he or she independent in using public transportation?

Ask parents about the wages and benefits they anticipate:

- What do you anticipate your child will earn?
- What benefits do you feel your child would have?
- What support can you provide in terms of financial assistance and benefits?

---

making assumptions about student and family wishes related to employment. Sample questions related to this format are presented in Action Steps 11.1.

Asselin, Todd-Allen, and deFur (1998) recommended the use of a "transition coordinator" to support students and parents during the transition from school to work and the community. Transition coordinators are a significant change in personnel roles for schools; rather than the typical secondary teacher role, the transition coordinator moves from instructional activities to meeting the challenges of providing quality and coordinated transition services. The transition coordinator is involved in (a) linking within the school, (b) connecting with agencies and businesses, and (c) providing for the assessment and career counseling of the students. In addition, the transition coordinator assumes responsibility for transition planning, and the educational and community training required by those transition plans. A transition coordinator may provide support and resources to the family as well as serving as a public relations contact for the community. Through program development and program evaluation, the transition coordinator can continue to develop opportunities for the students whom he or she serves.

PARENTS AND BEHAVIOR CHANGE

Linda tests with an IQ in the mid-forties. She still wears thick glasses (stylish ones now rather than the pink plastic ones purchased through Medicaid that she came to us with), and is still difficult to understand. She still takes a lot of different medications to manage her aggressive behavior. She still needs a lot of guidance—for example, when we picked her up at her house to come home for Thanksgiving, she packed her suitcase with all of her trophies from Special Olympics rather than with a change of clothes. No one had helped her pack, and she wanted to show them off.

Parent involvement is essential in working with adolescents' behavior in secondary school. Deslandes and Royer (1997) reported that adolescents whose parents provided supervision were less likely to have received disciplinary action than parents who did not provide supervision. In another parenting style, parent-adolescent interactions based on daily school matters occurred in response to inappropriate behaviors, and parent-teacher communication were related to students' behavior problems.

Families of youth with problem behaviors (such as aggression, property destruction, or self-injurious behavior) want an inclusive lifestyle for their children (Turnbull & Ruef, 1997). However, Turnbull and Ruef reported stressful and tenuous inclusive lifestyle supports. They report that families themselves have been the catalyst in most situations when any positive action has occurred related to attaining inclusive lifestyle supports. The majority of families were the primary "movers and shakers" for implementing the inclusive lifestyle supports for their children. The families had no regular or convenient access to state-of-the-art information, but sought out such information vigorously. Families wanted more genuine help, with professional and community members working with them collaboratively, to address the complex challenges across home and community. Families wanted professionals to do their job in a state-of-the-art, collaborative, and empowering way.

Many teenagers experience periods when keeping up with their work in school is difficult. Robertson (1997) said that teachers can help parents when students are struggling. She suggests that parents and teachers work together to do the following:

- Make time to listen to the teenager's fears or concerns;
- Set appropriate boundaries for behavior that are consistently enforced;
- Emphasize the importance of study skills, hard work, and follow-through at home and in school; arranging tutoring or study group support;
- Work with the home and school environment to demonstrate that education is valued;
- Encourage the teenager to participate in school activities;

- Encourage parents to become more involved in school activities by attending school functions, such as sporting events, concerts, science fairs and plays, to demonstrate their support for the school;
- Meet as a team with the student to share their expectations for the teenager's future and to identify ways to support the student;
- Help the student think about career options by arranging for visits to local companies and colleges, providing information about careers and vocational or college courses, and encouraging the teenager to participate in an internship or career-oriented part-time job;
- Encourage the teenager to volunteer in the community or participate in community groups.

TENSION IN THE TRANSITION PROCESS

We know she will never go to a university, but she will graduate from school and hold a job. She will live as independently as she can and be a tax-paying, contributing member of her community. She is happy. What more can a parent ask?

Barber (1997) described some of the issues involved in parent-adolescent relationships that may impact on engaging parents in the education of their children. He identifies three major areas: (a) the sense of connection with parents; (b) how well parents monitor the teenager's activities, and (c) the degree of the teenager's autonomy. If the parent-child connection is consistent, positive, and characterized by warmth, kindness, love, and stability, students are more likely to initiate social interaction with other students and adults. Teenagers who report that their parents are interested in their activities, and who are monitored, are more likely to avoid trouble. The children of parents who monitor their teenage children are less likely to lie, cheat, steal, or use alcohol and illegal drugs. Autonomy, a stressful area for parents, is nurtured when parents genuinely respect their teen's ideas, even when the ideas are contrary to their own. The opposite of psychology autonomy, psychological control, involves changing the subject, making personal attacks, withdrawing love, or inducing guilt to constrain the adolescent from expressing ideas incongruent with the parent's way of thinking.

One of the most difficult issues is monitoring, maintaining the balance between too much and too little. Chadwick and Top (1998) stated that the "prime directive of adolescence prohibits teenagers from admitting that having parents set firm boundaries is actually reassuring. Family rules and boundaries, however, can provide a sense of stability to teens who are struggling to understand themselves, relationships, and roles they may assume.

Students with disabilities are required by law to receive transition services. In planning the type of transition services, the IEP team considers options such as postsecondary education, vocational training, employment, independent living, and community participation. The services are meant to be a coordinated set of activities based on the student's needs. In addition, these services must take into account the student's preferences. Tension may arise from differences of opinions between parent and student.

IDEA 97 clearly delineated the transfer of parents' rights to the student when he or she reaches the age of majority under state law. Both parents and students must be notified of the rights that will be transferred at that time, with students receiving notification at least 1 year before they reach the age of majority. A statement must be included in the IEP that the student has been informed of these transferred rights. After the student reaches the age of majority, the school must provide any notices required by law, such as notice regarding upcoming IEP meetings, to both the student and the parents. In many states, however, all rights transfer, and parents receive no further information. If the student is determined to be incompetent under state law, rights remain with the parents or the appointed guardian. IDEA 97 recognizes that not all students may be able to provide informed consent with respect to their educational program even though they have not been determined to be incompetent under state law. Each state has procedures for appointing parents or another individual to represent the student's educational interests. This transfer of rights is an important step, and parents and students need to be prepared (NICHCY, 1999).

Self-Determination

One of the tensions in the transition process occurs as young adults with disabilities begin asserting themselves. Self-determination is a skill for all students, and is a valued educational outcome for students with disabilities (Holub, Lamb, & Bang, 1998). In inclusive settings, Holub, Lamb, and Bang reported that teachers integrate self-determination throughout general education classes, working with students with decision-making in various settings. Teachers also should provide concrete situations and materials, supporting students as they develop their self-advocacy skills. Campbell and Olsen (1994) provided more specific suggestions for teachers, including the following:

- Teach classroom rules consistently, using their own actions as models;
- Communicate consequences of behaviors, emphasizing positives;
- Teach students to manage their own behavior, assigning students individual responsibilities and holding them accountable;
- Have students sign in and out each day, encouraging them to manage their own behavior;
- Establish routines and procedures in order to encourage time-management.

Self determination and self-advocacy skills are necessary for students as they make the transition from school to work or the community. NICHCY (1993) suggested that four of the most fundamental skills related to self-determination and self-advocacy for students include the following:

- The ability to assess themselves, including their skills and abilities, and the needs associated with their disability;
- Awareness of the accommodations they need because of their disability;
- Knowledge of their rights through legislation such as the Americans with Disabilities Act and Section 504 of the Rehabilitation Act of 1973;
- The self-advocacy skill necessary to express their needs in the workplace, in educational institutions, and in community settings.

Social Interactions and Social Skills

Students with disabilities may confront unique challenges in view of social interactions and the development of their social skills. Participation in extracurricular activities may be key; Eder, Evans, and Parker (1995) in their study of the friendships of typically developing adolescents, found that participation in extracurricular activities strongly influenced seating patterns during lunch, far more than curricular tracking. Participating in activities made students more visible, and more visible people were more popular. Identification with a group or a team helps students increase their prestige among students.

In a study of how parent's facilitated friendships, Turnbull, Pereira, and Blue-Banning (1999) reported that among the families they studied, several themes emerged. There was the foundation theme that the family accepted the youth unconditionally, accepting the youth as "whole" rather than "broken." Next, the family worked hard to create opportunities for interaction. The families advocated for inclusion in their child's neighborhood school, rather than allowing the youth to be bussed across town. They supported participation in community activities, and set expectations consistent with those for their siblings (e.g., in light of how siblings call friends on the phone, encouraged the youth to call his or her friends in the same way). Families that facilitated friendships encouraged others to accept the youth, and worked hard to ensure that the youth dressed and groomed in a way that was likely to draw positive, appropriate attention. Finally, these families advocated for partial participation in community activities, and helped individuals in the community and friends to make accommodations.

Families From Diverse Ethnic, Cultural, or Linguistic Groups

A group with significant secondary school transition needs are immigrant adolescents. Learning the rules and practices of a new school system, and then managing the transition, is a challenge for immigrant families. Lucas (1996) suggested that workshops and seminars be held to inform families about school rules, procedures, extracurricular activities, and special support services. In addition, school documents and orientation materials should be translated into home languages, recognizing that parents may not be literate in their native language and that teachers cannot always rely on written documents. Structured relationships with school staff members can help provide key information to immigrant students and their families. Unfortunately, many English language learners are placed in vocational education classes that are not academically challenging. Rather, students and their families need career exploration, career guidance, cooperative education, service learning, and work-based mentoring.

SUMMARY

- Parenting any adolescent is a challenge.
- Transition plans become an issue for students when they reach 14 years of age and services are to be in place when the student reaches 16 years of age.
- School-to-work practices have been reported to have a significant effect on students and the classroom.

- Students may not receive the transition services they need to successfully become part of the community.
- Family involvement in the transition from school to work and the community is essential.
- Self-determination may cause tension between parents and students during the transition process.

REFERENCES

Asselin, S. B., Todd-Allen, M., & deFur, S. (1998). Transition coordinators: Define yourselves. *Teaching Exceptional Children,* 30(3), 11–15.

Barber, B. K. (1997). Introduction: Adolescent socialization in context—the role of connection, regulation, and autonomy in the family. *Journal of Adolescent Research,* 12(1), 5–11.

Blacher, J., Baker, B. L., & Feinfeld, K. A. (1999). Leaving or launching? Continuing family involvement with children and adolescents in placement. *American Journal on Mental Retardation,* 104(5), 452–465.

Borgen, W. A., & Amundson, N. E. (1995). *Models of adolescent transition.* ERIC Digest. No. ED401502. Greensboro, NC: ERIC Clearinghouse on Counseling and Student Services.

Campbell, P., & Olsen, G. R. (1994). Improving instruction in secondary schools. *Teaching Exceptional Children,* 26(3), 51.

Chadwick, B. A., & Top, B. L. (1998). *Rearing righteous youth.* West Valley City, UT: Bookcraft.

Cicmanec, K., & Boston, C. (1996). School-to-work transition in the K-12 classroom. ERIC *Review* 4(2), 12–13.

Clayton, K. (1993). *Family influences over the occupational and educational choices of Mexican American students.* Berkeley, CA: National Center for Research in Vocational Education.

Deslandes, R., & Royer, E. (1997). Family-related variables and school disciplinary events at the secondary level. *Behavioral Disorders,* 23(1), 18–28.

Devlieger, P. J., & Trach, J. S. (1999). Mediation as a transition process: The impact on postschool employment outcomes. *Exceptional Children,* 65(4), 507–523.

Eder, D., Evans, C., & Parker, S. (1995). *School talk: Gender and adolescent culture.* New Brunswick, NJ: Rutgers University Press.

Hollenbeck, K. (1996). In their own words: Student perspectives on school-to-work opportunities. Washington, DC: National Institute for Work and Learning.

Holub, T. M., Lamb, P., & Bang, M. (1998). Empowering all students through self-determination. In C. M. Jorgensen, *Restructuring high schools for all students: Taking inclusion to the next level* (pp. 183–208). Baltimore: Paul H. Brookes.

Hutchins, M. P., & Renzaglia, A. (1998). Interviewing families for effective transition to employment. *Teaching Exceptional Children,* 30(4), 72–78.

IDEA (Individuals with Disabilities Education Act) 1997. 20 USC 1401 300.1 et seq.

Izzo, M. V., & Shumate, K. (1991). *Network for effective transition to work: A transition coordinator's handbook.* Columbus: Center on Education and Training for Employment, The Ohio State University.

Johnson, J. R., & Rusch, F. R. (1993). Secondary special education and transition services. *Career Development for Exceptional Individuals,* 16(1), 1–18.

Kim, E. Y (1993). Career choice among Korean-American students. *Anthropology and Education Quarterly,* 24(3), 224–248.

Klimek, D., & Anderson, M. (1987). *Understanding and parenting adolescents. Highlights: An ERIC/CAPS Digest*

(No. ED291018). Ann Arbor, MI: ERIC Clearinghouse on Counseling and Personnel Services.

Lankard, B. A. (1995). *Family role in career development*. ERIC Digest No. 389878. Columbus, OH: ERIC Clearinghouse on Adult, Career, and Vocational Education.

Lehmann, J. P. (1998). Mothers' role: A comparison between mothers of adolescents with severe disabilities and mothers of vocational students. *Career Development for Exceptional Individuals*, 21(2), 129–144.

Lehmann, J. P., & Baker, C. (1995). Mother's expectations for their adolescent children: A comparison between families with disabled adolescents and those with non-labeled adolescents. *Education and Training in Mental Retardation and Development Disabilities*, 30(1), 27–40.

Lehmann, J. P., & Roberto, K. A. (1996). Comparison of factors influencing mothers' perceptions about the futures of their adolescent children with and without disabilities. *Mental Retardation*, 34(1), 27–38.

Lewis, M. (1997). *Characteristics of successful school-to-work initiations*. Information Series #370. Columbus, OH: ERIC Clearinghouse on Adult, Career, and Vocational Education.

Louis Harris, & Associates (1998). *Harris Survey on the current status of persons with disabilities in American life: Executive Summary of Survey Findings*. Washington, DC: Author.

Lucas, T. (1996). *Promoting secondary school transitions for immigrant adolescents*. ERIC Digest No. EDOFL9905. Washington, DC: ERIC Clearinghouse on languages and Linguistics.

Masino, L. L., & Hodapp, R. M. (1996). Parental educational expectations for adolescents with disabilities. *Exceptional Children*, 62(6), 515–523.

Middleton, E. B., & Loughead, T. A. (1993). Parental influence on career development: An integrative framework for adolescent career counseling. *Journal of Career Development*, 19(3), 161–173.

Millam, I. M., & Love, L. L. (1998). Leaving high school: An ongoing transition study. *Teaching Exceptional Children*, 30(3), 4–10.

Morningstar, M. E., Turnbull, A. P., & Turnbull, H. R. III. (1995). What do students with disabilities tell us about the importance of family involvement in the transition from school to adult life? *Exceptional Children*, 62(3), 249–260.

Mortimer, J. (1992). *Influences on adolescents' vocational development*. Berkeley, CA: National Center for Research in Vocational Education.

Mount, B. (1992). *Person centered planning finding directions for change using personal futures planning*. New York, NY: Graphic Futures.

National Information Center for Children and Youth with Disabilities (NICHCY, 1993). *Transition services in the IEP*. Washington, DC: Author.

National Information Center for Children and Youth with Disabilities (NICHCY, 1999). *Options after high school for youth with disabilities*. Washington, DC: Author.

O'Brien, J., & Lyle, C. (1997). *Framework for accomplishments*. Decauter, GA: Responsive Systems Associates.

Paris, K. (1995). *Critical issue: Improving school-to-work transition for all students*. Madison, WI: North Central Regional Educational Laboratory.

Peters, L. (1994). From school to work—and back again: Youth apprenticeships in Wisconsin. *Rural Audio Journal*, 2(3), Naperville, IL: North Central Regional Educational Laboratory.

Robertson, A. S. (1997). *If an adolescent begins to fail in school, what can parents and teachers do?* ERIC Digest ED415001. Washington, DC: Educational Resources Information Center, National Library of Education, Office of Educational Research and Improvement.

Turnbull, A. P., Pereira, L., & Blue-Banning, M. J. (1999). Parents' facilitation of friendships between their children with a disability and friends without a disability. *Journal of the Association for Persons with Severe Handicaps*, 24(2), 85–99.

Turnbull, A. P., & Ruef, M. (1997). Family perspectives on inclusive lifestyle issues for people with problem behavior. *Exceptional Children*, 63(2), 211–227.

Vandercook, T., York, J., & Forest, M. (1989). The McGill Action Planning System: A strategy for building the vision. *Journal of the Association for Persons with Severe Handicaps*, 14, 205–215.

Whitney-Thomas, J., & Hanley-Maxwell, C. (1996). Packing the parachute: Parents' experiences as their children prepare to leave high school. *Exceptional Children*, 63(1), 75–87.

CHAPTER 12

Parents and Families of Adults with Disabilities

Mary and Aaron

For the first twenty-five years of my life, I had never had a first-hand experience with a person with a severe disability. I attended segregated schools that were suburban, middle class, Catholic, Caucasian, and accepted children of average or better intelligence with no behavior problems. My high school experience was even more restrictive and was an institutional residential academy for girls who were going to be nuns and teachers. I finished my Bachelor of Science, with elementary education certification and taught in a public school. There were slow learners in my classes, but because this was before The Education of Handicapped Children Act (EHA), basically we just created open-ended activities and they repeated kindergarten until they became eligible for the newly created Developmentally Handicapped class.

In 1974, my son Aaron was born. When Aaron was-thirteen-months old, I enrolled him in the only infant stimulation class in our county. I was shocked to see children who could not walk, could not talk, and could not master even the most basic self-help skills. I did not know children like this existed, and now I had to admit that my precious baby belonged with this group of children. I was also shocked to learn that most of the children in the program came from families like ours. It was a crash course in disability, in learning about the law, and the involvement of parents in the educational process as well as dealing with the medical.

Tommy, our second son, was born in 1976. The fact that he developed typically helped normalize our family and put Aaron's life in a better perspective. A car hit Tommy in 1978 and we were forced to look at our dreams for both our sons and found out they were basically the same. The therapy specialists and medical doctors basically said there was nothing we could do medically for Aaron and we should put our energy into good educational programs.

When Aaron turned five (and was legally eligible for school), and we filed a due process appeal against the public schools for the right to attend a special class *in the public school and get therapy. In despair of ever getting a good program for Aaron, and of Tom not being harassed by fellow teachers, we moved to the only school district in five counties where both the boys could attend the same schools. On a family vacation near Flagstaff, Arizona, we were asked to leave a restaurant because someone complained they didn't like the way Aaron looked and made noises.*

Aaron had a community-based functional curriculum that focused on real life experiences and vocational jobs. We were working hard at attaining independence especially in his self-help skills like walking to the bus, ordering in restaurants, etc. We were focusing on Aaron and what HE needed to fix him so that he would be more normal. Aaron was getting some transdisciplinary therapy, but we were not searching for a cure for Aaron anymore. He had to be better than everyone else to be allowed into the mainstream classes. Other children could have bad days, but Aaron had to be perfect or he would be kicked out. He was going to be a "super crip" and be an inspiration to all. He was in regular classes for social goals, we were hoping someone would see his inner beauty and become his friend. Aaron was allowed to participate in Boy Scouts, and the school Track and Cross Country teams as long as Mom or Dad accompanied him. He could participate in gym, art and music because the teachers were agreeable and the aides went with him. We completed a personal future plan, looking at the world from Aaron's point of view. It became clear that concerns about Aaron took all the family energy and resources.

Aaron formed some friendships with some of the Boy Scouts in his troop. Facilitated Communication gave Aaron a voice, and we found out he was not severely retarded. The Medicaid Waiver brought attendants to take Aaron to inclusive activities and dramatically eased caregiving responsibilities. Aaron graduated in June 1997. Aaron was not notified of the time or date of the graduating class picture, leaving him out of one of the few senior activities he could participate in, and leaving him out of history (the school closed June, 1997).

Aaron is now an adult. After Aaron visited his brother Tommy's college dorm, he wanted to know when he was moving into his own place. Aaron and "Dave" moved into a condo in April, 1998. I had no idea how difficult the separation would be. The building is lovely, but it is 22 miles away in a different city, long distance to call. But it was "take this opportunity or wait and wait." Aaron's roommate is 57 years old, a very nice man, who never "qualified" for school, though his main hobby is to work 1000 piece jigsaw puzzles. Both of his roommate's parents have died, so he was at the top of the list for residential services, and Aaron had the Medicaid Waiver money, so, it was a match. Aaron works part-time at the local police department and has made some wonderful friends (Captain Tom came to his graduation party). Because Aaron is now in residential services and there is only part-time work, Aaron joins in some "handicap only" activities if he wishes. The good news is that Aaron seems to like the staff and his roommate and things are going pretty well.

Parents, family members, and significant others are all involved and affected by the transition of the young person to adult status. This transition is often problematic, with parents of young adults with disabilities reporting far greater discomfort and pessimism than parents of young adults without disabilities (Whitney-Thomas & Hanley-Maxwell, 1996). Suddenly, their children, who were so very recently in school, are expected to (a) identify, organize, plan, and allocate resources; (b) work with others; (c) acquire and use information; (d) understand complex interrelationships;

(e) work with a variety of technologies; (f) perform basic skills such as reading, writing, and arithmetic; (g) think creatively, make decisions, solve problems, know how to learn; and (h) demonstrate responsibility, self-esteem, sociability, self-management, integrity, and honesty (U. S. Department of Labor, 1991).

Learning Objectives

After completing this chapter, you will be able to discuss these topics:

1. Issues related to adults with disabilities
2. Engaging parents with their adult children with disabilities
3. How parents can continue to support their adult children with disabilities

ISSUES OF ADULTS WITH DISABILITIES

There is little information to assist parents into the transition of being the parent of an adult with disabilities (Arnold, 1984). Yet, as adults, individuals with disabilities often continue to need support. As they assume the roles of adults in their community, several issues emerge. Some of the more significant issues with which adults with disabilities and their families struggle include: (a) decision-making, (b) self-advocacy, and (c) community living.

Decision-Making

The ARC (1995) stated that the need for adults with disabilities to have support in their decision-making is much less than that perceived by policy makers, service providers, or family members. In addition, The ARC suggests that guardianship can be overused by those who want to have their views prevail over the wishes of the individual with a disability. Programs such as limited guardianship and powers of attorney have emerged as ways to have individuals with disabilities who require support in their decision-making retain some control over their lives.

Freedman (2000) indicated that the law assumes that all adults, including adults with disabilities, are legally capable of making decisions without interference, even if the decisions are irrational. Guardians, individuals who are legally appointed to make decisions for another person who has been determined to be legally incompetent to make decisions for him or herself, should not be appointed because of disputes between parent and child. When describing guardians, most people assume that a "general guardianship" is being discussed. The person requesting that another person be put under guardianship is called a petitioner. When appointing a guardian, the probate or family court judge must find that:

- The individual's disabilities are such that he or she is incapable of making informed decisions with respect to the conduct of his or her personal and financial affairs;

- Not appointing a guardian would create unreasonable risk to the individual's health;
- Appointing a temporary support individual, conservator, or guardian would not eliminate the risk.

Petitioners may also request a temporary guardian when a situation occurs that requires the immediate appointment of an individual. This temporary guardian cannot usually commit an individual to a facility for persons with mental illness or mental retardation. The temporary guardian also cannot agree to treatment with medication unless the court determines the individual would have agreed to treatment if he or she were competent.

Freedman (2000) stated that if the parents believe that a guardian is needed because of the severity of their adult child's disability, then the parents should draft a "memorandum of instruction." This memorandum addresses the parents' hopes and preferences for the living arrangements of their adult child with a disability.

There are less intrusive alternatives to guardianship, which vary from state-to-state or province-to-province. Among the typical options are the following:

- A health care proxy, in which a competent adult designates a person to make medical decisions on his or her behalf;
- A durable power of attorney, who is able to address decisions about the financial affairs of an individual with disabilities;
- A limited guardianship, in which the individual with a disability is allowed to make some decisions for him or herself;
- A conservator, who is authorized only to make decisions about someone else's property.

Self-Advocacy

The concept of self-advocacy has emerged because it is consistent with the idea that individuals should be judged incompetent only as a last resort. In self-advocacy, individuals with disabilities are trained in the skills needed so that they may speak on behalf of themselves and on behalf of issues that affect people with disabilities (Williams & Shoultz, 1982). Self-advocacy groups typically provide individuals with disabilities consistent opportunities to develop membership and leadership skills. In these groups, persons with disabilities can learn about their rights and responsibilities, develop confidence, and practice interpersonal skills (Shoultz, 1995).

Self-advocacy emerged in Sweden in 1968, during a parents' organization meeting for people with developmental disabilities. These individuals listed the changes they wanted in services for children with disabilities. In 1974, the "People first" movement was initiated. In this movement, individuals with disabilities asserted their desire to be known as people first rather than as labels, that is, a person with a disability rather than a disabled person.

Self-advocacy groups are often formed by individuals with disabilities with the support of parents or disability agency staff members. These groups typically have advisors who are chosen by the group. The first decisions made by the members of the group are generally about the group itself, that is, empowering the members to make decisions (Shoultz, 1995). As individuals, the self-advocates increase their decision-making skills and their knowledge of services and protections.

At times, self-advocacy programs have put individuals with disabilities in conflict with their support systems as well as their parents. Moseley (1999) suggested that this tension may have several sources. Case managers often act directly on behalf of the individual with disabilities, making their role that of advocate, friend, or employee. In addition, they work with the management of an agency to ensure the resources are cost-effective. At times the case manager may also provide direct service. All of these activities may be easier if the client, the individual with disabilities, is compliant and quiet.

When the individual is not compliant and quiet, self-advocacy may force changes in the system that currently provides services and supports to individuals with disabilities. Moseley and Nerney (1999) said that changes may occur in these areas:

- Programs that provide support also provide services. A case manager may be in a position to suggest certain services simply because they are available in the agency.
- Budgeting is often for programs, rather than individuals. Self-advocacy requires a shift in funding to flexible, individual budgeting.
- Supports are individually created, not assigned as part of a program.
- The individual with a disability, as a self-advocate, supervises and directs the staff members who provide their support.
- In planning, the individual is central, and authority for decision-making rests with the consumer.

Community Living and Supports

Many individuals with disabilities can live completely independently as adults. However, even individuals with high incidence disabilities, such as learning disabilities, may confront challenges living independently. Reiff and Gerber (1994) said that activities of day-to-day living "offer concrete evidence of the persistence of learning disabilities through the lifespan" (p. 78). Difficulties may arise around reading and spelling, visual perception, directionality, or organization. A disruption in daily routine may cause significant difficulties, because of difficulties in organization and self-management skills. The needs for support in living independently is related to the individual's disability, and can range from an occasional phone call from mom and dad, to a weekly visit from a caseworker, to 24 hour care. It can be short-term, such as respite care, or become the individual's primary living situation.

Respite care is short-term, temporary care provided to people with disabilities so that families may have a break from the daily routines of care giving (Ingram, 1991a). Respite services provide temporary relief of the stress that may be present while providing extra care for a son or daughter with disabilities. Ingram said that respite care

- How are the care providers selected and screened? How are they trained? Will there be training specific to my child?
- How are the care providers supervised?
- What happens while the individual with disabilities is in care? Are there planned activities? Are meals prepared?
- How does the program deal with medical emergencies? Medical needs?
- Can parents meet and/or select the caregiver?
- How far ahead of time do parents need to call to arrange for services? Is there a limit to the number of hours a person can use the services?
- Will the program also care for siblings without identified disabilities?
- Does the program include transportation?
- What is the cost of services? How is payment arranged?

Figure 12.1 *Questions to Ask About Respite Care. (adapted from Karp, undated)*

provides a "gift of time" (p.1) to families, enabling them to have relief for a few hours or for a more extended period of time such as a vacation.

Though respite care may sound like a boon to families, there are some difficulties. Services may be provided by chapters of national organizations such as The ARC, the Easter Seal Society, and United Cerebral Palsy, or may be arranged by families with neighbors or other people they know. Emergency respite services may also be available, allowing parents to access services on short notice in the event that an unexpected family emergency occurs. Ingram (1991a) cautioned, however, that accessing the system can be difficult. Programs may not be licensed, and the age, training, education, and licensing or certification of the staff may vary. Karp (undated) suggested that parents ask a series of questions regarding any respite care program. These questions are presented in Figure 12.1.

Respite care, however, assumes that individuals are living as adults with their families. Community living, however, has emerged as a more "normalized" alternative to adults with disabilities remaining at home. Community living is defined as the programs, services, and supports that enable individuals with disabilities to live in their community. Community living typically takes one of two forms: supported living and small group homes. Adults with disabilities who are not under guardianship are legally responsible for making decisions about and agreeing to their living situation. The state may, however, if there is a life-threatening or emergency situation, involuntarily commit an individual with disabilities to a specific program (The ARC, 1997).

One active movement for individuals with disabilities is that described as "A home of one's own" (Shoultz, 1998). This movement is grounded in the efforts of parents and individuals with disabilities to set up a "real" home, like other people create for themselves. A "home" involves both housing and support, which are individual issues. Choices for the individual are presented in terms of both location and living companions. Supports are flexible, and are designed for and with the person to respond to the person's changing needs and wishes. Funding for these supports may come from Medicaid, Medicaid Home and Community-Based Services waivers, state funds for residential services that become available by closing institutions, independent living funds from vocational rehabilitation, and other funds administered by state social service offices.

Individuals with disabilities may need daily assistance when living independently. Personal care assistants may provide this support. However, finding, hiring, and keeping personal care assistants is often difficult. Questions emerge in terms of payment, job descriptions, and hiring. Unfortunately, there is great turnover in personal care assistants (Craig Hospital, 2001). Personal care assistants may leave their jobs because of a changing job description, duties are not logically and efficiently planned, the work environment is unpleasant, there is inadequate pay and esteem, the client is too passive or aggressive, the employer is dishonest about the hours worked and salary owed, or there are unreasonable duties (DeGraff, 1988). Family members can provide significant assistance in interviewing, hiring, and evaluating personal care assistants.

In supported living, the individual with a disability lives either alone or, if it is their choice, with a roommate. Though the focus is on giving attention to the individual with disabilities' wishes, supported living often involves collaboration among the individual, families, and professionals. People in supported living may need very little support, or may need 24-hour support. Supports are designed to meet the individual's needs (The ARC, 1997).

In small group homes, up to six individuals live with 24-hour support. In these homes, staff may either live with the individuals with disabilities with outside relief, or three shifts of support may be scheduled daily. Individuals in group homes typically are in adult programs or are employed during the day (The ARC, 1997).

ENGAGING PARENTS WITH THEIR ADULT CHILDREN WITH DISABILITIES

Parenting an adult with learning disabilities may be in itself a challenge. People with learning disabilities are the largest segment of the disability population (Kerka, 1998), and there are some estimates that between 5% and 20% of the general population may be affected by learning disabilities (Gadbow & DuBois, 1998). But adults with disabilities may be assumed to have mental retardation, deafness, blindness (Roper, 1995), or not to have a real disability (Rocco, 1997). In addition, though schools and workplaces may offer accommodations to help with academic and vocational skills, little attention is paid to social skills (Kerka).

Thorin, Yovanoff, and Irvin (1996) described the issues related to parenting adult children with disabilities. They suggest that parent control and involvement is expected to decrease during this period. In reality, however, the individual with a disability's quality of life is deeply effected by the parents' resources. Thorin et al. identified a variety of dilemmas for adults. Parents wanted to create opportunities for the young adult to be independent while assuring that the individual was healthy and safe. They wanted a separate life while wanting to do whatever was necessary to assure a high quality of life for their adult child. In addition, parents wanted to provide stability and predictability in family life while wanting to meet the changing needs of the young adult and family. Parents reported that they wanted a separate social life for the young adult and wanted to maximize the young adult's growth and potential while struggling to accept his or her limitations. Finally, parents struggle with burnout while wanting to do everything possible for the young adult.

Self-Determination

Self-determination was first used by Nirje (1972) to describe the need for the adult with disabilities to manage himself or herself as a distinct individual, and in this way have his or her identity defined to himself or herself and others through the circumstances and conditions of his existence. Nirje identified making choices, asserting oneself, self-management, self-knowledge, decision-making, self-advocacy, self-efficacy, self-regulation, autonomy, and independence as the important features of personal self-determination. Self-determination was equated with dignity and respect.

Hughes and Agran (1998) suggested that self-determination represents a reversal of thinking and behavior for parents and professionals. As professionals and parents, we often speak and make decisions for our students. We are accustomed to functioning "on their behalf" and "for their own good." Self-determination is more than a basic human right. Self-determination becomes a systems change issue, forcing us to think and rethink about how we work with adults with disabilities and their families.

Wehmeyer (1998) clarified the issues of self-determination by identifying misinterpretations and discussing what self-determination is not. He suggests that self determination

- Is not independent performance; individuals with significant disabilities may have help, yet retain control over the decision-making process and participating to the greatest extent in the problem-solving process.
- Is not absolute control; an individual with a disability is an agent of change in his or her own life, an actor rather than being acted upon.
- Is not always successful behavior; not every decision a person makes is an optimal decision, and not every selection of a goal is the right goal.
- Is not self-reliance and self-sufficiency; self-reliance may mean relying on one's own judgment and resources to identify someone else who might better provide a desired outcome.
- Is not just skills or just opportunity; if you just look at skills, it may appear that someone with severe disabilities could not become self-determined.
- Is not something you do; self-determination is something you support, promote, and enable.
- Is not a specific outcome, but is specific to each individual.
- Is not just choice, but is taking control over one's life.

In their challenge to move beyond the complexity of self-determination, Brown, Gothelf, Guess, and Lehr (1998) challenged individuals in the lives of adults with disabilities to ask themselves the following questions to evaluate their commitment:

1. Are you prepared to recognize the opportunities to communicate choice and allow individuals with disabilities to take control of their lives, even if the choices are inconvenient or inconsistent with our desired outcomes?

2. Are you more concerned about being a controlling competent professional who must teach certain skills rather than empowering an individual to shape his or her life?

3. Are you committed to developing the communicative behaviors that would allow the individual to be truly self-determining?

Bambara, Cole, and Koger (1998) suggested that in work with adults with disabilities there are overlapping, interactive components of support. They contended that the most important way to encourage self-determination is to get to know the person, gaining knowledge about the individual's likes and dislikes, goals and values, communication style, and current opportunities. Professionals should build lifestyles that reflect the person's preferences, providing continuous options for choice and learning. In addition, specific communication, choice and decision-making, problem solving, personal advocacy, and personal autonomy skills may be taught. Perhaps most important, supportive social contexts should be created that support self-determining acts. Professionals can act as resources by interpreting and reframing situations, providing emotional support, and advocating on the person's behalf.

Another issue that may concern parents regarding self-determination is marriage. In her recent legal brief, Churchill (2000) presented the argument that depriving an individual of the right to marry on the basis of disability is a violation of his or her Constitutional rights. She argues that an individual with a disability has the right to marry and choose a spouse, as long as there is no objective evidence proving that the choice will result in their reasonable right to health or safety. States should encourage independence and a "normal life" for individuals with disabilities. A spouse may serve as a guardian. An adult with a disability is first and foremost an adult in the eyes of the law.

Ferguson (1998), the parent of an adult with a disability, said that her goal has not been self-determination, but a good life for her adult child with a disability. She provides an example that seems to exemplify the issues related to self-determination. Her son, who has lived in his own home for two years, invited his parents to his house on Christmas Eve. She asks: Did he somehow sense that it was time to shift holiday celebrations to his home? Did his housemates "support his choice" or shape his choice on his behalf? Did they teach him how and why he might want to invite his parents? Was he asserting his adulthood? Were his housemates asserting their competence as supports of his interdependent life? The results of his participation in the holiday were shaped by those who support his participation in the season. His housemates may have wanted company as much as her son with disabilities wanted to celebrate at his home. Perhaps his housemates wanted to share their decoration efforts. Ferguson uses the analogy that her son "participated as an 'author,' but how much was 'written' by him and how much by others of us must and will vary."

Parents with Disabilities

The relationships of children with their adult parents with disabilities are fraught with ambivalence (Ronai, 1997). But in their study of parents with learning disabilities, Booth and Booth (2000) found that many of their children demonstrated considerable adaptability in coping with difficult lives. Booth and Booth could identify no simple links between parent skills and child outcomes, and argued that relationships with parents lay at the heart of adult identify. They suggest, however, that their findings highlighted the part played by social exclusion in shaping the lives of adult children of individuals with disabilities. The challenges confronting these adult children could not simply be attributed to their parents' learning disabilities.

SUPPORTING ADULT CHILDREN WITH DISABILITIES

In addition to providing emotional and social support, parents of individuals with disabilities often must plan for the future and make financial arrangements for their adult child. NICHCY (1994) suggested that parents must consider several issues when planning for their son or daughter with a disability, including the following:

- The individual's disability and prognosis for future development. It may be best to take a conservative view to plan for unanticipated needs.
- Personal financial situation.
- Living arrangements after the parent's death. Prospective living arrangements have a great impact on planning.
- Earning potential of the individual with a disability, determining how much he or she can be expected to contribute financially.
- Eligibility for government benefits.

Government benefits usually take one of three forms. First, there are those benefits, such as Social Security Disability Insurance, in which beneficiaries receive their benefits without regard to financial need. Second, there are benefits for which one must qualify, such as Supplemental Security Income and Medicaid. If a person with a disability has too many assets or income, he or she is not eligible to receive these benefits. Finally, there are programs where payment of services is determined according to the person's ability to pay. Though government supports may be substantial to the individual's well-being, the actual cash benefits are generally very small and force the individual to live below poverty level (NICHCY, 1994).

Berkobien and Varnet (1998) advocated the use of a trust to support adult children with disabilities. If an SSI or Medicaid recipient has access to more that $2000 in available assets, he or she may lose eligibility. A trust can support the adult child without jeopardizing their eligibility for SSI and Medicaid. Parents may set up supplemental trusts, which are designed so that the principal and its earnings supplement the individual's care and doesn't replace the funds required to pay for the same care. The trust then provides funds for items, services, or expenses not covered by SSI and Medicaid. Some states allow a discretionary trust, in which the parents give the trustee full discretion in how much or how little of the trust to distribute. Some organizations have a "master cooperative trust" or a "pooled trust" in which families pool their sources with other families, reducing administrative fees. Beneficiaries of these trusts usually receive earnings based on their share of the principal.

Parents can set up trusts two ways. A testamentary trust is part of a will and does not take effect until after the person whose will it is dies. An "inter vivos" or living trust is set up by an individual who is still living. These trusts may be either revocable, meaning they can be changed or ended, or irrevocable. When an irrevocable trust is set up, the parents have little power to change or end it.

Another planning document for parents is the "letter of intent." The letter of intent is a document that describes the adult with a disability, his or her history and status, and the parents' hope for the future. Though the letter of intent is not a legal document, the courts can rely on the letter for guidance in understanding the individual and the wishes of the parents. The letter spells out the individual's history, present situations, and the parents' hopes, wishes, and desires for future care, and, if possible, the individual's opinions. NICHCY suggests that this letter include information concerning the following:

- Housing/residential care;
- Education;
- Employment;
- Medical history and care;
- Behavior management;
- Social environment;
- Religious environment.

Additional options include a discussion of who will look after, advocate for, and be a friend to the individuals, and who will manage the individual's supplementary income.

SUMMARY

- Adults with disabilities and their families struggle with decision-making, self-advocacy, and community living.
- The law assumes that all adults are legally capable of making decisions without interference, even if the decisions are irrational. An individual must be judged not legally competent in order to have another adult make decisions for him or her.
- Self-advocacy has, at times, put individuals with disabilities at odds with their parents or service providers.
- Many adults with disabilities can live independently; however, a range of supports may be needed by many individuals with disabilities.

- Parents are confronted with the challenge of supporting the individuals with disabilities and their efforts to be independent and their desire to see him or her safe.
- In addition to social and emotional supports, parents of individuals with disabilities often must provide financial support.

REFERENCES

Arnold, M. (1984). *The role of parents in transition planning and adult services.* Athens, GA: University of Georgia University Affiliated Facility.

Bambara, L. M., Cole, C. L., & Koger, F. (1998). Translating self-determination concepts into support for adults with severe disabilities. *The Journal of the Association for Persons with Severe Handicaps,* 23(1), 21–27.

Berkobien, R., & Varnet, T. (1998). *Future planning: Making financial arrangements with a trust.* Washington, DC: The ARC.

Booth, T., & Booth, W. (2000). Against the odds: Growing up with parents who have learning disabilities. *Mental Retardation,* 38(1), 1–14.

Brown, F., Gothelf, C. R., Guess, D., & Lehr, D. H. (1998). Self-determination for individuals with the most severe disabilities: Moving beyond the chimera. *The Journal of the Association for Persons with Severe Handicaps,* 23(1), 17–26.

Churchill, M. A. (2000). *Amicus brief supporting right to marry for a woman with a developmental disability.* Available at www.marthachurchill.com/

Craig Hospital (2001). *Personal-care assistants: How to find, hire, and keep them.* Denver, CO: Author.

DeGraff, A (1988). *Home health aids: How to manage people who help you.* Fort Collins, CO: Saratoga Access Publications.

Ferguson, D. L. (1998). Relating to self-determination: One parent's thoughts. *The Journal of the Association for Persons with Severe handicaps,* 23(1), 44–46.

Freedman, P. (2000). *Personal decision-making.* Boston : Boston University School of

Law, N. Neal Pike Institute on Law and Disability.

Gadbow, N. F., & DuBois, D. A. (1998). *Adult learners with special needs.* Malabar, FL: Krieger Publishing.

Hughes, C., & Agran, M. (1998). Introduction to the special section: Self-determination: signaling a systems change? *The Journal of the Association for Persons with Severe Handicaps,* 23(1), 1–4.

Ingram, D. (1991a). *Respite care.* Washington, DC: The ARC.

Ingram, D. (1991b). *Strengthening American families through grassroots support.* Washington, DC: The ARC.

Karp, N. (no date). *Respite care: A guide for parents.* Washington, DC: CSR, Incorporated and Association for the Care of Children's Health.

Kerka, S. (1998). *Adults with learning disabilities.* ERIC Digest No. ED414434. Columbus, OH: ERIC Clearinghouse on Adult, Career, and Vocational Education.

Moseley, C. (1999). "I'm not a case and I don't want to be managed!": Supporting self-determination. *Common Sense,* 2 (December), 1–6.

Moseley, C., & Nerney, T. (1999). Emerging best practice in self-determination. *Common Sense,* 2 (December), 7.

NICHCY (1994). *Estate planning.* Washington, DC: National Information Center for Children and Youth with Disabilities.

Nirje, C. (1972). The right to self-determination. In W. Wolfensberger (Ed.) *Normalization,* pp. 176–200. Toronto: National Institute on Mental Retardation.

Reiff, H. B., & Gerber, P. J. (1994). Social/emotional and daily living issues for adults with learning disabilities. In P. Gerber, & H. Reiff (Eds.), *Learning disabilities in adulthood: Persisting problems and evolving issues*, pp. 72–81. Boston: Andover.

Rocco, T. S. (1997). Hesitating to disclose. In S. J. Levine (Ed.), *Proceedings of the 16th annual midwest research-to-practice conference in adult, continuing, and community education* (pp. 157–163). East Lansing: Michigan State University.

Ronai, C. R. (1997). On loving and hating my mentally retarded mother. *Mental Retardation*, 35(6), 417–432.

Roper Starch Worldwide, Inc. (1995). *Learning disabilities and the American public*. New York: Roper Starch Worldwide, Inc. (ED389101).

Shoultz, B. (1998). A *home of one's own*. Washington, DC: The ARC.

Shoultz, B. (1995). *The self-advocacy movement*. Washington, DC: The ARC.

The ARC (1997). *Community living*. Washington, DC: Author.

The ARC. (1995). *Guardianship*. Washington, DC: Author.

Thorin, E., Yovanoff, P., & Irvin, L. (1996). Dilemmas faced by families during their young adults' transition to adulthood: A brief report. *Mental Retardation*, 34(2), 117–120.

U. S. Department of Labor (1991). *What work requires of schools*: A SCANS *report for America* 2000. Washington, D.C.: U. S. Government Printing Office.

Wehmeyer, M. L. (1998). Self-determination and individuals with significant disabilities: Examining meanings and misinterpretations. *The Journal of the Association for Persons with Severe Handicaps*, 23(1), 5–16.

Whitney-Thomas, J., & Hanley-Maxwell, C. (1996). Packing the parachute: Parents' experiences as their children prepare to leave high school. *Exceptional Children*, 63(1), 75–87.

Williams, P., & Shoultz, B. (1982). *We can speak for ourselves*. Boston: Brookline Books.

Index